T0131393

MYP – New Directions

Edited by
Mary Hayden, Jeff Thompson and Judith Fabian

A John Catt Publication

First Published 2016

by John Catt Educational Ltd,
12 Deben Mill Business Centre, Old Maltings Approach,
Melton, Woodbridge IP12 1BL

Tel: +44 (0) 1394 389850 Fax: +44 (0) 1394 386893
Email: enquiries@johncatt.com
Website: www.johncatt.com

© 2016 John Catt Educational Ltd

ISBN: 978 1909717 87 9

Contents

Part C: Leading the change

Foreword

It was in 2011 that an earlier book, *Taking the MYP Forward*, was published with the intention of stimulating discussion around the revision of the International Baccalaureate (IB) Middle Years Programme which was beginning at that time, by feeding into the ensuing debate the views and ideas of the contributing authors through what was an independent, non-IB, publishing initiative.

Encouraged by the part that the 2011 volume played in contributing to MYP developments, it is hoped that this 2016 book may help teachers to implement the new version. The new MYP curriculum came into effect in September 2014 and will bring the MYP more closely into line with the IB Primary Years Programme and IB Diploma Programme, facilitating greater continuity across the IB continuum and easing the step up to the IB Diploma Programme from the middle years of schooling. We believe that this publication will not only be timely with regard to the current period of preparation for implementation of the new programme in 2017, but will also provide support for those involved in the change process through the contributions of experienced practitioners who have written from a range of relevant standpoints about different aspects of the MYP.

The book opens with a chapter by Judith Fabian who, until recently, was the Chief Academic Officer of the IB Organization. She reminds us that the MYP now has over 20 years of history, and charts the progress of the programme since its adoption by the IB in 1994. Briefly tracing the history of the MYP, she refers to the impact that it has had in transforming middle years learning. Judith Fabian describes the current context in which the programme exists and highlights the changes that have been introduced by the IB in designing the new approach. She spells out clearly the challenges and opportunities faced by those responsible for the implementation of the programme in schools in the immediate future, and offers encouragement for their efforts in enhancing what is already widely regarded as a programme of excellence for middle years schooling.

What follows in Part A is a collection of chapters written by authors who have been involved in making direct contributions to the change process and who are experienced in presenting their views to others through workshops, meetings and their publications. Each has chosen to focus their contribution on one of the central features of the new curriculum framework; thus Conrad Hughes (*Concept Driven Learning*), Alexandra Holland (*Global Contexts*), Lance King (*Approaches to Learning*), Marjorie Lope (*Interdisciplinary Teaching and Learning*), Patricia Villegas (*School-based assessment*) and Gareth Hegarty (*eAssessment*) all draw on their experience in offering advice in support of those who are involved in the task of translating the objectives of the revised programme into successful practice.

In Part B, chapters are contributed by a number of experienced practitioners who share their views on the changes that have been introduced, and identify a number of opportunities and challenges that the implementation of the new framework will bring within the institutional context. The topics chosen by our authors include *holism in the current MYP* (Hege Myhre), *a concept-based approach to learning languages* (Michael Huber), *a case study of MYP in conjunction with IGCSE in Geography* (Oyndrilla Mukherjee), and *transition from the new MYP to the Diploma Programme* (Anthony Hemmens). We asked contributors to focus on different aspects of the programme arising from their own perspectives, and to review those aspects through a critical lens – where critical is used in the sense of an informed critique – and to share strategies for effective implementation which are likely to facilitate the promotion of good practice, through adopting interesting or innovative approaches.

Part C focuses on *leading the change*, where Gillian Ashworth has used the framework of the MYP Unit Planner to highlight five concepts which present challenges arising in ideas explored earlier in the book, and relates them more widely to other relevant leadership literature in order to identify suggestions for effective implementation of the changes.

We hope that readers across a wide range of institutional contexts and pedagogical practices will find the information, observations, issues and suggestions expressed by the authors in this volume to be of interest, support and encouragement in their personal endeavours to implement effectively the changes in the new MYP curriculum framework. We hope also that those who are not directly involved in the Middle Years Programme *per se* will encounter ideas that will stimulate their own work in engaging with an appropriate middle years curriculum that will serve the learning needs of students in developing the ability to deploy the knowledge, skills, dispositions and attitudes that their future lives, undoubtedly to be characterised by fundamental and rapid change, will demand.

Many people have been involved in the production of this book. We wish to express our gratitude and appreciation to them all; to all the authors who have demonstrated professional knowledge and skill in sharing with us insights borne out of their impressive experience and in exercising enormous patience in responding so generously to editorial demands, and to our colleagues in John Catt Educational Limited for their continued guidance and encouragement throughout a process in which we, as editors, feel privileged to have played a part.

Mary Hayden
Jeff Thompson
Judith Fabian

List of contributors

Gillian Ashworth has worked in various international schools as head of secondary, MYP and DP coordinator roles, and department head, in places as diverse as India, Azerbaijan, Africa, South America, Eastern Europe and China. She is a Lead Educator for professional development in the IB Asia-Pacific region, programme field representative for both MYP and DP workshops, consultant and school visits team leader for MYP, and team member for DP. She was one of the facilitators when the MYP 'Next Chapter' changes were introduced, and she took part in some of the MYP curriculum review work with eAssessments for Language and Literature.

Judith Fabian taught English and drama in secondary schools in London for 10 years, followed by 15 years as department head and principal in international schools in Jordan, Tanzania and Germany. She joined the International Baccalaureate (IB) in Cardiff in 2004 as Head of Programme Development, and in 2007 was appointed Chief Academic Officer leading the development of IB curriculum for students aged 3 to 19 years. Latterly based in The Hague, she left the IB in 2014 to return to her home in the UK to work as an educational consultant. She has presented to, and worked with, schools and educators all over the world.

Mary Hayden is Head of the Department of Education at the University of Bath, where she is also leader of the Internationalisation and Globalisation of Education research group. Her personal research interests relate to international schools and international education, an area in which she has published widely in research journals and books, as well as supervising Masters and Doctoral students. She is Editor-in-Chief of the Journal of Research in International Education, a Founding Trustee of the Alliance for International Education and a member of the advisory boards of a number of international education projects.

Gareth Hegarty is leading the new IB MYP Assessment team in Cardiff as they develop the new assessment provision for the MYP, including the on-screen examinations. Previously Gareth led assessment in individuals and societies, the arts and the core of the Diploma Programme, and prior to that was the subject manager for chemistry. Gareth joined the IB after 10 years of teaching and leadership in schools in the UK, the Netherlands and Russia.

Anthony Hemmens unwittingly made education his life-long vocation at the age of five when he joined primary school. He graduated with a degree in philosophy from the University of Hull in the UK in 1993 and then began a grand tour that would last 22 years. He has lived and taught in Hungary, Portugal, Japan, Malaysia and the UK. He is presently stationed at the University of Bath where he is a member of a team undertaking research into CAS for the IB Diploma programme; he is also completing a Masters degree in education and has published in the field of international education.

Alexandra Holland is currently the Curriculum Development Manager for the Aga Khan Academies. Based in Mombasa, she works with schools in Kenya, India and Mozambique to build IB continuum programmes that are relevant to students living in the developing world. Over the past 20 years she has also worked in schools in the UK, Hong Kong and South Africa, teaching history and humanities, and relearning her subject each time she has moved.

Michael Huber is a teacher of Music, German Language Acquisition and Language and Literature, at the International School of Zug and Luzern in Switzerland. Before joining ISZL in 2013, he taught at Munich International School in Germany and previously in the Czech Republic. In addition to his current teaching roles, Michael helps to coordinate the newly implemented Well-Being programme at ISZL. He is currently studying for a postgraduate degree in international education.

Conrad Hughes is Campus and Secondary Principal at the International School of Geneva's La Grande Boissière, where he also teaches Theory of Knowledge. He was educated in France, Swaziland and South Africa, holds a PhD in English literature from the University of the Witwatersrand and has worked in schools in France, the Netherlands and India. He has published articles on assessment, critical thinking, prejudice, learning and effective teaching in academic and educational journals as well as an English textbook for students pursuing the IB Diploma. He is currently studying for a professional doctorate in education with the University of Durham.

Lance King is an internationally recognised author, teacher and workshop facilitator who has worked in 22 countries with both students and their teachers and parents. He is the creator of the Art of Learning programme taught in over 200 schools worldwide, and is a specialist in the direct teaching of 'learning skills'. Within the IB, he was the principal designer of the Approaches to Learning (ATL) curriculum for both the MYP and DP. He is the co-author of two ATL Skills textbooks, and has delivered many workshops in IB schools on the topic. He lives in Raglan, New Zealand where he teaches and presents workshops for teachers, parents and students.

Marjorie Lope is the Global Head of the IB Educators Network. Before joining the IB in 2015, she served as Assistant Principal at Bethesda Chevy Chase High School, Maryland; prior to that she was the supervisor for the Division of Accelerated and Enrichment Instruction of Montgomery County Public Schools, Maryland, where she established a common vision for the IB in the district. Following her work in US public schools as a teacher and MYP Coordinator she was consulted on the latest revisions to the MYP. Her doctoral research was on the perceptions of international mindedness among teachers and students in the MYP.

Oyndrilla Mukherjee is Assistant MYP Coordinator and teacher of MYP and DP geography at the École Mondiale World School, Mumbai, India. Before joining Ecole Mondiale in 2006, she taught in The British School, New Delhi. She is an IBDP examiner and a member of the external curriculum review team for IBDP Geography. She has a keen interest in exploring international mindedness in the context of geography education and she is currently pursuing an MA in international education degree from the University of Bath.

Hege Myhre is the Principal at Kongsberg International School, an IB World School offering PYP and MYP. She has taught students from Middle Years Programme to university level, and her specialized focus on student-led curriculum design has resulted in working projects with schools and industry in Canada, North America, Europe and Asia. Hege joined the IB network in 2004 and is acting as an IB consultant as well as an IB team leader for synchronized CIS/IB visits. In addition she is a sitting member of the consecutive committee for FRI (Forum for Private schools) in Norway.

Jeff Thompson is Emeritus Professor of Education at the University of Bath with particular interests in the fields of international schools and international education. He has published many articles and books in this area, in which he also teaches and supervises Doctoral and Masters students. He has been involved with the IB since its earliest days in a number of roles, including Academic Director, Chair of the Examining Board and Head of Research. He is a member of a wide range of advisory boards for international education projects and holds governance positions for a number of schools.

Patricia Villegas has been involved in education in South America for 30 years, having worked in Colombia, Virgin Islands and Buenos Aries in a variety of IB posts. She has been a senior moderator for the Personal Project, an MYP site visitor, workshop leader and Online Curriculum Centre faculty manager for MYP projects. She consulted on the revisions to the MYP and the development of the eAssessments, and participated in the pilot MYP interdisciplinary eAssessment as examiner in English and principal examiner in Spanish. She holds a Master of Arts in Education (Leadership and Management) from the University of Bath.

Chapter 1

Revising the IB Middle Years Programme: In pursuit of excellence

Judith Fabian

Teaching young adolescents is, in turn, exciting, daunting, stimulating, challenging, energising, frustrating, exhausting and enormously rewarding. Between the ages of 11 and 16 young people experience huge changes in every part of their lives, including their brains, their bodies and the way they relate to all those around them. The reward for the teacher is to be able to influence and support those changes and help young people find their pathways into adulthood. What sort of education can help the teacher best accomplish this?

A surprisingly large consensus has emerged in the last decade as to what excellent middle years education should look like, surprising only in that such a consensus has not led to the significant change that might be expected. Lasting change in this sector of 11 to 16 year olds has been slow, to say the least. P. Gayle Andrews describes middle level education in the US as, 'occupying a shadowland historically … often overlooked, underserved and under resourced' (Andrews, 2013). This description could well apply to middle years education in many schools, private, public and international, and many districts, local authorities, commercial educational organisations and governments across the world.

Middle years education, for many, is betwixt and between. It does not have the obvious charm and certainty of the best primary/elementary education with its focus on child development, curiosity, creativity and discovering the world; nor does it have the impetus and status of the upper years of secondary school or high school with the drive for credentials and university admissions. Middle years teachers will more often than not be faced with the struggle to address the nature and needs of young adolescents, hugely diverse and extreme in range, while under pressure to prepare them directly for high school and the rigors of examinations and college entrance.

Largely because it has been expedient to do so, middle years education has lurched from one extreme approach to another: either being left entirely in the hands of classroom teachers to do the best they can, often individually and unsupported, or being mandated by national systems in sometimes reductive and mind-numbing detail, and then converted into text books of varying quality and questionable value.

On a global and national level, the picture of middle years education continues to be depressingly unchanged. Despite this, exciting and innovative work has been going on for many years in the middle years of schools all over the world, with enthusiastic and committed teachers converting the wealth of research and thinking that exists into outstanding classroom practice. So how can all that is good in middle school education be translated into a curriculum that can be implemented successfully in any school that wants to be excellent? And how can middle years education emerge from the shadows to be recognised as a joy for educators and vital for every community?

In this chapter I will provide an overview of the major changes in the International Baccalaureate (IB) Middle Years Programme (MYP), in light of what has been acknowledged to be best practice in middle years education, and argue that the revised MYP provides a great opportunity for schools to improve middle years' education. In itself it is not the 'silver bullet' or 'golden chalice', or any other metallic metaphor you care to use, but it provides the framework, support and educational imperative that schools and middle years' teachers need to finally get middle years education right.

As stated above, the consensus amongst educators, psychologists, neurologists and many others about what makes the best middle years education is remarkably strong. In order to provide a context for an overview of the revised MYP, I summarise below, at a high level, what I believe to be the key elements of such an education. The list is my own, based on a synthesis of ideas and good practice that have persisted and gained credence over many years. It is not a definitive list, and it can be argued that it applies to all students, not just middle years students, but it captures the elements of a great education that is particularly relevant for 11 to 16 year olds. I make reference, as a guide only, to some of the most influential thinkers and research for each element.

Elements of an excellent middle years education:

- Education for young adolescents needs to be student-centred and holistic. It must focus on the needs of students, individually, and address the full range of those needs: intellectual, physical, social, emotional, moral, aesthetic and spiritual (Peterson, 1987; Cohen, 1999; Gardner, 2006).

- Students must be involved in their own learning, construct meaning for themselves and engage with big and significant ideas that will challenge them (Erickson, 2007; Perkins, 2010).

- Students need to understand themselves as learners and develop the skills of learning that they will need for the rest of their lives in order to contribute to society and create a better world (Hattie *et al*, 2006; Costa and Kallik, 2000; Wagner, 2008).

- Learning must be dynamic and engaging: doing, as well as listening and thinking (Kolb, 1984).

- Education must provide young adolescents with the opportunities to encounter and engage with real and important issues, personal, local, national and global (Johnson, 2002; Edwards, 2009; Boix-Mansilla, 2010).

- Opportunities must be provided for students to contribute to their communities – local, national and global (Berger Kaye, 2010).

- Assessment of students must focus on learning as well as measuring standards, and be used as an important tool to improve learning (Wiggins, 1998).

The IB Middle Years Programme: 1994–2014

Origins

A student-centred, holistic curriculum for 11 to 16 year olds was the vision of a radical group of international school teachers in the 1980s, working through the International Schools Association (ISA). The MYP was the outcome of the work of these highly experienced, skilled, practising classroom teachers who collaborated to produce a curriculum that would provide the best learning environment and experience for 11 to 16 year olds and prepare them for the final years of high school, college and life beyond. In 1994 their work was adopted by the IB and became the MYP.

What distinguished this programme was that it was the product of classroom practice combined with current research from all over the world, without the influence of politics or commerce. The interest of these teachers was the middle years student, and no one or nothing else. What they developed and what the IB adopted in 1994, and continued to refine, was composed of all the necessary elements of an excellent middle years curriculum. Some of these elements required better articulation, more detail, more explanation, better support for teachers and greater coherence across the whole, but the elements were, and still are, all there.

Since 1994 the development of the MYP has been 'incremental and expansionary' (Harrison, 2015). Twenty years of growth and an increasingly diverse population of schools have resulted in more contributors from a wider range of backgrounds and contexts, and increased resources. In September 2014, the MYP was republished, resulting in a middle years curriculum that is clearer, more coherent, and provides more support for teacher. Is it perfect? Of course not. But it continues to be faithful to the elements of an excellent middle years education and may well expand that notion. It will provide middle years teachers with the structure, tools, aspiration and vision to continue the task of developing outstanding middle years education.

The first 20 years

The MYP is a broad-based, holistic programme of education, focused on the individual student and inclusive of all students. From the outset it had subject groups covering the arts, sciences, mathematics, humanities, technology and physical education, and required the study of two languages. One key element of the MYP that distinguished it from other middle years curricula was the 'Areas of Interaction' that connected the subject groups and which encompassed key areas of excellent middle years education including service learning, metacognitive skills and health and social education. The programme required teachers to collaborate with colleagues to address the big ideas and global issues in an inter-disciplinary way. The Personal Project in the final year of the programme was the culminating experience for students, bringing together the learning from the Areas of Interaction and focusing that learning on their personal interests and passions.

Until 2014 assessment was largely internal, with schools having the option to have their assessments in each subject group, from year 5 of the programme, moderated by the IB, to check the standards of the assessment tasks and the marking of the teachers. Students could be awarded an MYP certificate, but that certificate was not the outcome of externally assessed examinations.

The elements of an excellent curriculum and the bones of a workable structure were all there:

- a Learner Profile at the centre of the programme model, with the mission to develop internationally-minded young people, addressing the holistic needs of middle years students

- the full range of academic disciplines, including two languages, the arts and physical education providing academic rigour, breadth and balance

- threads connecting the disciplines making the curriculum challenging, coherent and relevant

- school-based, formative assessment covering a broad range of assessment tasks to support learning at all stages

- an exciting, culminating task allowing students to follow their passions and apply their skills and learning

- a constructivist pedagogy implicit in all elements of the programme ensuring students were active learners and given multiple opportunities to construct meaning

The bones were strong and continue to be so, but they needed fleshing-out and to be clothed, to extend the metaphor. This is what the recent changes to the MYP have tried to do.

The rationale for change

The IB MYP has been in existence for over 20 years. There are 1149 MYP schools as of August 2015, in 101 countries. Many of these schools are private international schools, situated in almost every corner of the globe. Over 50%

are state-run schools, most of them in the USA and Canada, but others are in countries as diverse as Australia, Poland and China. In these schools, teachers and school leaders who want to implement the MYP often have to contend with national or state requirements in the form of prescribed curricula and/or compulsory, standardised assessments. The private international schools usually have more freedom, but pressures from groups of parents or financial pressures can be equally challenging.

The MYP was designed to be flexible and therefore adaptable to individual schools and local circumstances, up to a point. Certainly the curriculum was designed to be able to address the needs of the students and the local community in their particular context, hence the lack of prescribed content in the eight subject groups and the requirement that teachers collaborate to produce their own units of work. The content of the curriculum could be adapted, but the structure – the bones – of the programme had to be in place if a school wanted to be an IB MYP World School – the title given to an authorised MYP school. How could one programme meet the needs of both state and private, national and international schools in multiple settings and contexts?

One of the biggest challenges for the IB, now and in the future, is how to ensure that the MYP continues to provide an excellent middle years education and also meet the needs of schools in varied social, economic, geographic and political contexts. How flexible could and should the MYP be? This was the question that stimulated a major review of the MYP which started in 2010 and concluded in 2014 with the publication of the revised programme.

In 1994, the MYP had rules that were designed largely around private international schools. These rules were intended to ensure that an MYP education was an excellent education and, to a large extent, this was successful. The international schools could, in most cases, adapt to the programme where they needed to as it was designed to meet their needs. In the following 20 years, some of the rules were changed incrementally, circumvented or massaged, to better help an increasing number and a greater variety of schools implement the programme, all with the best of intentions. But how much flexibility could be allowed without losing the essence and value of the programme?

The answer from the IB was that there had to be more flexibility in the programme so that more students could benefit from an IB education, but that flexibility had to be carefully designed with the aim of achieving greater consistency of implementation and higher standards in MYP schools. Achieving a healthy balance between the principles of an excellent education for 11 to 16 year olds and the practical needs of a diverse community of schools all over the world was always going to be more than challenging; it was going to be very hard.

The Middle Years Programme Post-2014: Key changes

The student at the heart of the programme: the IB Learner Profile and international mindedness

An excellent education for any young person will always have at its heart the healthy development of the whole child and that is expressed in the MYP through the IB Learner Profile which continues to sit firmly at the centre of the MYP model (see Figure 1), and lies at the heart of an MYP education. The Learner Profile consists of 10 attributes that, taken together, describe what it means to be an internationally-minded person: *inquirers, knowledgeable, thinkers, communicators, principled, open-minded, caring, risk-takers, balanced, reflective.* It was comprehensively reviewed in 2012 and, based on a consensus of the IB community, has been refined but is, essentially, unchanged.

Figure 1 – the MYP programme model

The IB holds that international mindedness is the desired outcome of the Learner Profile and the four programmes that make up an IB education: the Primary Years Programme (PYP) for 3 to 12 year olds; the Middle Years Programme (MYP) for 11 to 16 year olds; the Diploma Programme (DP), for 16 to 19 year olds, and the Career-related Programme (CP) also for 16 to 19 year olds but focused on career-related studies. The words 'international mindedness' now sit across the base of the circular programme models for all IB programmes; the words did not appear on the previous models. The preamble to the IB Learner Profile states:

> The aim of all IB programmes is to develop internationally-minded people who, recognising their common humanity and shared guardianship of the planet, help to create a better and more peaceful world (IB, 2014).

International mindedness, then, has a strong moral purpose – 'to create a better and more peaceful world' – and the education that this programme provides is aspirational and idealistic. Shouldn't the education of 11 to 16 year olds be aspirational and idealistic? Skills, knowledge and qualifications are certainly important but will have limited impact on an individual and society if they are not underpinned by aspirations and ideals. Young adolescents crave the opportunity to aspire to something greater than themselves. While the pressures on the MYP have resulted in some pragmatic changes to help schools implement the programme, the Learner Profile and international mindedness have been strengthened.

The academic disciplines

For the eight subject groups of the MYP, there have been some refinements to terminology, which now aligns with the DP, but they essentially remain the same. Before 2014, and from its earliest years, there was no prescribed curriculum for the MYP, instead the IB published broad guidelines and learning objectives to help teachers develop their own curriculum to best suit the students they were teaching, the school and the local context. Advice was also provided on teaching and learning in the subject group, and an optional planner was published to guide teachers in planning an effective unit of work. In other words the IB provided the tools, but it was the responsibility of the teachers, in teams, to plan the units of work and ensure the curriculum was vertically and horizontally coherent and of a high standard.

For the first MYP schools, many of which were international, this was ideal. There was a curriculum framework, there were guidelines, and the teachers had the freedom to create the curriculum they wanted and believed in. But some other schools, later adopters of the programme, found the lack of prescribed curriculum and the vagueness of the guidelines frustrating and problematic: it was not always easy to find teachers with sufficient experience and interest to write good curriculum, and finding time within the school day for teachers to collaborate on the units of work could be very difficult, especially if they also had to teach a national curriculum in addition to the MYP. Therefore concerns grew about standards of learning which, partly because of the curriculum freedom given to schools, could vary. The question for the IB was how to better support MYP teachers and to ensure high and consistent standards of curriculum. Furthermore, how could this be done without constraining the 'creative professionalism' (Hargreaves, 1998) that is the essence of a great middle school teacher?

The solution has been to introduce prescribed concepts: *key concepts* for subject groups that will connect learning across the academic disciplines, for example: change, identity, logic; *related concepts* that apply more specifically to the subject groups, for example in chemistry: movement, energy, balance (IB, 2014). The concepts are the organisers for the curriculum and units of work. Teaching through concepts has always been part of an IB education: there are eight key concepts in the PYP; MYP teachers have always been prompted to organise units of work around essential questions; and the depth and breadth of DP courses have always required conceptual understanding by students, implicitly, if not explicitly. Teaching through concepts means focusing learning on the big, significant, ideas that will have relevance to students' lives beyond school and that will provide depth of understanding. Learning conceptually will help students make sense of what they are learning, connect their knowledge and understanding, and transfer knowledge and understanding as required (Erickson, 2007). Teaching through concepts makes learning relevant, and 'life-worthy' (Perkins, 2014).

The theory and practice of concept-based learning is persuasive and there is no doubt that young adolescents are hungry to understand themselves and the world around them. However, teaching through concepts is not easy for those who haven't done it before. The choice of the content through which you teach the concepts becomes very important; it must be significant in every possible way, not just what is easy to teach or has been taught for many years. While the prescribed concepts will provide strong guidance for teachers they will also challenge them to select content that is significant and will produce 'life-worthy learning'. The prescribed concepts should serve to raise the standards of the school's MYP curriculum and make those standards more consistent across schools.

It is a bold move by the IB not to give into the call from some for prescribed curriculum in order that teachers can take the curriculum documents off the (virtual) shelf and just teach. The need for MYP teachers to collaborate to produce excellent units of work, based around concepts, that articulate across and between grades, is as important in the revised MYP as it was in the early days of the ISA. The prescription of concepts means that MYP schools, now more than ever, will need to train staff and provide ongoing support for curriculum development.

Connecting the academic disciplines

Prior to 2014, there were the five Areas of Interaction that provided thread or links across the eight subject groups: Approaches to Learning; Human Ingenuity; Health and Social Education; Community and Service, and Environments. These underwent some refine-ment in the intervening 20 years, but there was general agreement that the connecting and underpinning of the disciplines needed rethinking to ensure relevance and reflect re-search and current thinking. There are no Areas of Interaction any longer but there are clearer and stronger threads that connect and underpin the subject groups.

Global contexts

While international mindedness has always been central to an IB education at all levels, the MYP has, at various times, used intercultural awareness or intercultural understanding as a fundamental concept and as a thread to connect components of the programme. The revised version of the MYP replaces the Areas of Interaction, as a whole, with 'global contexts'. 'This decision offered a way forward that both simplified curriculum development and more explicitly integrated the development of international mindedness in the programme' (Harrison, 2015). The MYP's global contexts have been adapted and developed from the six transdisciplinary themes of the PYP, ensuring they are appropriate for young adolescents: Identities and Relationships; Orientation in Space and Time; Personal and Cultural Expression; Scientific and Technical Innovation; Globalisation and Sustainability; Fairness and Development.

There is no doubt this is an important shift for the MYP in terms of the IB being much more explicit about the structure and themes of global contexts and ambitious about the types of issues middle years students can handle. Schools still have the freedom to incorporate content that is relevant to their context, but they will not be able to avoid having to tackle the big issues of the day. It is a change to be welcomed, though it will take time to fully develop and realise the potential of such a change.

An excellent education for young adolescents needs to be relevant to them and their world, their world being the whole world as well as their families and local community; it needs to tackle the serious and important issues that adolescents have no trouble in recognising as being important to their lives, including the environment they live in, fairness to others, their culture, technology and their relationships with others.

Approaches to Learning

The importance of Approaches to Learning (ATL) has grown considerably in recent years with the popularity of the notion of 21st century skills. It could be argued that there are few skills in these multiple lists that are new to the 21st century, and that the skills that universities, employers, and parents are now lauding have always been important for learning, they just haven't been understood or recognised in the rush to cram knowledge into young heads. However, better late than never.

The IB has been engaged for over 46 years in promoting the skills of learning how to learn, the skills that will enable young people to have the desire and ability to learn throughout their lives. For the MYP, post 2014, ATL stands on its own as a major component of the programme and has been significantly strengthened and more thoroughly described and explained. The five sets of ATL skills: communication skills; social skills; self-management skills; research skills; thinking skills, as developed over the 20 years of the MYP, are now integral to all four IB programmes. The skills in the new ATL framework are certainly more contemporary, going way beyond the quite narrowly focused academic concerns of the original approaches to learning. They include, for example, mindfulness, practising delayed gratification, practising the ability to 'fail well', and being aware of body-mind connections, in addition to long recognised skills such as collaboration, time management and critical thinking.

Interdisciplinary learning

Interdisciplinary learning has always been an important part of the MYP. While ensuring the development of disciplinary knowledge through the eight subject groups, the programme also emphasised the making of connections between them, enabling students to develop greater understanding of the relationship between the academic disciplines and the nature of knowledge, and providing them with the opportunity to study complex world issues which are, intrinsically, interdisciplinary in nature.

It could be argued that the interdisciplinary dimension of the MYP was not strong enough and that the balance between disciplinary and interdisciplinary was not achieved in many schools. From 2014 the revised MYP framework significantly elevates interdisciplinary learning. It now has its own aims, objectives, unit planning structure and assessment. It can be implemented through multiple models, including the combining of subject groups, and it is designed to be simpler, clearer and more practical for day-to-day teaching. It is also designed to connect more explicitly to Theory of Knowledge in the DP. There is an inevitable tension in a curriculum which is structured around academic disciplines but also promotes interdisciplinary learning. This tension is exacerbated by the way most middle years teachers are trained – largely in the academic disciplines – and the time and effort required for teachers to collaborate across disciplines in a truly interdisciplinary way. However, the IB is making a clear commitment to ensure interdisciplinary learning in the MYP is strengthened; the new interdisciplinary eAssessment and, hopefully, the resulting 'backwash' effect of such an assessment is evidence of this commitment.

Assessment

How best to assess student learning in the middle years? There are regions of the world where externally assessing 15-16 year olds is sacrosanct. These countries are often those that are influenced by the education system in England and Wales of O Levels or General Certificate of Secondary Education (GCSE) examinations at 16; these examinations lead to credentials which can influence university admissions. Other regions of the world administer standardised assessments during the middle years as a way of ensuring schools maintain teaching standards, and also as a mechanism to stream or track students. There are also countries and private and international schools that do not assess externally and would argue that external assessment is not only unnecessary but detrimental to the education of middle years students. There are schools from all three groups that wish to implement the MYP.

The IB MYP in its first 20 years stood firmly opposed to external assessment at the end of the programme, and firmly for school-based, internal, teacher-led assessment throughout the five years of the programme. The MYP provided a voluntary system of moderation so that schools could get support to develop appropriate assessment tasks and could check the standards of teacher assessment. The IB provided moderation of teacher assessments only; it did not assess students. This was seen in some quarters as a weakness of the programme, in others as its great strength.

From May 2016 schools can opt to enter students for electronic assessments (eAssessments) in four subject groups (Language and Literature, Mathematics, Sciences, Individuals and Societies) plus an interdisciplinary eAssessment. These assessments are all taken on computers under examination conditions. Language Acquisition will be assessed through moderation of an ePortfolio, as will the Personal Project. An MYP Certificate will be awarded to students who achieve specific levels in all components. The introduction of external assessments, though optional, has caused controversy. It has been warmly welcomed by some schools but other schools fear the impact of end-of-programme examinations on student learning and the quality of teaching. Some practitioners have warned that pressure could be put on schools by governing bodies or parent groups to opt for the eAssessments even though the school does not wish to offer them. It remains to be seen what impact this innovative form of external assessment will have.

While the IB has acceded to the needs of some schools to offer external assessment and credentials at 16, it has also made great efforts to ensure the eAssessments reflect best practice in middle years education and will positively influence teaching strategies as opposed to constraining them. The eAssessments are concept-based, to reflect the concept-based nature of the revised MYP curriculum, not content-based. They are designed to assess skills and understanding. They are certainly innovative in that there is currently no other form of external assessment that assesses deep learning in a way that is true to the nature of the curriculum and the pedagogy of middle years education.

While much attention has been focused on the new eAssessments, internal assessment in the MYP has been clarified and simplified. There are now the same number of criteria for each subject group and a common language for the criteria across subjects. This should not only make the lives of teachers easier when assessing their students but should en-courage standardisation and collaboration across subjects to the benefit of teachers as well as students.

The Personal Project and the Community Project

The Personal Project still stands as the culminating event in year 5 of the MYP, and one of the defining components of the whole programme. Previously, external moderation of the school's internal assessment of the projects was optional; it is now mandatory for all schools. This has been done as a way of providing some form of standardisation across all MYP schools. It is hoped it may also become a unifying element, providing experiences and achievements all schools can share.

Middle schools that offer only the first three years of the MYP can now offer a Community Project at the end of year 3, as a culminating experience for students who may not have the opportunity to complete the MYP in high school. Community Projects will be assessed internally but it would make sense for the IB to provide mandatory moderation for these projects in the future and offer them to all schools at year 3 of the programme.

Pursuing excellence

An excellent middle years education must combine the creative energy and freedom of the best primary education with the intellectual rigour and challenge of a college-entry programme. The IB certainly understands this. It has resisted calls, both from within and with-out the organisation, to provide an off-the-shelf curriculum and external examinations that would satisfy a number of existing and potential MYP schools; providing such a programme would be relatively straightforward and more financially attractive for the organisa-tion. Instead the IB has persisted in providing a curriculum framework that insists schools and teachers focus on developing their students as rounded human beings, and that they collaborate closely to develop a curriculum that is coherent, reflective of their students and aspirational. While the IB will now offer external assessments to those who want them, it is developing the type of assessments that will, as closely as possible, assess the type of learning the programme promotes.

The IB has not taken any easy paths with this revised MYP, and the results are yet to be seen. What it has done is taken the best of the MYP, as evidenced by the last 20 years of successful implementation, and strengthened the elements that combine to create what is acknowledged to be an excellent middle years education.

Will this new programme bring middle years education out of the shadows? The IB organisation and IB MYP schools will need to implement the revised programme with confidence and determination. There are many in education who would prefer to take the easy educational paths with our 11 to 16 year olds, instead of educating them in the ways that research and practice have demonstrated to be best, thereby doing them a great injustice and society a great disservice.

References

Andrews, P G (2013): *Middle Grades education: emerging from the shadows,* from *Re-search to Guide Practice in Middle Grades Education.* Association for Middle Level Educa-tion, Westerville, Ohio

Berger Kaye, C (2010): *The Complete Guide to Service learning: Proven Practical Ways to Engage Students in Civic Responsibility, Academic Curriculum and Social Action.* Free Spirit Publishing, Minneapolis, Minnesota

Boix-Mansilla, V (2010): *Guide to MYP Interdisciplinary Learning,* International Baccalau-reate Organisation, Cardiff

Cohen, J (1999): *Educating Hearts and Minds: Social and Emotional Learning and the Passage into Adolescence.* Teachers College Press: Columbia, New York

Costa, A L and Kallic, B eds. (2000): *Discovering and Exploring Habits of Mind,* ASCD, Al-exandria, Virginia

Edwards, R (2009): Introduction: life as a learning context? in *Re-thinking Contexts for Learning and Teaching: Communities, Activities and Networks,* Edwards, R, Biesta, G and Thorpe, M, Routledge, eds. London and New York

Erickson, H L (2007): *Concept-based Curriculum and Instruction for the Thinking Class-room.* 2nd edition. Corwin Press Inc., Thousand Oaks, California

Gardner, H (2006): *Five Minds for the Future,* Harvard Business School Press, Boston, Massachusetts

Hargreaves, D (1998): *Creative Professionalism: the role of teachers in the knowledge society.* Demos, London

Harrison, R (2015): *Evolving the IB Middle Years Programme: Curriculum.* International Schools Journal, Vol XXXIV No 2, April 2015

Hattie, J, Biggs, J and Purdie, N (2006): Effects of learning skills intervention on student learning: a meta-analysis. *Review of Educational Research,* 66(2): 99-136

IB (2014): *MYP: From Principles into Practice,* International Baccalaureate Organisation, Cardiff

Johnson, E B (2002): *Contextual Teaching and Learning: What is is and why it's here to stay.* Corwin Press, Thousand Oaks, California

Kolb, D (1984): *Experiential Learning: Experience as the Source of Learning and Development,* Prentice Hall, Englewood Cliffs, New Jersey

Perkins, D N (2010): *Making Learning Whole: How Seven Principles of Teaching Can Transform Education.* Jossey-Bass Publishers, San Francisco, California

Perkins, DN (2014): *Future Wise: Educating our Children for a Changing World.* Jossey-Bass Publishers, San Francisco, California

Peterson, A D C (1987): *Schools Across Frontiers: The Story of the International Baccalaureate and the United World Colleges,* Open Court, Chicago, Illinois

Wagner, T (2008): *The Global Achievement Gap.* Basic Book publishers, New York

Wiggins, G (1998): *Educative Assessment. Designing Assessments to Inform and Improve Student Performance.* Jossey-Bass Publishers, San Francisco, California

Part A
Exploring new directions

Chapter 2

Concept-driven learning in the MYP

Conrad Hughes

In this chapter I explore concept-driven learning in three parts. Firstly, I discuss why concept-driven learning is fundamental for learning, discussing the role concepts have to play in cognitive architecture. Secondly, I investigate and critically evaluate the role of concept-driven learning in the revised IB Middle Years Programme, (MYP) with some background as to how this development has evolved in the programme. In the third part I suggest opportunities for the application of concept-driven learning in the classroom.

What is a concept?

Before taking this three-part journey, let us reflect upon what exactly we mean by a concept and concept-driven learning. The word 'concept' comes from the Latin *concipere*, meaning 'to take in', linked to the word 'conceptum', meaning 'a thing conceived'. A modern definition of a concept is as 'an abstract idea' (Oxford Advanced Learner's Dictionary, 2015).

A concept is an abstract idea that is conceived and taken into the mind. This notion will be important for the chapter as it is in the 'taking in' that an idea, or series of ideas, can be stored and later retrieved, something that is fundamental to concept-driven learning and learning in general. Furthermore, the word 'conceive' is helpful as it evokes being able to imagine something, to see it in the mind's eye and, therefore, grasp it mentally. This reminds us that concept-driven learning hinges on understanding. Checking the understanding of a concept is done by asking the learner to communicate his or her conception, what he or she has configured mentally.

However, a more precise definition of concept is needed for the purposes of this chapter, one that involves unpacking what we mean by 'idea' when referring to concepts, for there are several types of ideas and a concept is not a fleeting memory, a simple mental image or a phrase of meaning, it implies a special kind of idea or often a linking of many ideas: 'Concepts are the mental categories that help us identify, develop and classify objects, events or ideas, building on the understanding that each object, event or idea has a set of common relevant features' (Ecolint–IBE, 2014, p21). The relevant features that allow us to group elements under a conceptual category are usually functions or properties. For example, Ovid's classic *Metamorphoses* (8 AD) has as a fundamental concept the function of change, which runs through the different examples he treats, allowing the reader to synthesise the work with this concept in mind. Practically every verse in the *Metamorphoses* is about the concept of change. This is an illustration of the definition of a concept as 'an abstract or generic idea generalized from particular instances' (Merriam-Webster Dictionary). The 2014 guide to the revised MYP (*Middle Years Programme: Principles into Practice*), referring to Wiggins & McTighe (2005), describes a concept as a 'big idea' – a principle or notion that is enduring, the significance of which goes beyond particular origins, subject matter or a place in time (IB, 2014, p14).

Concepts, therefore, can be described as units of thought that operate at a high cognitive level; a learner cannot show understanding of a concept by iterating different examples alone, he or she must be able to describe the fundamental properties or functions of the thing in question to communicate understanding. For example, to describe the concept of a revolution in history, one cannot simply describe a series of different revolutions, one has to synthesise what these different revolutions have in common, exactly what it is about revolution that means it is not the same thing as change, reversal or rebellion. To grasp a concept is a marvellous learning moment; it is good education, education that ensures understanding.

In sum, to conceptualise is to group information, according to shared properties, into a system at an abstract level of thought, and to be able to carry that system in the mind as an idea. A concept is, essentially, a way of organising information but, as I will show in this chapter, it is an extremely powerful organising principle.

Part One: Why concept-driven learning is fundamental for learning

Cognitive architecture (long-term and short-term memory) and brain schemata

To appreciate the importance of concept-driven learning, we should first turn to the phenomenon of learning and make clear what it entails. The structuring of information in the mind, what we could call the mind's cognitive architecture, consists of working memory (also known as fluid intelligence) and long-term memory (also known as crystallised intelligence). (Baddeley, 1986; Just and Carpenter, 1992; Klahr and MacWhinney, 1998; Sweller, 2003, 2004).

Working memory

New information is perceived and configured by working memory. Working memory involves chunking information into manageable units but can also be used to apply knowledge to new situations. Problem solving, for example, involves mainly working memory capacity.

Working memory, therefore, has a dual function: to organise information and to apply knowledge. It stores and retrieves. To give an example, if someone is asked to find the third side of a right-angled triangle, he or she will use working memory to deduce this, not only by sorting the available information into a manageable unit but also by retrieving knowledge of Pythagoras' theorem and applying it to the new situation.

Working memory is a vital part of brain functioning and can be assessed through intelligence quotient (IQ) tests, particularly items such as non-verbal reasoning, patterning and problem solving requiring no prerequisite knowledge. Another way of describing working memory is as conscious information processing.

Long-term memory

Once information has been picked up and organised in working memory, it is stored in long-term memory. This is the place where information that has been learnt or 'known' is kept and lies dormant, so to speak, waiting to be activated and applied.

Whilst working memory is limited (most people can hold onto three or four chunks of information simultaneously, geniuses can go up to seven), long-term memory capacity is extremely important; there is almost no limit to the amount of information that the brain can 'know'.

Technically speaking, all of the information that has been recorded by the brain remains stored in long-term memory from childhood experiences to events encountered and lessons learned more formally. Subconscious information that makes itself apparent to the conscious mind in dreams, or spontaneously after sensorial stimuli, comes from long-term memory. The famous '*madeleine*' in Marcel Proust's masterpiece *Remembrance of Things Past* is an example of long-term memory. The protagonist, Swann, smells a *madeleine* (a type of French cake) and the olfactory sensations evoke deep memories from childhood that he had forgotten. These memories were stored in his long-term memory and it took the smell of the madeleine to trigger the information from his long-term memory.

Schemata (or schemas)

So learning, at least when it comes to cognition, is the overall system that involves the configuring, storing and retrieval of information through working memory into long-term memory. What has been learnt is what has been stored in long-term memory in such a way that it can be retrieved.

There are a number of ways of storing and retrieving information and these will vary according to the learner and the type of information being manipulated. However, when it comes to storing and retrieving knowledge, it is generally accepted that the most efficient and effective method is through schemata (also called schemas).

The term schema was coined by Bartlett in 1932 to describe the methods people used to reconstruct stories from a limited number of cues. Schemas are mental representations of linked information that allow clear understanding, storage and retrieval. As Pellegrino *et al* point out, referring to research by Wason & Johnson-Laird, 1972, and Cheng & Holyoak, 1985:

> It is well known that people have a good deal of trouble with the implication relationship, often confusing 'A implies B' with the biconditional relationship 'A implies B, and B implies A' […]. [P]eople are quite capable of solving an implication problem if it is rephrased as a narrative schema that means something to them. An example is the 'permission schema', in which doing A implies that one has received permission to do B; to cite a specific case, 'Drinking alcoholic beverages openly implies that one is of a legal age to do so'. [Research has shown]that college students who have trouble dealing with abstract A implies B relationships have no trouble understanding implication when it is recast in the context of 'permission to drink' (Pellegrino *et al*, 2001, p70)

This is an example of how information that might seem difficult to grasp because it is phrased too abstractly can be rendered easily comprehensible if phrased differently. The information has been conceptualised through a schema, a narrative.

Another example is the use of *être* (to be), as an auxiliary verb in French. For a learner to master this rule without any schematic structuring, the most likely path will be the extremely laborious, working memory-taxing method of rote learning (or learning off by heart): verbs that take *être* are *devenir, revenir, monter, rester, etc*). Note that this is not only a difficult way of learning the verbs but will also require large amounts of mental energy to retrieve as well. A better step would be to organise the information that must be learnt off by heart into a mnemonic such as the acronym Dr Mrs Vandertramp, for which each letter stands for a verb. This makes it easier to store and retrieve the information as each letter acts as a trigger to draw the information out of long-term memory.

Many acronyms are used to learn patterns off by heart such as Richard Of York Gave Battle In Vain (ROYGBIV) to learn the order of the colours of the rainbow. However, there is a simpler, more powerful and elegant way of grasping the verbs that take *être* as an auxiliary: understanding that they are verbs of movement or life. This is not an acronym but an idea, it is not a schema built on memorising, it is a schema built on understanding. This makes it infinitely easier to store and retrieve the information at hand because the schema used is a concept.

Extensive research by De Groot (1945/1965), who studied expert chess players' ways of storing and retrieving information (Egan & Schwartz,1979; Jeffries,Turner, Polson *et al*, Atwood, 1981; Sweller & Cooper, 1985), points out that expert learners use schemata in particularly dynamic ways as opposed to novice learners who do not have techniques or strategies to store information effectively into long-term memory. This is important for educational practice as we can learn from the ways that experts organise information and use this in pedagogical design: 'Results suggest that expert problem solvers derive their skill by drawing on the extensive experience stored in their long-term memory and then quickly select and apply the best procedures for solving problems' (Kirschner, *et al*, 2006, p76).

If the goal is to develop within learners educational strategies that allow for quick selection and application of information for the best problem solving procedure, then the most elegant schema for this is the concept since the concept ensures deep understanding and allows for the most pithy configuration of an idea, requiring the least working memory capacity.

Concepts as pattern builders and connectors of ideas

Patterning

Let us consider the concept of conflict. Within this mental category, many examples can be found, for instance conflict as a general concept can cover wars, battles, power struggles, bitter arguments, political tussles, strong disagreements and so on. If these phenomena are treated separately, storing and retrieving their fundamentals will be difficult and they will be learnt as isolated facts, which means that each one will have to be retrieved separately into working memory in order to apply them. However, if the theme of conflict is recognised within each of them, connections will be made and patterns will be built that will allow for easier schematic organisation and storing.

To give an analogy (so as to conceptualise the point!), imagine a student is asked to memorise the contents of a room with a broken statue in it. Rather than learn each piece separately ('this is a hand, this is an arm, this is a torso' *etc*), the concept of a broken statue of a human will allow the student to understand, identify and store the information almost seamlessly. This is because the phenomena at hand have been successfully grouped in an organising whole, a concept.

The human mind finds it easier to relate objects to one another in a sequence or pattern as we naturally seek global wholes, a phenomenon that has been studied extensively from its origins in 1890s Gestalt psychology through to the more recent field of cybernetics (the study of systems).

The concept as a higher level of thought

If we are to consider a hierarchy of elements in the structure of knowledge, going from facts to topics to concepts to generalisations, concepts operate at the cognitively high level of analysis and synthesis. The higher up the structure one goes, the more grouping and organisation can be found (Erickson, 2012).

At the highest level of intellectual activity we find theory, which is a series of concepts that has been yoked together to form a large system of meaning. Take, for example, Karl Marx's theory of class struggle which relies on numerous concepts (for example the bourgeoisie, the proletariat, mode of production and fettering) that have been linked together into a system that can be generalised across contexts: Marx suggested that all political strife was class struggle.

It is by generalising across all contexts that Marx's idea becomes theory; it implies universal truth, the highest level of human thought. Etymologically, the root of the word theory is *theorein* in Ancient Greek, meaning 'to gaze upon the divine', suggesting that theory is a God-like level of intellectual abstraction.

While it might be too ambitious to expect students to develop their own theories, we should not imagine that this is impossible, which means providing learning experiences that allow them not only to attain conceptual understanding, but to transcend the conceptual realms of understanding and break into an even broader scope of meaning.

The importance of concept-driven learning in 21st century learning

As we are living in an information-saturated world where the world-wide web offers a continuous flow of seemingly disparate information that make processing overwhelming and untenable, the ability to synthesise information is critical.

Concept-driven learning enables the process of synthesis since the learner can pattern information, see common threads, classify and categorise and make suitable connections that allow meaning-making:

> With the exponential growth of information we need to rise to a higher level of abstraction –
>
> 1. to create brain schemata for organizing, and patterning the information base;
>
> 2. to facilitate transfer of learning through time, across cultures, and across situations" (Erickson, 2013).

The 21st century also presents many higher-order concepts to learners such as derivatives, globalisation, offshoring and externalities, each requiring understanding at a demanding level. Furthermore, in an interconnected world where solutions to environmental and social problems can no longer be isolated to particulars but require coordinated action, being able to identify commonalities, build patterns and make interdisciplinary connections is increasingly important and should feature in a twenty-first century education.

Part Two: Concepts in the MYP

Big Ideas

From the initial draft of the MYP in 1987, where emphasis was placed on 'the understanding of concepts' (IB, 2008, p2), to the 2014 iteration of the programme (IB, 2014), concept-driven learning has been central as a driver of deep, interdisciplinary understanding in the MYP, as it has always been in the IB's Primary Years Programme (PYP).

Up until 2014, the role of concepts in the MYP was in the MYP unit planners, where concepts were the building blocks, ensuring that a unit was driven by a unit question that was conceptually based. In the 2008 MYP guide, in the section on Approaches to Learning, teachers and students had to ask themselves what were the 'big ideas' of each of the different subjects groups (p25), the aim being 'to ensure that students are not only knowledgeable about a subject area, but also develop a genuine understanding of ideas and an ability to apply these in new contexts, in preparation for further learning' (p16).

The 2012 IB document, *Teaching the disciplines in the MYP: Nurturing big ideas and deep understanding*, made it clear that teaching should be towards 'key underlying concepts or big ideas [...] A curriculum focused on big ideas strives to provide students not with definitions to remember but with conceptual tools for sense making'. Examples of big ideas included:

the theory of evolution (with its associated notions of natural selection and adaptation) in biology; the atomic theory of matter in physics; expressions (a way to represent, explore and reason quantitatively about situations) in mathematics; and the notion of polysemy (multiple meanings of terms) in language (IB, 2012, p4).

The evolution of concept-driven learning in the MYP

This conceptual focus of the MYP has been phrased differently over time, but with increasing importance and centrality. During the 1980s, as the MYP was drafted, there was a focus on concepts in the broadest sense (IB, 2010, p38). In 1994, the focus was on concepts and skills (p38), pointing out that one relies on the other for meaningful, knowledgeable action. In 2008 the idea of a 'significant concept' was prominent. What are the big ideas? What do we want our students to retain for years into the future? (p68), flanked by a concept statement (2008). Note that 'Since 2008, the MYP thinking in the area of developing significant concepts has been strongly influenced by Erickson, H L. 2002. 'Concept-based curriculum and instruction: teaching beyond the facts'' (IB, 2010, p34).

From 2014 concepts play a predominant role in the MYP guide. They are broken down into generic key concepts and subject-specific related concepts, and a detailed description of 'the nature of a concept-driven curriculum' is given (IB, 2014, p15).

Today, concepts are recognised as essential not only in the PYP and the MYP, but in the IB Diploma Programme (DP) too. Conceptual learning is described as a central feature of an IB education in general: 'conceptual learning focuses on powerful organizing ideas that have relevance within and across subject groups. Concepts reach beyond national and cultural boundaries. They help to integrate learning, add coherence to the curriculum, deepen disciplinary understanding, build the capacity to engage with complex ideas and allow transfer of learning to new contexts' (IB, 2014, p13). This programme-wide focus on concepts is expressed in the IB's Learner Profile ('IB learners strive to […] explore concepts […] and develop understanding across a broad and balanced range of disciplines' [IB, 2008, p8]).

By ensuring that students approach their learning through concepts, the MYP is aligned with much research in cognitive psychology and promises students intellectually stimulating, 'ideas centred teaching and learning' (IB, 2014, p15).

Key concepts and related concepts

A significant development in the MYP's approach to concept-driven learning is the notion of prescribed key concepts and related concepts:

MYP programme design uses two kinds of concepts:

Key concepts, contributed from each subject group, provide interdisciplinary breadth to the programme. Key concepts are broad, organizing, powerful ideas that have relevance within and across subjects and disciplines, providing connections that can transfer across time and culture.

Related concepts, grounded in specific disciplines, explore key concepts in greater detail, providing depth to the programme. They emerge from reflection on the nature of specific subjects and disciplines, providing a focus for inquiry into subject-specific content. (IB, 2014, p15)

The new MYP guide has listed the 16 key concepts that all MYP teachers, across the disciplines, are to use in their planning: 'Aesthetics; Change; Communication; Communities; Connections; Creativity; Culture; Development; Form; Global interactions; Identity; Logic; Perspective; Relationships; Systems; Time, place and space' (IB, 2014, p56).

The MYP guide suggests 12 related concepts per subject group for teachers' use in their planning and teaching (pp105-107). Schools are expected to address key concepts with relevant related concepts through the five years of the MYP in order to 'help to integrate learning, add coherence to the curriculum, deepen disciplinary understanding, build the capacity to engage with complex ideas and allow transfer of learning to new contexts' (p13).

Potential problems

At this point, I shall indicate three potential problems about the most recent developments in concept-driven learning in the MYP.

Over-stipluation

The first is that the subtle and often difficult mental process of arranging information into concepts, something that happens in the human mind and allows for powerful breakthroughs of understanding or 'aha' moments, might be hijacked by an approach that insists on a concept-driven approach, so much that it starts to turn concepts into things 'to be learned' and, perhaps, recited rather than discovered. There is something of an industrial level of reference to the word 'concept' in the 2014 guide (it appears no less than 134 times) and in the hands of a zealous teacher, it runs the risk of becoming a rather forced state of affairs.

To continue with this point, we should not lose track of the importance concepts have as schemata: they enable effective coding and retrieval of information in patterns. This process cannot be totally standardised or controlled. By specifying the key concepts that students should approach before they begin to learn the unit, there is a risk of determining too narrow a cognitive path. Even if the key concept is hidden from the student, there is a danger that the teacher's mind will have been engaged in one direction and not another. We must remember that 'concepts can be interpreted differently and explored from various perspectives and at different levels of complexity' (IB, 2014, p15).

Not only should we accept that certain individuals might have unorthodox ways of creating schemata (their own conceptual frameworks), but realise that it is often those who think differently and who conceptualise differently that are exceptionally creative. They should not be tied down by the key concept they were supposed to discover or, for that matter, any specified manner of discovering the concept.

Teachers should be mindful of this danger and scaffold in, accordingly, strategies to keep students' minds open, ensuring that the students are doing the thinking and not merely following a prescribed path.

Trivialising concepts

The second potential problem goes in quite the opposite direction, not to point out the danger of over-stipulating concepts for those students that might wish to fly to different intellectual pastures, but more the danger of trivialising concepts and dumbing them down through superficial treatment.

We have already seen that concepts are strings of facts, topics and ideas drawn together in systems. Each of these facts make up the fibre needed to flex conceptual muscle. An informed, intelligent account of any concept will use examples, anecdotes and explain processes in detail to elaborate and fully master the concept. Indeed, the old idea of demonstrating an argument, of building up to a conceptual high point with iterative steps through substantiation, is what makes for a rigorous analysis.

By offering a curriculum structure that is 'top down' so to speak, where we start with that which is most abstract and generalisable and then look for examples to pack into the concept, there is a risk that superficial or, worse, copied phrases, ideas and beliefs will proliferate and fundamental declarative knowledge will be skimmed over.

There is surely a danger of seeing numerous unit planners peppered with the 16 key concepts but leaving little guarantee of a powerful learning experiences behind them. All sorts of trite things can be said about 'identity', 'communication' or 'connections'. The situation becomes particularly difficult since concepts are primarily verbal constructs, usually single substantives. If students mention concepts and relationships between them, the discourse might be of a high, philosophical standard, but it might also be a sort of lazy man's hit-and-miss, built on throw-away statements such as 'identity depends on community' or 'communication is connection'.

Land *et al* (2005) point out the danger:

> The simplified interpretation of the concept, intended to some extent as a proxy for the fuller, more sophisticated understanding which it was intended to lead on to, was found to operate more frequently as a false proxy, leading students to settle for the naïve version, and entering into a form of ritualised learning or mimicry (p61).

Seeing through this danger, preventing it and assessing genuine conceptual understanding built on rigorous factual knowledge, is a challenge that teachers should engage in by ensuring that students are consistently drawn out of one word responses to explain their understanding fully.

Understanding the relationships between concepts

The third potential problem for teachers is that the relationship between related concepts and key concepts remains fuzzy in their minds, stopping purposeful course planning. The 2014 MYP guide is not entirely helpful in this regard. If related concepts are supposed to be disciplinary (or subject-specific), then one would expect the guide to give known examples of domain-specific concepts (force and gravity in physics, adaptation, metabolism and evolution in biology and so on). However, the related concepts given as examples are much broader and tend to be repeated across subject areas (for example: Genre, Innovation, Interpretation and Narrative for the arts or Evidence, Form, Function, Interaction, Models, Movement, Patterns and Transformation for the sciences [p106]).

One has to ask what the real difference is in the level of generalisability and abstraction, between the key and related concepts. In fact, some are repeated in both categories ('form' is a key concept and a related science concept for instance). Personally, I would argue that 'consequences' and 'patterns' (related concepts for modular science) are more generalisable and at a higher level of abstraction than 'global interactions', which is meant to be a key concept.

A way around this pitfall is to ensure that teachers discuss related concepts in planning groups in order to reach some common understanding on what is meant by them and how they can be interpreted, modified, adapted to context and related to key concepts effectively.

Part Three: Concept-driven learning in the MYP

Despite these potential problems, the MYP's focus on concept-driven learning is an opportunity for excellence in teaching and learning. In this last part of the chapter I offer some suggestions for meaningful teaching and assessment of conceptual understanding with reference to the International School of Geneva's *Guiding Principles for Learning in the 21st Century*, published jointly with UNESCO's International Bureau of Education.

Scaffolding

Teachers should take care to guide students' thinking (but not to do the thinking for them) so that as they learn the constituents of knowledge, they ascend its structure:

Students need to be taken through the process going from:

- factual knowledge (separate pieces of information);

- to topics (which are groupings of pieces of information);

- to concepts (ideas within and across topics that identify the common characteristics linking pieces of information to one another);

- to principle generalisations (laws);

- and, eventually, to theory, where broad statements can be made about the body of knowledge in question (Ecolint-IBE, 2014, p21).

An example can be given in English literature using Shakespeare's play *Macbeth*:

Level	Assessment tasks
Factual: understanding the characterisation of the play's major characters (Macbeth, Lady Macbeth, Banquo, Duncan, Malcolm, the witches)	Informal: reading, discussion, presentations, hot-seating (empathy exercise), acting Formal: textual commentary
Topic-based: establishing themes in the plot that can group traits, behaviours and statements (themes of jealousy, ambition, naiveté, fate, belief, knowing one's place in society)	Informal: discussion, acting with emphasis on themes, brainstorming Formal: thematic essay, research project, debate
Conceptual: yoking these themes into concepts (the Great Chain of Being; ambition; heroism) and then setting tasks for students to connect these concepts to the appropriate MYP key concepts	Informal: group work, discussion, brainstorming Formal: projects using multimedia (film, posters, creative writing)
Generalisation: setting tasks for students to generalise about the play	Summative essay on higher-order question
Theoretical: (extension) probing students for theoretical positions	More challenging essay, project, comparison with other Shakespearean tragedies

Threshold concepts

A threshold concept is a useful term for referring to those concepts that are so fundamental to understanding that the student will be unable to move on until they are fully grasped. Such a concept 'represents a transformed way of understanding, or interpreting, or viewing something without which the learner cannot progress' (Ecolint–IBE, 2014, p22). Teachers need to be sensitive not only to the nature of threshold concepts but the way that learners react to them. 'As a consequence of comprehending a threshold concept there may thus be a transformed internal view of subject matter, subject landscape, or even world view, and the student can move on' (Land *et al*, 2005, p53). Teachers need to identify those related concepts that are crucial for understanding within a domain and ensure that they have been well understood before moving on to the next set of concepts in the curriculum. Examples of threshold concepts include fractions, buoyancy, photosynthesis, gravity, analysis, and numerous examples from economics such as opportunity cost, price and value, equilibrium.

Often, a threshold concept is 'troublesome knowledge' (Land *et al*, 2005, p61) that takes a while to master. The time that a learner spends contemplating a concept, known as a "liminal space", often evokes hesitancy, frustration and self-doubt. When in a liminal space:

> One outcome is that students present a partial, limited or superficial understanding of the concept to be learned which we have characterised as a form of 'mimicry'. A more serious outcome is that students become frustrated, lose confidence and give up that particular course. (p55)

So patience is needed, as is encouragement and a classroom environment where students are given the space, time and support to appreciate concepts, particularly difficult ones, in such a way that they have been fully mastered and the student has left the liminal space, crossed the threshold and entered into a zone of better understanding.

We should also note that concepts are difficult because they cover not only knowledge but contexts that can be highly destabilising. Perkins points out that the understanding of concepts relies on entire circuits that can evoke variable levels of predictability, called 'underlying games' (2005). The underlying game is not the concept itself but the conditions that lie beneath the concept. For example, students might grasp the necessary concepts in physics when applying them to electrical circuits but will experience difficulty when confronted with the underlying game of the 'highly unpredictable and surprising ways in which complex circuits might behave' (Land *et al*, 2005, p55). Similarly, 'in computer programming [...] students may grasp the concepts of class, objects, tables, arrays, and recursion, but they may not appreciate [...] the underlying game, of the interaction of all these elements in a process of ever-increasing complexity' (pp55-56)

This points to the importance of conjugating conceptual learning with applications that allow not only for applied skill development, but richer understanding of the relationships between contexts and concepts and, therefore, the degrees of mutability that can be expected or tolerated when handling concepts.

Assessment

There are numerous ways of testing understanding of threshold concepts but, like all quality assessment, they should involve a range of learning experiences and types of evidence of learning. The MYP general grade descriptors (IB, 2014, p93) are useful for establishing a gradation of conceptual thinking from 'limited' to 'comprehensive, nuanced understanding'. Typical strategies for the testing of conceptual understanding include:

- conceptual essay questions: requiring students to substantiate their understanding of a concept (command terms such as 'analyse', 'evaluate', 'compare and contrast', 'explain' are helpful);

- transposition tasks: whereby understanding is to be represented in a number of forms, verbal and non-verbal (diagrammatic, figurative, verbal, narrative, musical, mathematical, theatrical). Projects, presentations or creative assignments work well for this;

- analogy: whereby students show understanding of a concept by comparing it to something, usually an object, situation, system or image. Projects, creative assignments or reflective statements can evoke this type of thinking;

- models: where a concept is structured physically or mentally by giving it tangible form. This could be done by students designing, programming, drawing or explaining their models through presentations and projects;

- verbalising: done in class debates, interviews, viva voces, requiring students to articulate their understanding of a concept;

- application of a concept to a new situation through a creative assignment (designing a political system, peace treaty, transportation system, *etc*).

The assessment question is critical and will be one of the first things that teachers should reflect upon as they design units of work. The chapters in this book on eAssessments and school-based internal assessments should be read in conjunction with this chapter to enable the design of the most valid and reliable assessments for conceptual understanding.

Conclusion

Concept-driven learning is a powerful way of managing information, developing higher-level understanding, generalising across contexts and disciplines and preparing students for a complex interrelated world. The MYP gives teachers many tools to do this. IB publications that are particularly useful for more reflection on the development of concept-driven teaching and learning include Erickson's *Concept-based teaching and learning* (2012) and the IB's *Teaching the disciplines in the MYP: Nurturing big ideas and deep understanding* (2012).

The potential pitfalls mentioned earlier in this chapter can be overcome by careful, coordinated and thoughtful approaches to the teaching of conceptual understanding so that the core knowledge involved in each concept is well understood and scaffolded pedagogically for each student.

At the International School of Geneva, our guiding principles state that we 'should ensure that the curriculum [...] is structured around concepts-focussed learning objectives; interdisciplinary projects should have a clear conceptual focus; there should be continuous appropriate professional development in concepts-focussed learning [and] the school administration should ensure that time is set aside for teachers to collaborate and plan together in order to teach interdisciplinary projects' (Ecolint-IBE, 2014, p23).

Some of the steps that we have taken to embed concept-driven learning more fundamentally in teaching and learning are:

- ensuring that big ideas or concepts feature prominently in learning objectives so that learning experiences are not described as a series of procedures or list of topics but conceptually.

- working with renowned experts in the field of concept-driven learning.

- designing units of work that have a conceptual focus. Examples of such units at our *Campus des Nations* include 'the importance of water for human settlement' (Humanities, MYP 1); Heroes in Literature (Language A, MYP1); 'Revolution' (Humanities, MYP 3) and 'Diseases and Immunity' (Science, MYP 2).

- designing units of work that allow students to climb up the ladder of abstraction to the conceptual space that is the high road of transfer, but without dictating to students what those concepts or theory-making connections should be once they are in that space. In other words, anticipating concept-formation but not prescribing it.

For a truly conceptual focus to be sustained in learning, an effort is required by the teacher and learner to engage with thought at a consistently high level and not to lapse into trivia. This requires the teaching body to behave as a community of lifelong learners, constantly researching higher-order thinking, up-skilling in cognitive psychology and reading around the topic. At the International School of Geneva we run a Masters in Education course in collaboration with Durham and Geneva Universities through our Institute of Learning and Teaching, this allows colleagues to follow a post-graduate level study of education as they teach.

In the final analysis, if a thought is to be retained, it is that teaching concepts is not an end in itself, it is part of a larger design stated eloquently in 1972 by Alex Peterson, the first Director General of the IB:

> What is of paramount importance in the pre-university stage is not what is learned but learning how to learn … What matters is not the absorption and regurgitation either of fact or pre-digested interpretations of facts, but the development of powers of the mind or ways of thinking which can be applied to new situations and new presentations of facts as they arise (Peterson, 1972, cited in International Baccalaureate, 2012, p2).

References

Baddeley, A. (1986): *Working memory.* Oxford: Clarendon Press/Oxford University Press.

Bartlett, F.C. (1932): *Remembering: a study in experimental and social psychology.* New York: Macmillan.

Cheng, P.W., and Holyoak, K.J. (1985): Pragmatic reasoning schemas. *Cognitive Psychology, 17*(4), 391-416. Academic Press.

De Groot, A. D. (1965): Thought and choice in chess. The Hague, Netherlands: Mouton. (Original work published 1946)

Egan, D. E., & Schwartz, B. J. (1979): Chunking in recall of symbolic drawings. *Memory and Cognition,* 7, 149–158.

Ecolint-International Bureau of Education (2014) *The Guiding Principles for Learning in the Twenty-first Century,* page 21. http://www.ecolint.ch/sites/default/files/document_files/guiding_principles_brochure.pdf

Erickson, H.L. (2007): *Concept-based Curriculum & Instruction for the Thinking Classroom.* Corwin Press Pub.

Erickson, H.L. (2012): *Concept-based teaching and learning.* International Baccalaureate Organization.

Erickson, H.L. (2013): Concept-based Curriculum and Instruction– *Engaging the Child's Mind.* Presentation at the 9th Annual Education Conference at the International School of Geneva.

Land, R., Cousin, G., Meyer, J.H.F & Davies, P. (2005): Threshold concepts and troublesome knowledge (3)*: implications for course design and evaluation. Rust, C (ed) (2005) Improving Student Learning Diversity and Inclusivity. Oxford: Oxford Centre for Staff and Learning Development.

IB (2008): MYP: From principles into practice. Cardiff: International Baccalaureate Organisation.

IB (2010): History of the Middle Years Programme. Cardiff: International Baccalaureate Organisation.

IB (2012): Teaching the disciplines in the MYP: Nurturing big ideas and deep understanding. Cardiff: International Baccalaureate Organisation.

IB (2014). MYP: From principles into practice. Cardiff: International Baccalaureate Organisation.

Jeffries, R., Turner, A., Polson, P., & Atwood, M. (1981). Processes involved in designing software. In J. R. Anderson (Ed.), Cognitive skills and their acquisition (pp255–283). Hillsdale, NJ: Lawrence Erlbaum Associates, Inc

Just, M.A., and Carpenter, P.A. (1992): A capacity theory of comprehension. Individual differences in working memory. *Psychological Review, 90*, 122-149.

Kirschner, P.A, Sweller, J., Clark, R.E. (2006): Why Minimal Guidance During Instruction Does Not Work: An Analysis of the Failure of Constructivist, Discovery, Problem-Based, Experiential, and Inquiry-Based Teaching. Educational Psychologist. 41(2), 75–86, Lawrence Erlbaum Associates, Inc.

Klahr, D., and MacWhinney, B. (1998): Information processing. In W. Damon, D. Kuhn, and R.S. Siegler (Eds.), *Cognition, perception, and language (5th Edition, Volume 2)*. New York: Wiley.

Land, R., Cousin, G., Meyer, J.H.F. and Davies, P. (2005): Threshold concepts and troublesome knowledge (3)*: Implications for course design and evaluation. In C. Rust (Ed.), *Improving student learning diversity and inclusivity*. Oxford, UK: Oxford Centre for Staff and Learning Development.

Ovid. *Metamorphoses (8 AD)*. Trans. A. D. Melville (2008): Oxford: Oxford University Press.

Oxford Advanced Learner's Dictionary, 8th edition (2015). Oxford, Oxford University Press.

Pellegrino, J. W., Chudowsky, N., and Glaser, R. (2001:. *Knowing What Students Know: The Science and Design of Educational Assessment.* Washington, DC: National Academy Press.

Peterson, A.D.C. (1972): *The International Baccalaureate: An experiment in International Education.* London. George Harrap.

Sweller, J., & Cooper, G. A. (1985): The use of worked examples as a substitute for problem solving in learning algebra. Cognition and Instruction, 2, 59–89.

Sweller, J. (2003): Evolution of human cognitive architecture. In B. Ross (Ed.), The psychology of learning and motivation (Vol. 43, pp. 215–266). San Diego, CA: Academic.

Sweller, J. (2004).:Instructional design consequences of an analogy between evolution by natural selection and human cognitive architecture. Instructional Science, 32, 9–31.

Wason, P.C., and Johnson-Laird, P. (1972): *Psychology of reasoning: Structure and content.* Cambridge, MA: Harvard University Press.

Wiggins, G, and McTighe, J. (2005): *Understanding by Design.* Expanded 2nd edition. Alexandria, Virginia. Association for Supervision and Curriculum Development.

Chapter 3

Making a difference: Achieving the IB mission through Global Contexts in the MYP

Alexandra Holland

Introduction

I remember the moment clearly, although it was over 25 years ago. I was in a mathematics lesson, toiling away on a rare hot summer's day in the UK. We were working on matrices and a whole page of problems needed to be solved before we could escape to the cool of the school field at lunchtime. I enjoyed the process of solving the problems as a mathematical exercise, there was a neatness to it that was quite satisfying when you got the correct answer. But I couldn't understand what this was for, beyond keeping me from a chat with my friends under the shade of a tree. So, I put up my hand and asked the question all teachers have heard at one time or another: 'Why are we doing this?' Back came the timeless, frustrated response from my teacher: 'Because it's on the exam.'

Of course I've since had students ask me the same question, on topics ranging from Stalin's agricultural policies, to the Mfecane in Southern Africa, to the New Deal. It's an aggravating question, it implies disengagement with the lesson that is easy to take personally, but it is a valid one. The answer my teacher gave me can be a tempting response at times, but we need to go beyond this if we want to maintain the credibility and integrity of our classrooms.

The question arises from students' need to see the relevance of what they are learning to their current or future lives. While the focus of the revised IB Middle Years Programme (MYP) on conceptual learning creates a curriculum that is highly transferable, giving students considerable flexibility to adapt their learning to new ideas and situations, it is through contextual grounding that students will see the immediate or long-term relevance of what they are studying.

The six Global Contexts of the revised MYP provide a structured approach through which we can bring together conceptual understanding, content and practical skills, to explore real-life issues and the challenges facing our societies. They allow for an inter-disciplinary approach to significant ideas, highlighting the connections between different academic disciplines and the ways that they work together to create our understanding of the world. The Global Contexts are also crucial in building students' intercultural understanding. These elements all respond to the IB mission 'to develop inquiring, knowledgeable and caring young people who help to create a better and more peaceful world through inter-cultural understanding and respect' (IB, 2013).

However, building a curriculum that develops students with the contextual understandings they will need to make a difference in the world, requires thought and planning at a whole-school level. When approaching the Global Contexts, MYP schools need to work in an inter-disciplinary way, coming together across subject group boundaries to answer the following questions:

- How can we establish what is a 'significant' issue for our students?

- How can we build passion for these issues, which will inspire students to make a difference both now, and in the future?

- How can we ensure that the understandings we build in this area reach the level of complexity that will allow students to effectively create positive change?

By answering these questions we can leverage the Global Contexts as a means to create a curriculum that will both equip and inspire students to address the key challenges of the 21st century.

The Global Contexts

The Global Contexts emerged from the three fundamental concepts of the original MYP from 1994: Holistic Learning, Intercultural Awareness, and Communication. Introduced with the review of the MYP in 2014, Global Contexts replaces the old 'Areas of Interaction' and builds on the transdisciplinary themes embedded within the IB Primary Years Programme (PYP). They form a key element of the inquiry process and provide a common structure for students to think holistically, making links between the concepts and content covered, and students' own experiences of the world around them. The six Global Contexts, each composed of a pair of complementary concepts and overarching focus questions, are:

- Identities and Relationships – Who am I? Who are we?

- Orientation in Space and Time – What is the meaning of 'where' and 'when'?

- Personal and Cultural Expression – What is the nature and purpose of creative expression?

- Scientific and Technological Innovation – How do we understand the world in which we live?

- Globalisation and Sustainability – How is everything connected?

- Fairness and Development – What are the consequences of our common humanity?

(IB, 2014b)

The questions help teachers and students to identify the big ideas inherent in each context. Schools may add further contexts to this list if they wish to, to include ideas of specific relevance to their own context. (IB, 2014a)

Each of the contexts is designed to promote the building of intercultural understanding and global engagement, thus ensuring that the curriculum meets the mission of the IB. They cover the broad spectrum of human activity and, while some subject groups will find more congruence with some contexts than with others, it is hoped that through the five years of the MYP subject groups will venture into less obvious connections, allowing for the exploration of varied perspectives (IB, 2014a).

Linking concepts and contexts

The MYP rests upon the balance of conceptual and contextual learning. Abstract concepts are important building blocks for the future transfer of ideas and understandings, but it is the contextual learning that gives these concepts immediate relevance to students' current and future lives. Many researchers have focused on the critical importance of students being able to see the connections between the knowledge they have gained and its practical application, with Wim Westera concluding that 'decontextualisation of education tends to produce "arm-chair scholars", who may well obtain high marks, but lack meaningful insights and under-standing that are required for using the knowledge in a productive or creative way' (Westera, 2011). It is therefore essential that curriculum planners within the MYP place equal emphasis on the concepts and the context to be explored through the unit of inquiry (the name given to the planner for units of work published by the IB), ensuring that balance is maintained be-tween these two approaches.

Linking concepts, context and skills requires careful planning, but when done well can lead students to much deeper levels of thinking. Erickson and Lanning describe this as 'synergistic thinking', where students are able to step back and think critically about material to arrive at a larger conceptual understandings. They suggest that although this thinking specifically demands the synergy of factual and conceptual content, the process partly derives from work that engages students intellectually and emotionally, as this fosters students' fascination with the subject (Erickson and Lanning, 2014). The importance of linking the cognitive and affective, the heart and the head, is fundamental to successful education of young people. This engagement comes from students learning about issues that have relevance to them, again showing the importance of using the Global Contexts to build a curriculum with explicit connections to students' lives.

The Global Contexts within the curriculum

Every MYP unit needs to be based around one of the Global Contexts but this should not add extra content or detract from the time to be spent on building factual or conceptual under-standings. By linking the Statements of Inquiry and Inquiry Questions in the unit planner to the Global Context, teachers can embed it within the fabric of the unit, rather than creating an 'add-on' that would demand extra teaching time. The key to including the Global Context can often come through asking the 'Why are we doing this?' question, which will start to highlight the relevance of the learning to real-life issues. The Global Contexts are therefore an opportunity to enrich the learning taking place, stimulate discussion, and address complex or controversial ideas. There will be many inquiries that can link to more than one of the Global Contexts but it is often desirable to develop one context in depth, whilst acknowledging other relevant questions and ideas, as this allows for the development of more nuanced under-standings.

The Global Contexts provide a bridge between academic disciplines, creating opportunities for links to be developed between subjects. The framework they provide allows students to make connections and to combine their conceptual understanding from different areas in organised ways, thus providing coherence and structure. The culmination of this process is the creation of inter-disciplinary units, where two or more subjects will come together to explore an idea or issue through the common lens of the Global Context. In doing so students approach knowledge in more authentic ways. It is rare that complex real-life problems are solved by one discipline working in isolation.

With the introduction of the Global Contexts as a fundamental part of the MYP electronic assessments (eAssessments), summative assessments in five subject groups offered at the end of year 5 of the programme, this area of the programme is taking on more prominence than the Areas of Interaction had in the original MYP. The eAssessments for each session will be centred on one Global Context, announced to schools approximately six months before the assessment. The Global Context will anchor the assessments, tying each to a common idea and leading students into the culminating Interdisciplinary eAssessment. Students will need to be familiar with the process of exploring ideas from multiple disciplines and the Global Contexts will allow them to build this skill throughout the five years of the MYP. The Global Contexts also play an important role in grounding the Personal Project, the culminating experience of the MYP, in a real world context, ensuring that it does not remain an ab-stract act of creation, but maintains a sense of relevance and purpose.

International Mindedness

The terms international and global address slightly different, but connected, points of view, which are explained in a key IB document *What is an IB Education?* (IB, 2013). Whilst 'international' focuses on how different nation states relate with one another, 'global' looks at the planet as a single entity and deals with ideas that affect us all, regardless of context (IB, 2013).

International mindedness has been defined in different ways, but is commonly seen as a willingness to be open to understanding difference within the world, particularly in terms of mindset, and the ability to engage in productive ways of bridging these differences. The Global Contexts were specifically designed to embed into the MYP curricular framework the idea of our 'common humanity and shared guardianship of the planet', as stated in the preface to the IB Learner Profile (Harrison, 2015).

The Global Contexts are a vital tool in building students' international mindedness, through the use of 'the world as the broadest context for learning' (IB, 2013). They allow schools to expose students to relevant national, international and global issues and encourage consideration of these from a variety of perspectives. The issues covered may well be global but can be linked to local or national concerns. Students will need to consider the experiences and perspectives of people different from themselves, perhaps from other national, religious, geographic, ethnic or chronological contexts, in order to truly engage with these issues. They can also see how the application of concepts can alter in different contexts, building a more flexible and open-minded approach to knowledge.

There is a need for us to take a more 'global' perspective in approaching many of the challenges of the 21st century. From migration, to combating infectious disease, to intellectual property rights, we are increasingly faced with issues that cannot be solved by the efforts of any one nation state working alone. It is essential that we are able to bridge our differences to find co-ordinated strategies and responses if we are to move forward successfully (Rischard, 2002). By creating learning experiences that make students aware of their own assumptions, and that force them to think beyond them, the Global Contexts can be vital in building the mindset that will allow for successful pluralistic engagement, preparing students to go beyond passive tolerance, and to actively engage in collaborative work with people who are different from themselves.

The Global Contexts therefore play a crucial role in breaking down boundaries and forcing us to venture beyond the limits that both disciplinary boundaries and national perspectives can place on our thinking. They ensure that we are exploring ideas in all their complexity, and effectively preparing students to apply their learning in real-life contexts.

How can we establish what is a 'significant issue'?

Whilst key concepts are prescribed by the IB, context is largely left up to the school to determine. Freedom from great lists of prescribed content continues to be one of the most rewarding aspects of working with the MYP. However, there is only a finite amount of curriculum time and we must therefore make choices as to which ideas and issues are most worthy of attention in our particular contexts. Such choices need to be weighed carefully, considering the location of the school and the demographics of the student body. In schools where students come from a wide variety of nationalities it is important that they are able to explore their own cultural origins, however it is also essential that they are able to make meaning from the context in which they are growing up, as this has immediate relevance to their daily lives. In schools with a more homogenous student body, choices need to be made about the most relevant international examples to be included, ones that will add complexity to their understanding of their context and the world.

Establishing what is 'significant' for students is no straightforward task, but is essential for all curriculum designers, whether or not they work with IB programmes. Take the complex variety of students who make up any classroom today, add in a rapidly changing world and a growing roster of challenges brought on by the increase of globalisation, and there is a huge number of different issues vying for inclusion. It is important that we make choices about which issues to focus on, or we face the danger of trying to do far too much and, as a result, covering none of the issues in a sufficiently deep and nuanced way. If each subject area simply decides for itself what to focus on and when, we can end up with in incoherent mish-mash of different ideas being explored, with students hopping from one to the other with little coherence or progression in their thinking. Teachers therefore need to come together, perhaps also with students, to decide what the most significant issues are for their particular context and student body, and map a coherent progression of these issues within the curriculum.

How can this be done? In our own context in Mombasa, Kenya, we approached this by bringing interested teachers together from a range of curriculum areas. They worked in small groups to brainstorm ideas about what an 'informed Kenyan' should know about his or her own country and the world. Through asking the questions, 'Why does this matter?' or, more brutally, 'So what?' we were able to narrow down the wide range of ideas by prioritising some and combining others. The resulting list included a range of global, international, national and local issues that we felt were important for students to have engaged with during their time in the school. The focus was on understanding their local context, and ways in which quality of life could be improved for individuals and groups, whilst adding global issues that could enrich their understanding of Kenya. A few examples of issues linked to understanding the Kenyan context included:

- the importance of storytelling and oral traditions to the Kenyan identity
- the impact of the Indian Ocean on Kenyan culture and economy
- Kenyan technological innovations, and their impact on society
- the success of Kenyan runners
- the strengths and weaknesses of Kenya's new constitution

Members of the curriculum team then worked to coordinate coverage of the range of issues within the curriculum as a whole, linking to the relevant Global Contexts.

This process did not lead to universal answers, or a definitive list of 'what to teach', but it did give teachers a chance to come together to consider the role of the Global Context in building students' larger understandings. It also enriched our own sense of the larger goals of an MYP education, beyond simply preparing students for the IB Diploma Programme (DP). David Perkins has written about this process as being 'intrinsically educative' for teachers and a step on our own 'way to wisdom.' (Perkins, 2014)

How do we build passion for these issues in students?

It is all very well learning about the world and the key questions facing civilisation today, but knowledge and engagement are two separate things. An important challenge we face is turning the Global Contexts into living themes that students can identify in the world around them, and within which they find issues that they feel passionate about. It is only through sparking this passion that we will help create students who will be willing and able to achieve positive change in the world. Methods to kindle this individual interest will be different for every student, each will have their own 'spark' that ignites their curiosity, but there are ways that we can organise the curriculum and learning to help students engage personally with the Global Contexts, making explicit their connection with our local environment.

It is therefore essential that schools give students the opportunity to build connections within their local community that will transform learning from the abstract to the concrete, and stimulate students' curiosity. To build genuine engagement students need to get out from behind their textbook or screen and see and experience the real world. By observing the real-life relevance of their learning to their own lives, or those of others, students come to understand the relationship between academic learning and practical action.

Through the 'Fairness and Development' Global Context a school might decide that students should understand how people can, as members of civil society, influence others to make change. This would link to ideas about our rights and responsibilities as members of communities, and peace and conflict resolution. Students could study activism and protest within subject groups such as Individuals and Societies, Language and Literature, and Arts, focusing on the reasons that people desire change, and the methods they use to achieve this. This is an interesting inquiry, with some engaging stories for students to follow, but it is through real-life application that students can begin to be passionate about speaking up on the issues they believe to be important. Taking a local issue that is relevant to their own lives, or those of people around them, and working in different ways to lobby for change can allow students to experience the process first-hand and bring the learning alive.

Service and experiential learning can be very influential here. A strong service learning programme, that gets students actively involved in their local community, can bring the Global Contexts alive in very real ways. How better to understand the links between individuals and civilisations, or the different ways we express ideas and feelings, or the impact of technology and economic activities on society, or the ways that groups of people make decisions, than by practical engagement with our wider community? Through mixing with people who are different (and sometimes age or socio-economic differences within our own cultural context can be the most challenging differences to overcome) students can come to better understand the Global Contexts. In tandem their classroom learning of the Global Contexts can better inform their work within the community.

Cathy Berger Kaye has written extensively on this symbiotic relationship, showing how the combination of intellectual and emotional engagement, the link between the head and the heart, can lead students to greater understanding and the connecting of previously disparate ideas (Berger Kaye, 2010). An example of this occurred with a group of students from an IB school who became involved in a community service project at a local Kenyan girls' school. Fewer than 50% of girls in Kenya are able to progress to secondary education, with a variety of educational, social, and economic factors standing in their way. (UNICEF, 2012) A group of MYP and DP students visited the school each week, working with the girls to try to help them get the exam results they needed for admission to secondary school. They soon found a complex web of issues that needed to be addressed, going well beyond the academic tutoring that they had begun with. The project deepened their understanding of both 'Fairness and Development' and 'Globalisation and Sustainability'. They saw that education in this context was a finite resource and there were differing ideas about what was a 'fair' distribution of this resource. This led to questions about the interconnectedness of the systems and communities that placed barriers in the way of girls' education. Students became passionate about trying to remove these barriers which led to a greater determination to understand them.

The Personal Project, undertaken in year 5 of the MYP, is another key area in building students' personal engagement with, and thus passion for, issues connected to the Global Contexts. In grounding their project within a specific area, students are able to delve into it in depth, so building more sophisticated understandings. A student who chooses to create a water filter or a poetry anthology needs to build his or her technical understanding of the field, but the addition of the Global Context means that thought must also be given to how science and technology or literature can be used to impact the lives of individuals and communities. The Global Context ties the Personal Project to a real world issue or application, ensuring that students connect with their context. Whilst students often start the Personal Project with a particular product in mind, it can help to clarify their direction if they think in the very early stages about what their learning will be in connection to the Global Context. This gives the creation of their product relevance and purpose, hopefully deepening their commitment to their project. In the best cases students can also go on to build a commitment to change within their wider communities, setting a strong foundation for their later work in the Creativity, Action and Service (CAS) of the IB Diploma Programme.

Community and Service, and the Personal Project are two of many areas of the MYP that allow students to build passion for the ideas and questions raised by the Global Contexts, but it is important to explicitly guide them towards this outcome. This process cannot be left implicit, nor should it be assumed that students will be able to see these connections for themselves (Berger Kaye, 2010). As students engage in these activities we need to give them opportunities to pause and reflect on their learning, to articulate their experiences and to consider the impact these have had on their understanding of the Global Contexts. This will make the links to the Global Contexts far more clearly understood by both students and teachers, and will allow for deeper learning to be achieved in the future.

Ensuring effective action: How can we ensure that the understandings we build in this area reach the level of complexity that will allow students to make a difference?

We can identify significant issues, and also work to build engagement and passion in students, but this can only go so far unless the curriculum is planned in a way that ensures students are sufficiently challenged. Students in the 11-16 age group are in the process of forming their view of the world and we have to ensure that this view is both complex and nuanced. With each curriculum area bringing its own slant to the Global Contexts it can be hard to co-ordinate and it is too easy for the approach to become scattered, with fragmented ideas and little coherence between them. Planning is necessary to build a longitudinal approach to ensure that the ideas and issues chosen by the school are developed in a way that allows students' ideas to progress, and become more complex, as they move through the five years of the MYP.

This issue becomes more challenging for schools that offer all the IB programmes and more challenging again for those schools whose students arrive from other schools and other programmes. The Global Contexts build on the transdisciplinary themes of the PYP, and when teaching students who have completed the PYP, MYP teachers must have a good knowledge of the ideas they have covered so that they can acknowledge and build on their prior learning; it should not be assumed that teachers are starting from scratch in these areas. It is possible to build spirals through the curriculum where students touch upon aspects of each context in age appropriate ways, with each interaction contributing to the complexity of their understanding.

One student's journey through the concepts of 'diversity and inclusion' within the Fairness and Development Global Context

Level	Central Idea/ Statement of Inquiry	Jane's experience
PYP 2	Children around the world encounter differences and similarities in their daily lives.	Jane first encounters the idea of diversity by learning about variety in the lives of children from around the world. When looking at how and why these differences occur she considers the role of both culture and geographical features in creating differences in people's lives. She comes to see diversity as something that occurs naturally between societies, adding to the richness of our world.
PYP 4	Children are a group with specific rights and responsibilities	In thinking about children's rights, Jane starts to consider the idea of inclusion. Through reading the novel 'Out of My Mind' by Sharon Draper, Jane encounters the challenges faced by children with disabilities, and learns how the prejudices they face can lead to them being excluded from social and educational opportunities. She visits a centre for children living with cerebral palsy and takes part in activities with the children there.
MYP 2 – Individuals and Societies	There are things that bind us together in communities, despite our differences.	Jane learns about the diversity that is present in Mombasa, and starts to consider what makes someone a member of the community there. She thinks about whether people mix together to make a blend of cultures, or whether they co-exist, each maintaining their own cultural identity.
MYP 4 – Mathematics	Governments can use statistical tools to make society fairer	Jane considers a scenario in which she is a government minister who has extra funds that could be used by two Kenyan counties to improve education. By analysing data from the two counties she decides which is the best way to allocate the funds using her own definition of what will be the most inclusive or fair distribution. She has to report on and justify her choice.
MYP 5 – Arts	Encounters between cultures can lead to the fusion of ideas and collaborative innovation.	Jane engages with the work of artists who have produced Art that blends cultural traditions from their home and adopted countries. Questions are posed about what it means to be 'included' within a society. Does this mean adopting another culture and shedding your own? By what criteria might people decide how far to adapt their culture to a new context?
MYP – Personal Project	Inclusive activities for children with cerebral palsy	Inspired by her reading of 'Out of my Mind' and her visit to the centre for children with cerebral palsy, Jane plans and runs a series of integrated activities for the children at the centre and students from her school encouraging mutual understanding and co-operative work.

DP Language and Literature	The use of multiple narratives allows us to explore themes from different perspectives.	Jane reads Toni Morrison's novel, 'The Bluest Eye', using this to consider how societies' ideas about beauty can lead to the exclusion of individuals and groups. She thinks about the ideas of conformity and alienation.
DP – Theory of Knowledge	Language can be used intentionally and unintentionally to create inclusive and exclusive environments.	Jane and her class discuss ways that language can be used to include and exclude. Through looking at the use of words to describe minority groups that have become taboo, and have sometimes been 'reclaimed', they think about the power of words, and the ways that language shifts and evolves over time.

In planning in this way, teachers are able to make explicit links to similar ideas students have encountered elsewhere in the curriculum, clearly articulating the connections between inquiries from different parts of the programme. Through making this apparent to students we can draw on the opportunities to get students thinking in more divergent ways, moving beyond the 'boxes' created by subject based or national perspectives. This requires teachers to have knowledge of and build upon one another's work, creating a necessity for strong vertical and horizontal planning.

We have to recognise that simple answers are not enough when thinking about the global contexts in which we live. There are endless nuances, shades of grey, which need to be considered to form a full appreciation of our own experiences and those of others. Issues that face us are not binary and need multi-faceted approaches if they are to be effectively tackled. The ability to tackle complexity cannot be built through a single curriculum iteration or one subject group; such an approach will only result in a series of simple issues viewed in isolation.

Beyond the MYP

The inclusion of the Global Contexts within the revised MYP has created a continuum for students aged between 3 and 16 years, which then halts as students enter the DP or the IB Career-related Programme (CP). How could, or should, these ideas be continued into the final stage of an IB education? These are obviously considerations for another forum, but there are immediate opportunities that schools could take advantage of whilst waiting for formal developments by the IB. Within the DP the Extended Essay allows students similar opportunities to the MYP's Personal Project, and the introduction of the six categories for the DP World Studies Extended Essay, whilst not directly mirroring the Global Contexts, do provide key areas of overlap. Similarly, the Reflective Project in the CP places importance on exploring an issue in context and considering ethical implications, again areas where there is synergy with the Global Contexts. Creativity, Activity, Service (DP) and Community and Service (CP) also provide clear ways to extend practice into these areas, by creating opportunities for students to explicitly link their experiences to their academic learning. Schools that have graduates from the PYP and MYP could easily make these links explicit to students, allowing them to extend their prior learning in these areas and continuing the reflective process.

Similarly when planning curriculum in DP and CP courses there is nothing to stop teachers using the Global Contexts to invite broader and more complex discussion of the material covered. For example, when teaching the Cold War we can make reference back to relevant Global Contexts, considering how far the conflict arose from Identities and Relationships, or how it impacted people's ideas about Fairness and Development. Similar opportunities arise in all curriculum areas and, as most teachers will already link curriculum to real-world contexts, creating connections with the Global Contexts could be relatively straightforward.

Conclusion

George Walker stated that, 'schools must offer an education that strives unashamedly for the highest intellectual standards but connects them to a concept that has become thoroughly unfashionable during the 20th century, that of obligation. It has been assumed in the West that a good education will be the passport to a materially comfortable life. In future a good education, one that connects the intellect to human compassion, must be perceived as the means of providing, as well as receiving, material wealth' (Walker, 2007). Once again, the importance of the connection between the head and the heart, between academic learning and real-world actions, is shown as key to engaging students and achieving the mission of the IB.

The Global Contexts are an opportunity to make learning relevant, to ignite passion for important issues, and to develop students who are willing and able to make a positive difference in the world. They pull together the different elements of the MYP and show students how their learning is applicable to life. It is only through a whole-school approach and deliberate planning that we can fully realise the potential of this area to build a curriculum that will inspire our students to address the key challenges of the 21st century.

References

Berger Kaye, C (2010): *The Complete Guide to Service Learning: Proven, Practical Ways to Engage Students in Civic Responsibility, Academic Curriculum & Social Action.* Minneapolis: Free Spirit Publishing.

Erickson, H L and Lanning, L A (2014): *Transitioning to Concept-based Curriculum and In-struction.* Thousand Oaks, CA: Corwin.

Harrison, R (2015): 'Evolving the IB Middle Years Programme: Curriculum' in *International Schools Journal Volume* XXXIV No.2 April 2015 Pp 45-58.

IB (2013): *What is an IB education?* Cardiff: International Baccalaureate.

IB (2014a): *Further guidance for developing MYP written curriculum.* Cardiff: International Baccaluareate.

IB (2014b): *MYP: From Principles into Practice.* Cardiff: International Baccalaureate.

Perkins, D N (2014): *Future Wise. Educating our children for a changing world.* San Francis-co: Jossey-Bass.

Rischard, J F (2002): *High Noon. Twenty Global Problems, Twenty Years to Solve Them.* New York: Basic Books.

UNICEF (2012): Statistics for Kenya. From: www.unicef.org/infobycountry/kenya_statistics. html [Accessed 10th June 2015].

Walker, G (2007): *"Educating the Global Citizen" – An argument for the case for an interna-tional education, irrespective of whether it takes place in international or national schools.* Speech made at The British Schools of the Middle East conference. Oman. 31st January 2007.

Westera, W (2011): 'On the Changing Nature of Learning Context: Anticipating the Virtual Extensions of the World.' in *Educational Technology and Society* 14(2) Pp201-12.

Chapter 4

Implementing Approaches to Learning: Key strategies for all schools

Lance King

Introduction

Intrinsically motivated learning is achieved through the application of a dynamic, internally controlled set of metacognitive, cognitive and affective processes that positively influence a student's tendency to approach, engage with, expend effort on, and persist in tasks of learning in an ongoing, self-regulated manner (McCombs, 1986). Exactly what everyone does when they are learning something new in which they are intensely interested.

Metacognitive processes are those that focus on the self-management of learning, planning, implementing and monitoring learning efforts, as well as gaining the knowledge of when, where, why and how to use specific learning strategies in their appropriate contexts. Cognitive processes are those which focus on developing the particular skills necessary to facilitate the acquisition of knowledge or skill. Affective processes are those that focus on such non-cognitive aspects of learning as motivation, resilience, emotional management, perseverance and concentration.

> PISA 2012:
> Students who use appropriate strategies to understand and remember what they read, perform at least 73 points higher in the PISA assessment – that is, one full proficiency level or nearly two full school years – than students who use these strategies the least (Programme for International Student Assessment, 2012).

Within such curricula as the UK-based GCSE (General Certificate of Secondary Education), International GCSE, and the New Zealand national qualifications NCEA (National Certificate of Educational Achievement) and many other curricula, there is implicit support given to the direct teaching of learning skills, but only within the International Baccalaureate (IB) is that support explicitly differentiated into a specific subject of its own, Approaches to Learning (ATL), originally formulated for the MYP but now percolating through all four IB programmes.

When the MYP was first conceived in 1980, the driving force at the heart of all thinking was the development of learning to learn skills. This later became known as ATL (Approaches to Learning). Over 30 years later, we know that developing a good ATL programme in schools is possibly the most important feature in preparing students to become lifelong learners, regardless of their educational pathways (IB, 2010).

The overall aim of the ATL component of the MYP is to provide the skills base necessary for any student to become a self-regulated learner and develop all the attributes described in the IB Learner Profile. Such a student, by the time they finish school, will be able to learn effectively and efficiently from any person or any information source, in any format, at any time, in any place, under any conditions, through any media, using any technology, for themselves or others, and by themselves or with others. They will have all the most important 21st century skills of effectively thinking and learning at the highest level of proficiency, that is the level of *self-regulation*, so they can be fully independent in all their learning should they want or need to do so.

The ATL implementation cycle

Having run ten or more IB ATL workshops in the last two years, my greatest concern is the possibility that we are all re-inventing the same wheel. All schools seem to me to have the same concerns and the same key issues, in the initial stages of ATL implementation anyway, and in order to make everyone's process more efficient I want to outline here all that I have learned in the last two years.

I see the whole ATL implementation process as following Kolb's (1984) experiential learning cycle which itself is embodied throughout the IB, from the Primary Years Programme (PYP) through to the Diploma Programme (DP) and now the Career-related Programme (CP), in both the inquiry learning cycle and the design cycle, and which can be simplified down to:

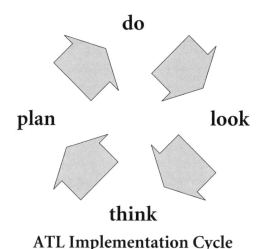

do

plan **look**

think

ATL Implementation Cycle

One thing I have noticed in the last two years is that some schools are getting stuck at different points in this cycle and not getting to the actual implementation phase of ATL. They are getting stuck at the **Think** stage and spending endless committee meetings working through some of the ATL documentation, paragraph by paragraph, or they are getting stuck at the **Plan** stage and spending countless hours designing wonderful horizontal and vertical ATL skills articulation documents. But very little is actually changing in the classroom. No ATL skills are being effectively taught. One key thing I have learnt in the last two years is to start with **Doing**. This is what I intend to outline here: how to get change happening tomorrow; how to start teaching ATL skills tomorrow!

One major mistake I made early on in this whole ATL process was calling the ATL skills framework a *curriculum*. Please do not make this mistake yourself when describing ATL skills to any of your colleagues. Unfortunately when teachers see or hear the word curriculum they immediately build a mental model of subject matter – stuff to teach. That idea leads them to the idea of assessment, and then they start to be concerned about two things: how am I going to teach this stuff when I know nothing about it and how am I supposed to assess this stuff that I know nothing about?

Both concerns tend to create unnecessary blocks and can even derail the whole ATL process before it starts. Both issues are worth addressing but by using different terminology maybe we can get all teachers on board with the ATL skills idea first. I would suggest you describe ATL as a 'framework' or 'structure' for the skills needed to be an effective learner, rather than a 'curriculum'.

The ATL skills framework

For this chapter I will be broadly following the structure of my one day ATL1 workshop, the Powerpoint slides for which you can access at http://taolearn. com/atl_resources/article174.pdf

The full MYP ATL skills framework has three levels of descriptors. I will be using the following words to differentiate between levels of ATL skills:

Categories

There are five categories of ATL skills which are now promulgated through all four IB programmes:

- Communication skills
- Social skills
- Self-Management skills
- Research skills
- Thinking skills

Clusters

These five categories of ATL skills, at the MYP level, are then broken down into 10 clusters:

Communication skills	1. Communication – Interactive and Language
Social skills	2. Collaboration
Self-Management skills	3. Organisation
	4. Affective
	5. Reflection
Research skills	6. Information Literacy
	7. Media Literacy
Thinking skills	8. Critical Thinking
	9. Creative Thinking
	10. Transfer

Practices

The 10 clusters of skills are then broken down within each cluster into over 160 examples of skills practices. For example, within the organisation skills cluster, the first few skill practices are:

3. Organisation: a. Get to all classes on time

b. Plan short and long-term assignments; meet deadlines

c. Create plans to prepare for summative assessments

On my website you can access this full framework at http://taolearn.com/atl_resources/article159.docx

In this document I have numbered all the skill practices to make it easier for teachers to discuss skills by using the same system to identify them, *eg*:

Self-Management (skills category)	
3. Organisation skills (skills cluster)	
Managing time and tasks effectively (skills practices)	
How can students demonstrate organisational skills?	a. Get to all classes on time
	b. Plan short- and long-term assignments; meet deadlines
	c. Create plans to prepare for summative assessments (examinations and performances)
	d. Keep and use a weekly planner for assignments

Please note that this whole ATL framework is not to be considered as either totally exclusive or totally inclusive. It was designed to be a guideline for schools to use to design their own ATL framework. No one will ever be required by the

IB to teach all these skills and practices, or to include all the clusters of skills in their planning. Individual schools and individual teachers are welcome to include more skills, to take out irrelevant skills, and to modify this framework to suit their context.

Why do we need an ATL skills framework?

At some point, early on in the process, it will be important to demonstrate to teachers, students and parents that implementing ATL skills will help all three parties to achieve all their goals more effectively and more efficiently.

Teachers are of course often very sceptical about what they may see as a new *flavour of the month* and sometimes suspect that a new initiative like this is actually a thinly disguised mechanism to get them to work longer, harder or to increase their assessment or accountability burden. It is very important that teachers realise that:

- Helping students to learn more effectively is what good teaching has always been, and will always be, about. Good teachers have always helped students to achieve subject objectives by focusing them on the processes they are using and how to improve those processes. Every teacher is already a teacher of ATL skills, the only real change is to make these skills more explicit, more directly addressed in every classroom.

- Implementing ATL skills will not increase the assessment burden for teachers. There is no requirement from the IB for the assessment of discrete ATL skills.

- There is good evidence to show that students at school often do not have good learning skills and that the teaching of learning skills improves academic, social and behavioural performance – see my literature review for the evidence http://taolearn.com/atl_resources/article156.pdf

- Helping students to improve their ATL skills will improve their classroom performance, help eliminate re-teaching and make teaching both easier and more effective.

- Teachers do not need to be experts in the skills of effective learning, all they have to learn how to do is to make more explicit all the learning processes that are already happening in every classroom.

Students are very pragmatic, if they can see a direct benefit in improving a certain process or skill then they will do so without hesitation. Students need to be made aware of the skills that they use in all learning tasks, and the skills that the best students in school have. They then need to realise that they could all learn the skills of the best students and improve both the efficiency and the effectiveness of their own learning. Once students realise that focusing on skills could make their learning easier, quicker and more effective they will be intrinsically motivated to improve those skills. I suggest surveying students, both present and past, and involving them in designing a programme of skills that they see as being most useful for them.

Parents are the key players in this tripartite relationship. Parents need to be made aware of a few key points:

- The secret of success for their children in the 21st century lies with skills, not content. Skills programmes teaching *21st Century Skills* are presently being implemented in many countries, businesses and schools.

- The IB is leading the way with a comprehensive skills-based framework permeating all IB programmes.

- There is good evidence to show that many students today do not have good learning skills and that such skills can be taught – http://taolearn.com/atl_resources/article156.pdf

- Improving learning skills will also improve subject based and exam based outcomes and prepare their children well for the world beyond school. See https://www.youtube.com/watch?v=mnGoJwBoIrM for a presentation to parents, the slides for which are available at http://taolearn.com/articles/article138.pdf

Process not content

Teachers need to realise that ATL is not a subject in itself, it is a collection of the processes, skills, techniques and strategies needed to learn any and every subject. ATL skills are not more content to be learned; they are processes to be noticed, experienced and improved.

From this point of view, any lesson can be oriented towards the ATL skills students are using, without taking away from the subject matter being taught, simply by adopting a dual focus on both what the students are learning and the skills they are using to learn that subject.

ATL skills architecture

If we look at all the ATL skills a students will need to succeed at school and beyond, and the way those skills are gained through schooling, we can group them into two groups:

- Core generic ATL skills: those which every student, in every class, in every school will need in order to cope with learning in a school environment

- Subject specific ATL skills: those which are involved in the processes of thinking, data capture, information research, representation, manipulation and delivery that are specific to particular subject disciplines

Different types of ATL skill lend themselves to different structures of teaching:

- Explicit teaching means teaching ATL skills outside subject based lessons – teaching a lesson specifically, for example, on time management, note making or concentration, focused on strategies, practices and techniques, using content that exists outside of subject lessons

- Implicit teaching means embedding the teaching of the ATL skills within the subject focused lesson, using the subject matter being taught as the focus of ATL skill practice and development

In order to make the best use of available resources and make sure ATL implementation is not a burden on any one person's shoulders (usually the MYP Coordinator), it is important to find within the school a range of ATL skills champions who will:

- have a particular interest in one particular ATL skill practice

- develop a model of development of that skill: definition, what to teach, how to teach, how many lessons etc.

- seek agreement from peers as to who will teach the skill first, when and where, how to reinforce the skill across all subjects

- take responsibility for the implementation of a particular ATL skill across the school

Core generic ATL skills

These are the ATL skills that apply to every student, that are essential to the learning process and are, therefore, not age specific. These are skills that persist throughout the life of the learner as the most fundamental skills; they do not change in nature, but may well increase in complexity with the age of the learner. For example, research skills are needed by students of all ages, but research for a 7 year old looks quite different to research for an 18 year old. It is the same group of skills but there is a big differences in the complexity of the skill practice.

There are many ways within your school that you could generate a list of your most important core generic ATL skills:

- Different year groups or subject groups of teachers could get together and consider possibilities, and then compare lists. However, I have found that this is usually an inefficient process which creates incomplete lists that often need to be modified later.

- Students can be surveyed at critical points in their school careers and asked what skills they have noticed they need at what points in their schooling, but often they don't know what they don't know, and they are not aware of the skills they are using every day in classes at different levels.

- You could start with a generic list like I have provided below and modify it as needs be.

This is my list of what I consider to be some of the most important core generic ATL skills. It is only a suggestion, a place to start. I have tried to make it as simple as possible, only focused on very basic skills that apply to all students. Please feel free to change the list, take some out and add in different ones, whatever suits your school, your students, your cultural environment and your country. I have grouped the skills under 11 general headings and added in brackets the skill descriptors from the IB MYP ATL skill description framework – available with all these core generic skills highlighted (in yellow) at http://taolearn.com/atl_resources/article160.docx.

1. Managing time – get to school on time; get to class on time; plan and timeline the completion of assignments; plan out study for tests and assignments (3a, 3b, 3c, 3d)

2. Listening – listen actively to others' perspectives and ideas; follow instructions accurately; ask questions to facilitate understanding (2.i, 1.1a, 8.d)

3. Note making – take accurate notes in class; make effective summary notes for studying (1.2i, 1.2j)

4. Staying on task – concentrate, focus, overcome distractions, persevere, persist with specified tasks (4.1a, 4.1b, 4.1c, 4.2a)

5. Working well in a group – listen actively; work collaboratively through different media; build consensus; negotiate effectively (1.1h, 1.1j, 2f, 2h, 2j, 2k)

6. Being organised – bring all necessary equipment to class; keep all notes and information well organised (3g, 3h)

7. Setting goals – set academic and personal goals; plan strategies and take action to achieve goals (3e, 3f)

8. Researching – select appropriate information sources; collect, verify and record information; make connections, process data and report results (6a, 6c, 6h, 6i)

9. Reflecting – reflect on understanding of subject matter, changes in proficiency of ATL skills and effectiveness of learning strategies utilised (5e, 5f, 5g)

10. Remembering – use memory techniques and regular reviews of subject matter to improve retention and recall (3j, 6e)

11. Learning from mistakes – practise analysing and accurately attributing causes of failure; practise 'bouncing back' after failure; practise failing well (4.4a, 4.5a, 4.5b)

If you look closely at this list you will notice that it is made up of examples from each of the three different skill types:

Cognitive – managing time, listening, note making, working well in a group, being organised, setting goals, researching and remembering

Affective – staying on task, learning from mistakes

Meta-cognitive – reflecting

The distinction becomes important when we start to consider how these skills will be taught because each type of skill lends itself to a different method of teaching.

Putting core generic skills into practice

Having decided at your school what the most important core generic ATL skills are for your students, I think the next step is to move directly to the *Doing* phase of the implementation cycle, to where these skills are actually being taught.

To do this try the following process:

Step 1 – Define the ATL skill practice to map out:

First, decide which one of your list of core generic ATL skills is most important for your students. Which one can teachers agree is vitally important for all students and of which there is a demonstrable lack in your students? To demonstrate the process I will use the example of *Taking effective notes in class (1.2.i)*

Notice first that the skill isn't defined as just *note-making* which is a very general skill which could encompass making summary notes for studying, writing scientific reports, creative writing etc. It is just one ATL skills practice as defined in the framework – 1.2.i. It is very clear and precise.

Step 2 – Decide on the appropriate models of skill practice:

Decide, by discussion with relevant teachers, on a few models of note-making in class that would encompass all experiences students could have across the school, in all subjects, from the lowest to the highest levels. After much discussion, the group I was working with most recently decided on six models or methods of note-making in class:

- Mind mapping – known sometimes as spider diagrams

- Linear notes – headings, sub-headings, bullet-points

- Visual note making – picture series, storyboard, cartoon strip, flowchart

- "Cornell" notes – page divided 1/3 2/3, notes written on 2/3 side in class, summaries added in 1/3 column at a later date

- Annotation – highlighting the minimum key words and significant concepts and ideas in printed text

- Fill in the blanks – teacher hands out printed matter with gaps for students to fill in appropriate words

Step 3 – Decide when it is important to teach each model:

Decide when in a child's life at school they will need to be able to take coherent notes in class in each particular way in order to succeed, or when, if they weren't able to do this, would their learning be likely to suffer?

Within the group I was working with, they decided that each one of these six techniques was suitable for a different grade level of student, and so they could be taught in a progression across the years:

- Year 3 – Fill in the blanks

- Year 4 – Visual note making

- Year 6 – Mind mapping

- Year 8 – Linear notes

- Year 9 – Annotation

- Year 10 – Cornell notes

The key decision at this point being when does each note-making method need to be taught? Before it is needed or at the point that it is needed? Keep in mind that students are very pragmatic and there will be no improvement in any ATL skill if it cannot be used and practised immediately. Each note-making method needs to be taught at the point that it will then be used by students.

Step 4 – Find skills champions:

- Survey teachers and find out who already teaches these note-making methods within their normal teaching and when

- If no one does, call for volunteers

- One person with an interest in this area could become the 'Note-Making in Class' skills champion or each different note making method could have its own skills champion

- Each skills champion is then responsible for making sure the particular skill practice is taught to every student at the appropriate time

Step 5 – Get agreement from all teachers on reinforcement:

Once a plan is in place for the direct teaching of each of these note-making methods, by specific teachers at specific times, agreement needs to be reached with all teachers on reinforcement of the appropriate note-making methods. Once all teachers are clear on when a certain note-making method was taught to their students, then after that point directing a student to write classroom notes in a certain way should be the only reinforcement needed in all subject lessons.

Step 6 – Generate visual resources:

Print up a poster showing all six note-making methods clearly, with a diagram and an explanation of each method, clearly showing when each will be taught with year level expectations of skill practice. Post one in every classroom.

Step 7 – Allow for personal difference:

The aim of this exercise is not to become rigid about how notes are taken in class; the aim is to make sure that every student has been specifically taught, and had reinforced, some methods of note-making which will serve them well in all areas of learning at school. One proviso: I would also make sure that teachers in every class allow for personal difference. If a child can demonstrate that they have their own method for note-making in class, which is different from the basic six but works well for them and produces effective notes, then they should be allowed to use that method. Maybe that method could even be included in next year's round of strategies for everyone.

Step 8 – Get it happening – tomorrow!

Get teachers to start teaching and reinforcing these methods – tomorrow. Once the first core generic ATL skill is in place across the whole school, after a suitable time of teaching and reinforcement, then I suggest you get the core ATL group back together again, reflect on the success of the implementation of the process to date, think about what the next one should be, make a suitable plan then repeat the process. If I have learned anything at all about this process in the last two years it is to start small. Get one in place and working well, then move onto the second. This way you start by doing and immediately the experience for the student changes, but only in a small and manageable way.

Subject-specific ATL skills

These are the skills that are involved in the processes of thinking and learning specific to particular subject disciplines. The practise of these skills will of course rely on the development of all of the skills already identified as core generic ATL skills, but to avoid duplication, if we look here only at the ATL skills applicable to different subjects *outside the core generic framework*, then they might include:

- In all language learning – reading, writing for different purposes, key word summarising, paraphrasing

- In Science – creating research questions, designing experiments, gathering and analysing data, drawing conclusions, reporting findings

- In Mathematics – logical, analytical thinking

- In the Arts – creativity, imagination

- In Design – software management skills

- In Physical and Health Education – co-ordination, balance, physical skills

Planning and mapping subject specific ATL skills can be a very similar process to that outlined above for the core generic skills but obviously this process would need to be undertaken by subject specific teams. The important tasks for these teams will be:

1. Deciding what the particular ATL skills are that students need in order to think and learn like a chemist, biologist, artist, geographer *etc.*

2. Identify where and when within the existing framework of the subject these skills are specifically taught at present; map out any existing progressive development of these skills through the school life of a student, as specified in the unit plans or subject guides, and identify any gaps in skill development.

3. Decide by when each subject specific ATL skill needs to be developed, in order for that student to cope with the complexity of the subject at each level.

4. Look to the existing unit plans to find any opportunities to teach these skills within existing lessons.

5. As in the core generic example, identify what model of skill to use, and identify who is going to teach it and when will they teach it. Also plan how you will get buy-in and reinforcement from all subject teachers.

Just as with the core generic skills example, the important factors are getting agreement from all the subject teachers on what model, method or technique to use, teaching the skill, and gaining agreement on reinforcement by all teachers once the skill has been taught. Just as with the core generic skills, my advice would be to start small; just start with one, the most important subject specific ATL skill first. Get that in place, reflect on its success, think, plan and move on to a second skill.

If schools are well down the track with creating MYP units of work then including ATL skills in those plans will have already happened; a lot of subject specific ATL skill mapping can be drawn directly from the existing units of work.

ATL and MYP unit planners

- ATL skills statements are now a requirement that must be written into all units.

- Potentially, many skills may be developed within the teaching and learning in any unit, so it is important to be strategic by considering the criterion command terms, the objective strands, the summative task and the nature of the learning experiences that build to the summative task, each of which can be used to give clear pointers to the ATL skills descriptors at increasing levels of complexity across the years.

- For learning experiences that you plan to deliver within any unit, consider which ATL skills must be practised in order to successfully achieve the objective and access the learning.

- The skill is manifested through the successful completion of the summative task.

- Once the skill is identified in the ATL section of the unit planner the complexity of the use of the skill can then be specified in the ACTION section of the unit planner.

How to teach ATL skills

ATL skills can be taught in many different ways, but the significant distinction in teaching methods that I make is between teaching cognitive and affective ATL skills.

With cognitive skills we can propose a model for students to use, we can point them at the best practice of the best students in the world, we can directly train them in proven strategies and techniques, we can give them exercises to demonstrate the skill and we can help them to practise and practise until they get it right. A basic, explicit, *installation* pedagogy.

Teaching cognitive skills

1. Define the parameters of the skill and engage students in a discussion about what the characteristics of the skill are. How could you tell that someone was an expert in this skill? What would they be able to do that someone who was not very good at it would not be able to do? What are practical examples of high and low proficiency in this skill?

2. Describe best practice in the field. What are some of the models, techniques, strategies that people who are good at this skill use? How do the best students do it? Try asking those students in the class who are good at it how they do it. Get senior students in to explain how they do it.

3. Break each skill down into a straight-forward series of steps, strategies and techniques.

4. Teach your students through practical examples; get them to practise the skill in simple situations, or on simple subject matter first, until they feel they are gaining some mastery of the skill, and then move them onto more complex content or situations.

5. Allow for personal difference. If someone can come up with a different way to achieve the same skill that works as well or better than the prescribed way, it would be good to allow them to do it their way.

Teaching affective skills

Affective skills, such as perseverance, resilience and concentration, can be taught the same way as cognitive skills, using installation strategies, but there are other ways which can be more effective. These are methods which rely more on an *extraction* pedagogy than on *installation*.

a. Drawing out and transferring internalised strategies

1. Define the parameters of the skill, as with cognitive skill teaching, but first be very clear about the definition of the skill because there are sometimes only subtle differences between affective skills, and they often overlap. For example, what is the significant difference between perseverance and resilience? The key characteristic of resilience is getting back up each time you fall down, physically or metaphorically, whereas perseverance can be characterised as 'keeping on keeping on' no matter what. The two often go together but they are not the same. Having defined it, then engage students in a discussion about what the characteristics of the skill are. How could you tell that someone was an expert in this skill? What would they be able to do that someone who was not very good at it would not be able to do? What are practical examples of high and low proficiency in this skill?

2. Then ask students to remember a time when they were exhibiting this skill. This can be done as a straight memory exercise or with eyes closed as a visualisation exercise.

3. Ask them to describe their experience in detail, in writing, focusing on sensations, images, thoughts they remember from that time, ways of talking to themselves, strategies and techniques they employed then.

4. Once they have a description of how they manifest this particular skill, the teacher needs to set up an experience for the students where they can deliberately practise this skill.

5. The more they practise it the more aware of the skill they become and the better at it they become.

6. Then when they need it they are able to do it with purpose.

b. Experientially

Teachers can also sometimes set up experiences for students that bring about the development or use of affective skills like self-motivation, resilience, perseverance, concentration, focus, leadership, 'bouncing back' after mistakes and learning from failure.

- Physical education – many aspects of PE can be used to highlight the development of affective skills

- Outdoor Education – taking students out of the classroom can create opportunities for the development of affective skills

In these situations it is most important for the teacher to simply notice instances of the manifestation of the skill and draw attention to it, maybe asking a student to think about how they did it in order to make it more explicit. For example, 'I noticed in that basketball game that you got knocked down several times, but each time you got straight back up again and joined back in with great energy. Do you know what that is called? That is called resilience. How did you do it? Did you notice what you said to yourself or what you imagined that helped you to get back up again straight away? That is a great skill and all the students in our team could learn from your example. How do the rest of you do this? The same way or differently?'

The point with this type of extraction pedagogy is that it implies for the student several things that I think are very important: I, as the teacher, don't know the best way to do this skill; everyone already knows how to do it and does do it sometimes; everyone does it differently. I can't teach you how, all I can do is to help you to understand how you do it for yourself and then help you to practise it until you get really good at it. Once you are good at it you will have that skill as a resource you can call on any time that you need it.

For more information on teaching all the affective skills please see http://taolearn.com/atl_resources/article148.pdf

Assessing ATL skills

Within your subject guides and your unit plans you will already have standards of assessment for many ATL skills, most commonly the subject specific ATL skills. The question is then, is it necessary to have measurable standards for all ATL skills?

This is a very important question because I am seeing a lot of effort, in many parts of the world, being put into creating sequential frameworks of age appropriate ATL skill standards that children can be measured against to determine their ATL progress, in much the same way as their mathematics proficiency or their biology or languages understandings might be measured. The problem with this approach is that if ATL is a collection of skills of effective learning, then in assessing ATL what we are attempting to assess is the efficiency and effectiveness of learning itself. The process of effective, efficient learning is a very complex amalgam of the influences of many skills, techniques, strategies, aptitudes, attitudes, understandings, motivations, environment, culture and context. It is very difficult, arguably impossible, to objectively and externally measure improvements in the effectiveness and efficiency of the learning process. I think only the students themselves are in any position to measure this at all, maybe by noticing an improvement in the end result.

Of course some ATL skills are measurable and do lend themselves to objective measurement, and many are already measured within standard curriculum subjects.

eg 1.1.d. Use appropriate forms of writing for different purposes and audiences

It is perfectly reasonable with this ATL skill for a teacher to define *appropriate* in terms of age appropriateness, and to generate standards to suit and measure against them.

But for many ATL skills there is no simple objective measure and what I am seeing in some areas are standards being produced for assessing ATL skills which are something like:

1.1.f – Use a variety of media to communicate with a range of audiences

Level 1 – occasionally uses a variety of media to communicate with a range of audiences

Level 2 – usually uses a variety of media to communicate with a range of audiences

Level 3 – often uses a variety of media to communicate with a range of audiences

Level 4 – always uses a variety of media to communicate with a range of audiences

Unfortunately what is being measured here is not an improvement in the individual's skill proficiency but an increase in their frequency of use. They are not the same thing. Increasing proficiency means getting better, more capable in the execution of the skill, not simply using the skill more frequently. Just because some ATL skills can be measured and are measured, it does not mean that they all need to be measured and assessed. The last thing ATL needs to be is another assessment burden for teachers.

The best way to assess a well-structured ATL framework is to use student self-assessment of the efficiency and effectiveness of their own learning, based on their practice of useful ATL skills in their own learning of their school subjects.

To help with this I have developed a simple four level structure of assessment of skill proficiency which runs from the Novice to the Expert where the increasing levels of skill proficiency can be simply described as **Watch, Copy, Do, Teach** (with thanks to Barclay Lelievre).

Self-Assessment:

Novice *Watch*	Learner *Copy*	Practitioner *Do*	Expert *Teach*
Can watch others performing tasks and using the skill. High levels of scaffolding from teacher needed	Can copy others' performance of the skill. Medium level of scaffolding needed	Can demonstrate the skill on demand. Minimal teacher scaffolding required	Can teach others the skill. No teacher scaffolding required

I have then taken the **Do** section of the rubric and broken it into three subsections I call **Practising, Getting there**, and **Got it!** This then makes up a simple format for students to use for self-assessment of ATL skills.

ATL Skill	Novice	Learner	Practitioner			Expert
	Watch	Copy	Do			Teach
	Watch	Copy	Practising	Getting there	Got it!	Teach

My suggestion is that for all the ATL skills not presently assessed you use this form of self-assessment, the aim of which is to create a mechanism through which students can develop self-confidence in their proficiency in any ATL skill. This pro-forma or anything like it can also be used for reporting home to parents, for gathering parent feedback and as a discussion tool for parent/teacher interviews.

I hope this brief overview will help you and your school to avoid some of the pitfalls I have seen and get through the initial stages of ATL implementation and into the exciting stuff – seeing improvements in student learning. When all students have all the skills of effective learning, everyone's job becomes easier, more efficient and more effective.

Please feel free to send me any feedback or questions to lance@taolearn.com.

References

IB (2010): History of the IB Middle Years Programme. Cardiff, International Baccalaureate Organization

King, L. http://taolearn.com/articles/article138.pdf

King, L. http://taolearn.com/atl_resources/article148.pdf

King, L.http://taolearn.com/atl_resources/article156.pdf

King, L. http://taolearn.com/atl_resources/article159.docx

King, L. http://taolearn.com/atl_resources/article160.docx

King, L. http://taolearn.com/atl_resources/article174.pdf

Kolb, David A (1984): Experiential learning: experience as the source of learning and development, Englewood Cliffs, NJ, Prentice Hall, www.learningfromexperience.com/images/uploads/process-of-experiential-learning.pdf

McCombs, B. L. (1986): The role of the self-system in self-regulated learning. Contemporary Educational Psychology, 11, 314-332.

PISA (Programme for International Student Assessment), 2012. http://www.oecd.org/pisa/keyfindings/pisa-2012-results.htm

Youtube. https://www.youtube.com/watch?v=mnGoJwBoIrM

Chapter 5

Interdisciplinary teaching and learning in the MYP

Marjorie Lope

Introduction and overview

Whether a child goes to school in Beijing, China, Kabul, Afghanistan, or Baltimore in the United States, she is being educated in an ever-changing, complex, diverse and interconnected world. Children are growing up in a world that is grappling with an unprecedented flow of knowledge, power, technology, and global migration. This enhanced global interconnectivity is just one of the facets of the multidimensional phenomena of globalisation, which is expanding and transforming societies in ways and speeds never seen before by humankind. As a result, globalisation has the potential to expand and transform the critical, imaginative, and ethical dimensions of education (Heilman, 2009). With that in mind, in recent years, scholarship on education and globalisation has evaluated ways in which we can best prepare children to address these global challenges and opportunities. The findings suggest that interdisciplinary teaching and learning is one of the ways to prepare children for the ever-changing world. The world in which children are now growing up requires that they both innovate and address challenges using more than singular, disciplinary knowledge. The multi-faceted problems we are facing today and in the future will require students to solve problems using interdisciplinary knowledge, understanding and ingenuity.

Interdisciplinary teaching and learning is a central component of the curriculum framework of the IB's Middle Years Programme (MYP). It has emerged as a consequence of the challenges and opportunities of educating students in, and for, a complex, diverse, and interconnected world. As the MYP has evolved, interdisciplinary teaching and learning has taken a more prominent place in the curriculum framework. Schools and teachers are now required to include interdisciplinary teaching and learning in the planning, teaching, and assessment in a more defined way. The aim is to help students develop the knowledge, attitudes, and skills they need to participate actively and responsibly in a constantly changing world. To that end, the IB is committed to students learning in an interdisciplinary way, that is, their ability to make meaningful connections across subjects in order to understand and act in the world.

This chapter will explore interdisciplinary teaching and learning in the revised MYP. Firstly, a definition and explanation of interdisciplinary teaching and learning will be provided, followed by an explanation of why interdisciplinary teaching and learning has evolved to a more prominent place in the MYP curriculum framework. The chapter will include some examples of how interdisciplinary learning is being implemented in IB schools, a discussion of some of the issues arising with implementation, and some potential strategies to deal with the challenges. The chapter will conclude with some questions to consider when evaluating the impact of interdisciplinary teaching and learning.

What is interdisciplinary learning?

In the MYP, interdisciplinary learning is generally defined as 'the process by which students come to understand bodies of knowledge and modes of thinking from two or more disciplines or subject groups and integrates them to create new understanding' (IB, 2014). Students demonstrate interdisciplinary understanding when they can bring together concepts, methods, or forms of communication from two or more disciplines or established areas of expertise to explain a phenomenon, solve a problem, create a product, or raise a new question in ways that would have been unlikely through a single discipline (Boix Mansilla, 2010). There are three key qualities that distinguish interdisciplinary teaching and learning: it is purposeful, grounded in the disciplines, and integrative (Boix Mansilla, 2010).

Interdisciplinary teaching and learning is purposeful

It effectively integrates two or more disciplines or areas of expertise as a means to deepen students' understanding of the world and become more competent in it. Therefore, integrating the disciplines is not the goal; rather it is the means to get to the deeper learning and application of learning. For example, the goal of teaching and learning about World War Two could be for students to understand the dimensions of power. Students in year 2 in an MYP school learned about power via World War Two in two subject groups – Individuals and Societies and Language and Literature. In Language and Literature the students read *The Diary of Anne Frank* and learned about perspective, questions, and interview techniques. For the culminating task students had to interview someone who lived in that time period, and then apply their learning about power in an unfamiliar situation using the writing techniques learned in Language and Literature. The students had to use knowledge from both subject areas to successfully engage in the task. They then chose from a list of people in leadership positions to write a persuasive piece (persuasive speech, letter to president, letter to student government leader, or another leader) to address a current power struggle. The written piece had to include a recommendation with lessons learned from history. Interdisciplinary teaching and learning is needed when challenges and opportunities cannot be fully understood from one disciplinary perspective alone. When it is purposeful it gives direction and meaning to student effort. Additionally, it gives a clear purpose for inquiry within broader global contexts. On the other hand, when interdisciplinary learning does not include a clearly articulated purpose, contrived connections and fragmented learning are more likely to occur (IB, 2014).

Interdisciplinary teaching and learning is deeply grounded in the disciplines

It is represented within the MYP subject groups. It does not replace MYP subject groups, it builds on disciplinary objectives in meaningful and connected ways (IB, 2014). In the previous example, using power as the key concept, the students explicitly learned history, context and relationships in Individuals and Societies. They learned about perspective, interview techniques and persuasive writing in Language and Literature. Then, they used the learning as the foundation for engaging in the culminating or summative task. In interdisciplinary teaching and learning the disciplinary learning is explicitly taught and assessed. Disciplinary grounding is an essential feature of the MYP interdisciplinary approach in which students work across disciplines and areas of expertise to build from disciplinary learning to deeper interdisciplinary understanding.

Interdisciplinary teaching and learning is integrative

This means that both teachers and students integrate disciplinary perspectives and concepts, and they do so deliberately and productively. Interdisciplinary units of work are not disciplines juxtaposed around a 'theme', neither are disciplinary connections made haphazardly (IB, 2014). Rather, interdisciplinary teaching and learning integrates the concepts, knowledge, attitudes and skills across disciplines to create a productive relationship with one another. Following the example of MYP year 2 students studying power as the key concept, they integrated understanding of power and perspective using knowledge of World War Two and the book The Diary of Anne Frank as the vehicle for learning. The skills and attitudes were reinforced in both subject groups and had to be used in an integrated way to engage in the culminating task, and students achieved a new, deeper and more compelling or nuanced understanding of the topic (IB, 2014).

The aims of MYP interdisciplinary teaching and learning

They describe very clearly what a teacher may expect to teach and what a student may expect to experience and learn as a result of engaging in an interdisciplinary unit:

- develop a deeper understanding of learning skills and apply them in meaningful contexts

- integrate conceptual learning, ways of knowing, and methods of inquiring from multiple disciplines

- inquire into compelling issues, ideas and challenges by creating products or explaining phenomena

- reflect on and communicate understanding of the interdisciplinary learning process

- experience the excitement of intellectual discovery... including insights into how disciplines complement and challenge one another
  (IB, 2014).

The objectives of MYP interdisciplinary teaching and learning

These provide required targets. The objectives describe what the student will be able to accomplish as a result of experiencing interdisciplinary teaching and learning, and are directly aligned with the assessment criteria for interdisciplinary learning.

- Disciplinary grounding: students should be able to demonstrate relevant, disciplinary factual/ conceptual and/or procedural knowledge.

- Synthesising: students should be able to synthesise disciplinary knowledge to demonstrate interdisciplinary understanding

- Communicating: students should be able to:

  - Use appropriate strategies to communicate interdisciplinary understanding effectively

  - Document sources using recognised conventions

- Reflecting: students should be able to:

  - Reflect on the development of their own interdisciplinary understanding

  - Evaluate the benefits and limitations of disciplinary and interdisciplinary knowledge and ways of knowing in specific situations

These objectives are designed to be used together to create a holistic experience for students to develop interdisciplinary understanding. In each of the five years of the MYP schools must address all four objectives of interdisciplinary learning in every interdisciplinary unit that is taught.

Why has interdisciplinary learning become so important in the MYP?

Regardless of whether one perceives globalisation as a positive or negative phenomenon there is widespread agreement that current education systems need to consider both what they should be teaching and how they are preparing children for globalisation and the interconnected world in which we now live. In order to function effectively not only in their own societal contexts but also in international contexts, students need knowledge of languages and other cultures and the ability to function in cross-cultural situations (Stewart and Kagan, 2005). In the *Global Achievement Gap* (2008), Tony Wagner describes the seven new skills students will need for careers, continuous learning, and citizenship in an increasingly complex world:

1. Critical thinking and problem solving

2. Collaboration across networks and leading by influence

3. Agility and adaptability

4. Initiative and entrepreneurship

5. Accessing and analysing information

6. Effective oral and written communication

7. Curiosity and imagination.

Wagner goes one step further and suggests that all students need these new skills for college, careers, and citizenship if they are to engage in a highly competitive 'knowledge economy'. The failure to give all students these new skills leaves both the students and the country (in reference to the United States) at an alarming disadvantage (Wagner, 2008).

In the 21st century students need much more than the knowledge of a discrete set of basic skills in reading, writing, and mathematics (Wagner, 2008). Students need the opportunity to develop global mindedness, shared responsibility, and cultural pluralism to facilitate the development of a 'global-mindset' that may assist them with the realities of an ever-more complex world (Hett, 1993; Walker, 2008). Today's students need the knowledge, attitudes and skills to live in a world that is more interconnected than anyone has ever known. To better prepare students for the multi-faceted nature of globalisation, teachers must build on a holistic view of students and ensure all students have the educational opportunities that emphasise the development of the knowledge, attitudes, and skills that are necessary to be adaptable problem-solvers and life-long learners.

Interdisciplinary teaching and learning has always been a part of the MYP curriculum framework. However, as the MYP has evolved, interdisciplinary teaching and learning has assumed a more prominent place and more is required of schools, teachers and students. Schools are now required to show they are providing opportunities for collaboratively planned interdisciplinary learning at least once per year at every level of the MYP by submitting completed interdisciplinary unit plans. Additionally, the interdisciplinary learning must include at least two subject groups, and all four assessment criteria must be used to assess student learning that results from the interdisciplinary teaching. While this requires the school to produce more evidence of implementation, the underlying goal of this change is that schools will see the value of interdisciplinary teaching and learning and will implement multiple units per year, per grade level. While we know what is measured has value, the hope is that because of this 'measurement' more value will be placed on interdisciplinary teaching and learning.

Prior to 2014, interdisciplinary teaching and learning was part of the curriculum framework and schools were required to select and submit to the IB one interdisciplinary unit that represented the interdisciplinary teaching and learning that happened at the school. This was done at the point at which the school was authorised by the IB to teach the MYP, and again when it was evaluated by the IB, which happens every four-to-five years. Now the MYP has provided more clarity on what is meant by interdisciplinary teaching and learning. In the past, teachers might have attempted to teach an interdisciplinary unit from a singular disciplinary perspective. The MYP has made it very clear in the 2014 documentation that interdisciplinary teaching and learning is required across a minimum of two subject groups. It must be purposefully integrated and the content of each subject should be clearly identified. With the revised description of interdisciplinary teaching and learning, teachers should be able to answer the following questions in order to ensure they are implementing it in the way in which it was intended by the IB:

- What is my justification for planning and teaching the interdisciplinary unit?

- Why is it worth understanding this issue or idea from an interdisciplinary perspective?

When teachers answer these questions clearly there is a greater chance that the teaching and learning will be purposeful, grounded in the disciplines and integrative. Time will tell if these requirements will have has the desired impact or if the IB should have gone further with its requirements.

How can interdisciplinary learning be implemented?

There is a multitude of approaches that can be used to support interdisciplinary learning that are, to a large extent, dependent on the comfort level and familiarity of the teaching strategies of the teachers involved in the planning, teaching and assessing. However, as long as the learning is relevant for students, requires purposeful inquiry, is grounded in disciplinary expertise, and integrates disciplinary perspectives productively then the approach to planning, teaching and assessing can vary greatly.

Planning

When planning interdisciplinary units of work teachers should work collaboratively to clearly distinguish which disciplines will be involved, then use the interdisciplinary unit planner provided by the IB which has multiple entry points. Teachers can start their planning with the key concepts, the global context, or even the content. The key to successful planning is to be clear about the entry point and collaborate across disciplines on the development of multifaceted questions that will frame the unit. Next, it is important to identify and communicate to students the specific approaches to learning that will be focused on in the unit. It is crucial that the approaches to learning identify how the students will learn, are appropriate for the age-level and align vertically with other approaches to teaching and learning.

The culminating performance of understanding required of the students should be age-appropriate and address the interdisciplinary objectives and assessment criteria: disciplinary grounding, synthesising, communicating, and reflecting. The assessment of interdisciplinary learning promotes a collaborative approach among teachers that often generates powerful conversations in which teachers have the opportunity to further develop their understanding of the subject groups and how they interact. Finally, it is recommended that a specific, detailed timeline for implementation be developed and shared with the students.

Mathematics and Design

There are many approaches that can be used in a variety of settings to plan, teach, and assess interdisciplinary learning. A teacher or group of teachers could collaborate on the development of an interdisciplinary unit with relevance for students as the starting point. For example, MYP year 3 teachers wanted to connect a relevant and current global trend with mathematics and technology. They gave students the global context, concepts, content, approaches to learning and a list of potential unit titles. 'Globalisation and sustainability' was the global context. The key and related concepts were the rate of change and algebraic equations in mathematics. In their design course the students were studying advancements in technology with a focus on function. The approaches to learning were communication and media literacy. The students chose the title that seemed most engaging to them and the rest of the unit was developed and delivered by the teachers. Students chose from the following unit titles: 'What if everyone in the world was connected?', 'Cellphones: the great equaliser', or 'Everybody doesn't win with globalisation'. The choice of title was a way of hooking students; the teachers already had the unit developed. Students were intrigued that teachers might have something positive to say about cellphones and so chose 'Cellphones: the great equaliser', and thus they were drawn into learning about globalisation and sustainability.

Science with Language and Literature

In another school, the MYP year 4 science teachers collaborated with the Language and Literature teachers to develop an interdisciplinary unit with purposeful inquiry as the common starting point. From there, they ensured it was grounded in disciplinary expertise, that the disciplinary perspectives were integrated productively, and that they were relevant for the students. The teachers wanted to provide their students with a genuine opportunity to inquire. The disciplinary grounding in science was biology and the process and consequences around adaptation. In Language and Literature the students read the novel *Life of Pi*, by Yann Martel, and engaged in analysis of the narrative with a focus on character.

To start the unit the students read an excerpt from Charles Darwin's *The Origin of Species* (1859) as a means of inspiration to promote further study on the similarities and differences among communities and the individuals that function within them. The global context was 'Scientific and technical innovation'. The key concept that brought the entire unit together was development and the approaches to learning were communication and critical thinking. The disciplines were integrated so students would have the opportunity to develop connections between human society and biological concepts. Students developed their own questions about the extent to which genetics and environment shape an individual's identity. As year 4 MYP students explored the effect their decisions have on their own lives and the skills they need to survive and thrive in high school and beyond, the exploration of how humans adapt and the amount of control human beings have over their responses to the environment were both personally, as well as intellectually, significant.

As a culminating activity students had options: they could write a letter to Charles Darwin explaining the extent to which we are products of our environment, using their new learning and examples from the primary sources studied in the unit. Or, students could write the transcript of an interview they would conduct with Charles Darwin on who is in control of evolution, using the same sources. Alternatively, they could write a narrative with the development of a character the demonstrated understanding of the extent to which we are products of our own environment. Although the final product looked different, depending on student choice, all student work was evaluated on the prescribed MYP criteria: disciplinary grounding, synthesising, communicating and reflecting.

Just as with disciplinary teaching and learning it is important for the teachers to ask themselves the following questions when planning an interdisciplinary unit:

1. What is the multifaceted unit question? (consider purpose)

2. What are the disciplinary concepts, knowledge, attitudes and skills students will develop to address the question of study and can they be easily identified by the teachers and the students? (disciplinary grounding)

3. How are the disciplinary insights productively integrated to deepen understanding of the topic at hand?

4. What might students learn or gain from the experience? (relevance)

5. How will teachers and students know interdisciplinary understanding is being developed or has been achieved?

In order to effectively answer these questions teachers will have to have collaborative discussions. When there is little collaboration or the interdisciplinary unit is not developed within the context of vertical articulation there is a risk that the unit will not be purposeful, relevant or age-appropriate for the students.

Teacher collaboration

Both explicit and implicit in this discussion is the importance of teacher collaboration. Interdisciplinary teaching and learning requires the integration of a minimum of two subject areas. Teachers that teach single subjects have to plan together to develop interdisciplinary units, while those teachers that teach more than one subject area should seek out other teachers with whom to plan. Even if one teacher teaches the entire unit, the collaboration amongst teachers provides an opportunity for development from multiple perspectives. The IB requires schools to provide teachers with time to collaborate and interdisciplinary unit development is what can be done during that time.

While the IB requires that collaborative time must be provided to teachers, it does not say how or what should be done during the collaborative time. From observation of many schools and teacher collaboration time, it is recommended that the teachers who are collaborating establish an agreed upon definition of what effective collaborative time will look like and what the final product of the collaborative time will be. In addition, even though some might take it for granted, it is helpful to ensure teachers know how to plan collaboratively, even if that means showing them how or giving guidelines from the start. When the expectations are clear to teachers and they know how to make the best use of the collaborative time, teachers are more likely to feel it is a good use of time and they will enjoy and grow from the professional development opportunity. It is incumbent upon the school leadership to ensure that teachers not only have time to collaborate but know how to do so meaningfully.

In order to avoid some of the practical problems that could arise, it is recommended that schools assess the extent to which teachers understand the purpose and value of interdisciplinary teaching and learning. If teachers don't have a firm grasp of the purpose and value they could struggle with implementation and impact regardless of the amount of time they have for collaboration. When it comes to the students, it is important that they also understand the purpose and goals of interdisciplinary learning at the start of the unit. Students will engage and be inspired when the expectations are clear, the learning is relevant, and the task is engaging. Effective interdisciplinary teaching and learning challenges not only the students, it often requires teachers to go beyond the more traditional ways of planning, teaching and assessing learning. Interdisciplinary teaching and learning can offer teachers a genuine opportunity for professional development, requiring them to have conversations and collaborate across subject areas and grade levels.

When effective collaboration takes place, teachers have time for, and engage in, important conversations around what they want students to achieve as a result of the interdisciplinary teaching and learning, and how they will know if students have achieved the objectives. This aspect of interdisciplinary teaching and learning might be the hardest to detail and measure. Although to some the idea of teacher collaboration may seem simple, it is not as easy as it sounds, and it has the potential to be a reason why interdisciplinary teaching and learning will not have the desired impact on student development.

As mentioned above, the IB requires that teachers collaborate in MYP schools with little guidance. On one hand, that could be good in that is left to the schools to figure out how collaboration can best be organised in their context. On the other hand, collaboration, and finding collaborative time, can be very hard and frustrating for teachers and schools. The IB has not yet developed and shared any training on collaboration, nor have they provided advice on how schools could effectively develop schedules that include collaborative time. The intent that interdisciplinary teaching and learning be a more prominent part of the MYP will be more likely to happen if schools have teachers that collaborative effectively during a designated collaborative planning session. Additionally, it will be important that the teachers understand the value and potential impact of interdisciplinary teaching and learning because they will more likely give it more time and attention in their busy schedule; this is more likely to happen if teacher collaboration is effective. The challenge will be if teachers get discouraged because of lack of training or don't see the value of interdisciplinary teaching and learning, the end result being that students will not have positive experiences of interdisciplinary learning.

Interdisciplinary learning can be seen in the final product students develop and/or it may be seen more deeply as student understanding develops with additional learning and maturing. There could be times when interdisciplinary learning might not be evident when the unit ends. Students may still need time to develop their ideas and conclusions. It is important, therefore, for teachers to consider this possibility while developing the unit; they might consider evaluating the process of developing interdisciplinary learning, rather than only evaluating a culminating product or conclusion that a student might draw. Teachers must be clear from the time the unit is developed as to what they want students to achieve and how they will know students have achieved it.

Assessing interdisciplinary learning

While the MYP Personal Project, the culminating experience of the MYP, has the potential for students to demonstrate interdisciplinary learning, the MYP now also has an optional interdisciplinary eAssessment that students may take at the end of year 5 of the MYP. Not only will this be a good opportunity for students to demonstrate their interdisciplinary understanding but it will also be an opportunity for schools to consider the effectiveness of their interdisciplinary teaching based on how students perform. This will also be one way the IB will be able to evaluate, globally, the extent to which schools and students are developing their understanding of interdisciplinary teaching and learning. The interdisciplinary eAssessment will be driven by a global context and MYP concepts; it will combine a minimum of two MYP subjects and will be relevant, require purposeful inquiry, and be grounded in disciplinary expertise;

it will use the MYP assessment criteria as explained above. The interdisciplinary eAssessment is an innovative approach to assessing interdisciplinary learning across all MYP schools and is the first interdisciplinary assessment of its kind. It has the potential to drive teaching and learning in positive and significant ways.

It is important to note that there isn't necessarily a known market for the interdisciplinary eAssessment so its potential for use and impact is unknown at this time. While the idea of assessing student ability to demonstrate interdisciplinary understanding sounds valuable and aligns with current thinking around best practice for teaching and learning, this assessment comes at a time when the notion of another assessment on top of all the current national or state assessments students experience in today's schools may not be seen as positive for schools, teachers, or students. There could be an unintended consequence of offering this assessment in that schools may feel that the IB is feeding into the current desire of politicians and others to evaluate education through administering many tests (particularly standardised tests) as a way of assessing student progress. The end of the final year of the MYP – grade 10 – is not a critical point for most students on the path to college and career. At this time, it is not clear what the results of this eAssessment of interdisciplinary learning would be used for, except to provide feedback to the students and teachers. There is no guarantee that it will be successful for the IB from a business perspective, however, in the first pilot session of the IB eAssessments in May 2015, the interdisciplinary assessment was the most popular in terms of the number of students who took it.

Summary and conclusion

The more prominent focus on interdisciplinary teaching and learning in the revised MYP indicates the commitment of the IB to students learning how to innovate and address the challenges of our ever-changing world, using knowledge, attitudes and skills developed from multiple disciplines. Teachers and schools, therefore, need to provide students with multiple and varied opportunities to develop interdisciplinary understanding. Interdisciplinary understanding is more likely to be developed by students when teachers work collaboratively to develop units that are:

- relevant to students
- require purposeful inquiry
- grounded in disciplinary expertise
- integrate disciplinary perspectives productively.

When evaluating student learning as a result of teaching the interdisciplinary unit the following four criteria must be used:

- Disciplinary grounding
- Synthesising

- Communicating
- Reflecting

The new expectation for interdisciplinary learning in the MYP provides greater clarity of expectation for students and schools and gives the IB an opportunity to innovate and create an interdisciplinary eAssessment that has the potential to strengthen interdisciplinary learning, not only in the MYP, but in international education in general. In time, students, teachers, schools, and the IB will be able to better evaluate the impact of interdisciplinary teaching and learning. The ultimate intention of this clarity and focus is that students will be better equipped to innovate and solve the great challenges that lie ahead of them. However, as with most valuable changes made to teaching and learning, if it is not done with careful planning, proper training, and thoughtful follow-through and commitment, it will not have the desired impact.

References

Boix-Mansilla, V. (2010): *MYP Guide to interdisciplinary teaching and learning.* UK: Anthony Rowe.

Heilman, E. E. (2009): Terrains of global and multicultural education: What is distinctive, contested, and shared? In T.F. Kirkwood-Tucker (Ed.), *Visions in global education: The globalization of curriculum and pedagogy in teacher education and schools* (pp25-46). New York, NY: Peter Lang.

Hett, E. J. (1993): The development of an instrument to measure global-mindedness. *Dissertation Abstracts International, 54,* 3724.

IB (2009): *Middle Years Programme guide to interdisciplinary teaching and learning.* United Kingdom: Anthony Rowe.

IB (2014): *Fostering interdisciplinary teaching and learning in the Middle Years Programme.* United Kingdom: Anthony Rowe.

Kagan, S. L., & Stewart, V. (Eds.) (2005): A *new world view: Learning from education in other countries [Special issue].* Phi Delta Kappan.

Wagner, T. (2008): *The global achievement gap.* New York, NY: Basic Books.

Walker, G. (2011): *The changing face of international education: challenges for the IB.* Wales, UK: International Baccalaureate.

Zhao, Y. (2009): *Catching up or leading the way: American education in the age of globalization.* Alexandria, VA: Association for Supervision & Curriculum Development.

Zhao, Y. (2010): Preparing globally competent teachers: A new imperative for teacher education. *Journal of Teacher Education, 61,* 422-432.

Chapter 6

Assessing the MYP: Key changes to school-based assessment for years 1–5

Patricia Villegas

Assessment is central to educational policy in most countries and generations of young people have been directly impacted by the decisions of policy makers, good and bad. There is now recognition in both state funded and private schools, and by employers, that young people need to develop different skills and knowledge for the future, skills and knowledge that cannot be effectively or readily measured through traditional forms of testing. For the past twenty years, the International Baccalaureate (IB), through the Middle Years Programme (MYP), has tried to address the need for such skills, often referred to as 21st century skills, through an assessment system that has been largely internal (teacher-led) and focused on the process of learning, as opposed to more common assessment systems that are externally set and focused on a narrow set of learning outcomes.

Our globalised, interconnected world certainly needs people who can demonstrate twenty-first century skills. Pink (1995) says that, 'The future belongs to… creators, and empathizers, pattern recognizers, and meaning makers…', while Baker (2008) stresses the need to develop students' '… ability to analyse, synthesize, and apply what they've learned to address new problems, design solutions…'. A number of organisations have developed frameworks that attempt to identify the skills that students need to acquire and to help educators integrate these skills into their existing educational programmes. For example, the Organization for Economic Cooperation and Development (OECD, 2005) describes a set of key competencies which it summarises as: 'The ability to consider the wider context of decisions and actions – that marry the need for basic literacy with essential deep conceptual understanding'.

Recognising these developments, many state systems and educational organisations are trying to integrate these skills and competencies into teaching as they recognise them as imperative for educational systems that want to compete effectively, and it is clear that '…meeting the demands of today's world requires a shift in assessment strategies to measure the skills now prized in a complex global environment' as Partnership for 21st century skills (2007) clearly states.

MYP Assessment 1994–2014

Philosophy and framework

The ideas that guided the assessment of the MYP from its beginnings can be traced back to scholars such as Alec Peterson who, in the 1970s, envisioned a complex future ahead of us:

> What is of paramount importance in the pre-university stage is not what is learned but learning how to learn ... What matters is not the absorption and regurgitation either of facts or pre-digested interpretations of facts, but the development of powers of the mind or ways of thinking which can be applied to new situations and new presentations of facts as they arise (IB, 2010)

Thinking such as this nourished the philosophy of the MYP and helped to guide the pedagogical mind shift that the programme sought to bring about. The assessment model of the MYP was, from its earliest days:

- organised and structured by schools/teachers

- internal (conducted by teachers)

- embedded in the curriculum

- integral to teaching and learning

- a continuous process (every year of the programme)

- focused on subject-specific objectives (MYP prescribes subject objectives which can be used to address any national standards or content mandated by governments)

- criterion-related (assessment process based on determining levels of achievement against previously agreed criteria.)

The MYP approach to assessment valued, and continues to value, the processes of learning as much as the products of learning and aims to integrate both. The model insists on strong formative assessment where students are assessed and monitored throughout the five years of the programme and are provided with timely feedback that encourages them to become aware of their learning skills, strategies and processes and to improve on them. In the MYP students have the opportunity to demonstrate what they learn; the assessment focuses on the growth and the performance of a student and assesses higher order thinking skills.

The challenges of the MYP assessment framework

Criterion-related assessment

The MYP stresses the benefits of embracing criterion-related assessment for the learning process, arguing that it:

- corresponds to subject-specific objectives and is not subject to teachers' judgment

- provides clear and specific standards of expected student achievement
- fosters self-assessment and improvement
- shows the state of students' conceptual understanding, knowledge and skills
- gives flexibility for curriculum design
- can be applied in a variety of circumstances and contexts, and with a range of assessment tasks
  (IB, 2014)

The MYP assessment framework demanded that MYP schools undergo a paradigm shift in terms of letting go of the traditional view of assessment in which 'Instruction was driven by traditional assessment, which was speed-based, norm- referenced and one- shot, as they measure what learners could do at a particular time' (Bailey, 1998). To which Brualdi added that 'It focused on the students' ability to memorise and recall and most assessment tools required learners to display their knowledge in a predetermined way' (1996).

A lack of understanding of criterion-related assessment, and of the criteria themselves, has been of one the challenges identified by many MYP schools (NFER report, October 2012). This may be related to the fact that traditional assessment is still embedded in many schools. The MYP model demands a strong programme of support for teachers to help them to develop a thorough understanding of the assessment framework and to transfer it successfully to their classroom (Jackson, 2006), this support can be challenging to implement.

Assessment as the driver of unit planning

The MYP assessment framework requires teachers to employ a variety of assessment tools such as performance-based assessment tasks, process journals, selected response and open-ended tasks, in order to demonstrate the students' range of knowledge, skills and understandings. Teachers choose the appropriate tools to develop assessment tasks that address the MYP subject objectives. So assessment is planned from the start of a unit: it drives the learning process.

This method of planning follows the 'backwards design model' (Wiggins, 1998): 'One starts with the end – the desired results/goals – and then derives the curriculum from the evidence of learning (performances)'. While this planning method gives a clear objective to the teacher and helps him/her to effectively focus both planning and teaching, it also means that some teachers have to implement a completely new approach to unit planning which can result in anxiety and resistance.

Reporting on assessment

Implementing criteria-related assessment, making professional judgments and reporting it to the community has also brought some challenges for MYP schools.

The MYP requires that schools:

- develop assessment procedures based on MYP assessment guidelines
- share assessment principles and criteria with teachers, students and parents
- provide evidence of work assessed against subject-specific criteria
- ensure an effective MYP reporting system

In order to communicate the final achievement levels in each of the criteria, teachers have to collect evidence from a range of assessment tasks to enable them to make a professional and informed judgment. 'In gathering the evidence for the judgment to be made, teachers will analyze the achievement levels of students over the course of the marking period or year, which represents their summative performance for that period, paying particular attention to patterns in the data (such as an increasing level of performance), consistency and mitigating circumstances' (IB, 2008).

In addition to communicating achievement levels, some schools also have to communicate grades to meet their national, state requirements which may mean aligning or converting grading scales which can be time consuming and difficult to explain to parents.

Despite its challenges, the criterion-related MYP assessment framework can bring transparency and accountability for the parties involved and fosters metacognition as students become aware of where they are in the learning process and what to do to improve it. The layers of complexity, however, cannot be underestimated.

Some of the critics of the MYP assessment framework have pointed out that it is quite complex (Jackson, 2006) and is dependent on a strong professional development system to support it. It is also time consuming (Denver Public Schools, 2007), particularly with regards to collaborative planning and the time needed for the internal standardisation of assessments which are all IB requirements. These challenges were taken by the IB as areas of opportunity for change and development and paved the way for the changes to come in the revised MYP.

MYP Assessment from 2014

Overview of the changes

For those practitioners who believed that the programme as a whole was too complex, there are now fewer layers. With regard to the assessment framework, all eight subject groups and the MYP projects now share only four objectives and criteria; previously the objectives and criteria varied between subject groups. This will have a significant impact in terms of simplifying the implementation of assessment for teachers, and helping schools communicate about MYP assessment to students and parents.

For those that required external recognition of MYP assessment, optional external assessments have been introduced in the final year of MYP for all eight subject groups and interdisciplinary learning, along with the introduction of compulsory moderation of the Personal Project.

For those that saw the programme as belonging to elites, accessible mainly for private schools, the changes facilitate greater access by public/state schools by simplifying the MYP requirements so that they combine more easily with national/state requirements.

For those schools that offer other IB programmes and expected a better IB continuum, the changes to the MYP support further articulation of the programmes, for example by making the Approaches to Learning (ATL) skills a core component of all IB programmes, thus helping students to acquire the skills needed for the 21st century.

Major changes in MYP assessment

Optional moderation of subject groups replaced by optional eAssessment

The IB presents the eAssessment on its website as follows: 'The new optional MYP eAssessment provides external evaluation for students in MYP year 5 (15-16 years old) that leads to the internationally recognized IB MYP certificate. MYP eAssessment represents a balanced, appropriately challenging model that comprises examinations and coursework.

'There are three kinds of MYP eAssessments:

- externally marked onscreen examinations for selected courses in Language and Literature, Individuals and Societies, Mathematics, Sciences and Interdisciplinary Learning

- an externally marked ePortfolio for Language Acquisition courses in selected languages

- internally marked and externally moderated ePortfolios for selected courses in physical and health education, arts and design.

'In the past the moderation service was linked to the validation of schools' results in a specific subject, it was optional and schools had to pay a fee depending on the number of registered candidates. Now with the introduction of these optional eAssessments, the IB expects to gain recognition from governments and universities.'

Concept-based teaching and learning assessed in the optional eAssessment

This is one of the major changes of the revised MYP and it strengthens one of the main principles underpinning the MYP as a framework that addresses the 21st century.

The MYP has always had a focus on developing conceptual understandings and making the teaching of concepts explicit. However, for the first time the MYP now prescribes a list of concepts for each subject group which are to be assessed internally through summative tasks and which will be externally assessed in the optional eAssessments. Concept-based assessments will measure what students know, understand and can do through complex tasks that combine content and process skills. These concept-based eAssessments will 'allow students to move beyond factual learning to a level of understanding where knowledge transfers readily to new situations and thinking become integrated' (Erickson, 2012). It is to be hoped that there will be a positive back-wash effect on the teaching of concepts as teachers will have to assess student understanding of concepts throughout the five years of the programme.

Assessment of interdisciplinary work

An important change in the revised MYP is the inclusion of objectives and assessment criteria for the interdisciplinary units. Prior to 2014, the MYP described in general terms the qualities of good assessment of students' interdisciplinary understanding and what constituted adequate evidence, but no specific assessment criteria were defined. This lead to some confusion in MYP schools when having to assess the interdisciplinary units of work and report it to the community. Now the MYP addresses the problem with the introduction of four objectives and assessment criteria for interdisciplinary learning for years 1, 3 and 5 of the programme. It provides clarity on how to assess the units of work, and record and report interdisciplinary assessment. The IB has also introduced the option for schools of having their students' interdisciplinary understanding examined externally through an eAssessment in year 5 of the MYP.

Approaches to Learning (ATL) and assessment

In order to prepare students effectively for life beyond school, the ATL component of the revised MYP has been considerably strengthened, focusing on the development of cognitive, metacognitive and affective skills. These ATL skills are grouped into five interrelated categories in all IB programmes: communication skills, social skills, self-management skills, research skills and thinking skills, providing a framework that addresses all the necessary skills for the 21st century learner. They also provide a common language that students and teachers can use throughout the process of learning.

In the revised MYP, ATL takes on a more pivotal role in terms of the way that teachers plan their units and the way they assess the formative and summative assessment tasks. For example, skills that are embedded in the subject objectives are identified and developed through formative assessment tasks in order to scaffold the summative task chosen to address the objective.

In the past, ATL was an area of interaction that 'interacted' with all subject groups throughout the learning process but in many cases skills were taken for granted and not explicitly taught. There is now much more explicit guidance about the role of ATL and assessment: 'ATL skills help students prepare for, and demonstrate learning through, meaningful assessment. Every MYP unit identifies ATL skills that students will develop through their inquiry and demonstrate in the unit's formative (if applicable) and summative assessments. Many ATL skills directly support the attainment of subject-group objectives' (IB, 2014). The explicit teaching of these ATL skills and their close relationship to the command terms (see below) will surely bring far better results in all MYP assessments, including the new eAssessments and, hopefully, in the Diploma Programme for those MYP students that go on to study it.

Mandatory moderation of the Personal Project

As the Personal Project is the culmination of the MYP, there is now a requirement that all schools offering a five-year MYP undergo moderation – a mandatory process of external validation of teachers' internal assessment of the Personal Project. Prior to 2014, MYP schools could opt out of all external moderation by the IB. Optional external moderation was a way for the IB to provide students with external, international recognition of their achievements should they need it. Now with the mandatory moderation of Personal Projects, beginning in 2016, students' work will be externally and internationally recognised by the IB which will create a reliable standard of achievement that will inform the teaching and learning in MYP schools across the world.

Introduction of the Community Project

Schools that end their MYP programme in years 3 or 4, usually because of the way the school is structured, have to introduce a new project called the Community Project, which will provide students in the final year of the programme in that school with a culminating experience similar to the Personal Projects. With the introduction of the Community Project, there will be an opportunity for younger students to consolidate their learning guided by specific MYP objectives and assessment criteria. 'The community project focuses on community and service, encouraging students to explore their right and responsibility to implement service as action in the community. As a consolidation of learning, the community project engages students in a sustained, in-depth inquiry leading to service as action in the community' (IB, 2014).

Assessment criteria

Prescribed objectives and criteria for MYP years 1 and 3, in addition to those for year 5, for all subject groups, projects and interdisciplinary work. In the past the MYP provided only year 5 objectives and assessment criteria for each subject group. Schools were expected to develop their own objectives and criteria for years 1 and 3. This could be an an arduous task for teachers, involving extensive collaborative planning in order to vertically articulate the objectives, for each subject group, from year 5 to year 3 and then to year 1. The newly mandated objectives and criteria in years 1, 3 and 5 will simplify practice for schools and provide a level of global standardisation for MYP schools.

MYP assessment criteria are now equally weighted (see Figure 1). The MYP assessment criteria are now aligned across all 8 subject groups so that there are four assessment criteria in each subject group, in MYP projects and for interdisciplinary work.

All criteria have four bands and a maximum of eight achievement levels. Each of which represent two levels of achievement. The level descriptors for each band describe a range of student performance in the various strands of each objective. At the lowest levels, student achievement in each of the strands will be minimal. As the numerical levels increase, the level descriptors describe greater achievement levels in each of the strands. The criteria for each subject group include the knowledge, understanding and skills that must be taught. They also encompass the factual, conceptual, procedural and metacognitive dimensions of knowledge (IB, 2014).

	A	B	C	D
Language and literature	Analysing	Organizing	Producing text	Using language
Language acquisition	Comprehending spoken and visual text	Comprehending written and visual text	Communicating	Using language
Individuals and societies	Knowing and understanding	Investigating	Communicating	Thinking critically
Sciences	Knowing and understanding	Inquiring and designing	Processing and evaluating	Reflecting on the impacts of science
Mathematics	Knowing and understanding	Investigating patterns	Communicating	Applying mathematics in real-world contexts
Arts	Knowing and understanding	Developing skills	Thinking creatively	Responding
Physical and health education	Knowing and understanding	Planning for performance	Applying and performing	Reflecting and improving performance
Design	Inquiring and analysing	Developing ideas	Creating the solution	Evaluating
MYP projects	Investigating	Planning	Taking action	Reflecting
Interdisciplinary	Disciplinary grounding	Synthesizing	Communicating	Reflecting

Figure 1 – MYP assessment criteria (IB, 2014 p80)

Grade boundaries

Recommended grade boundaries (see Figure 2). Prior to 2014, there were a different number of criteria and achievement levels in the eight subject groups and Personal Project which resulted in a convoluted process whereby teachers had to assign MYP grades by checking different grade boundary tables. Now there will be only one grade boundary table for all MYP subjects, projects and interdisciplinary work.

Grade	Boundaries	Descriptor
1	1–5	Produces work of very limited quality. Conveys many significant misunderstandings or lacks understanding of most concepts and skills. Very rarely demonstrates critical or creative thinking. Very inflexible, rarely using knowledge or skills.
2	6–9	Produces work of limited quality. Expresses misunderstandings or significant gaps in understanding for many concepts and contexts. Infrequently demonstrates critical or creative thinking. Generally inflexible in the use of knowledge and skills, infrequently applying knowledge and skills.
3	10–14	Produces work of an acceptable quality. Communicates basic understanding of many concepts and contexts, with occasionally significant misunderstandings or gaps. Begins to demonstrate some basic critical and creative thinking. Is often inflexible in the use of knowledge and skills, requiring support even in familiar classroom situations.
4	15–18	Produces good quality work. Communicates basic understanding of most concepts and contexts with few misunderstandings and minor gaps. Often demonstrates basic critical and creative thinking. Uses knowledge and skills with some flexibility in familiar classroom situations, but requires support in unfamiliar situations.
5	19–23	Produces generally high-quality work. Communicates reliable understanding of concepts and contexts. Demonstrates critical and creative thinking, sometimes with sophistication. Uses knowledge and skills in familiar classroom and real-world situations, and, with support, some unfamiliar real-world situations.
6	24–27	Produces high-quality, occasionally innovative work. Communicates extensive understanding of concepts and contexts. Demonstrates critical and creative thinking, frequently with sophistication. Uses knowledge and skills in familiar and unfamiliar classroom and real-world situations, often with independence.
7	28–32	Produces high-quality, frequently innovative work, Communicates comprehensive, nuanced understanding of concepts and contexts. Consistently demonstrates sophisticated critical and creative thinking. Frequently transfers knowledge and skills with independence and expertise in a variety of complex classroom and real-world situations.

Figure 2 – General grade descriptors (IB, 2014, p93)

This change will help simplify the school-based assessment process and will be particularly beneficial for schools when having to communicate and report student achievement, as there is one sole grade boundary guidelines table for schools that want to use the IB 1-7 scale to report MYP grades. All schools are required to organise learning and assessment so that it is consistent with the prescribed MYP objectives and criteria. When assessing a task, teachers use their professional judgment and choose the achievement level that represents the students best achievements at that point in the learning process. The teacher can share the achievement levels with the students or parents and/or determine the IB grade by using the grade boundary table. As this practice will take place in all 8 subject groups, interdisciplinary work and MYP projects, teachers should find it much easier to apply.

Embedding of MYP command terms

These are "instructional verbs that indicate the level of thinking and type of performance (or behaviour) that is required of students, for example, 'describe', 'explain', 'analyse'. They are closely related to general and subject-specific Approaches to Learning skills, and they make explicit a shared academic vocabulary that informs teaching and learning in the MYP (IB, 2014).

Command terms are now embedded in the objectives and assessment criteria for all subject groups, MYP projects and interdisciplinary work. In the past some subject groups had command terms included in the descriptors of the achievement levels but it was not a common pattern that could be found throughout the subject group guides. Now with the systematic use of command terms in every subject group, in the projects and interdisciplinary work, students will be able to understand what is expected of them in a particular task and respond effectively. The consistent use of command terms throughout the five MYP years will also enable students to apply them in their optional eAssessment exams and later in their study of the IB Diploma Programme or IB Career-related Programme where the same command terms are used.

Implementing the revised MYP assessment model

Emerging good practice

Some MYP schools started implementing the changes described above prior to September, 2014 (the launch date for the revised programme), as they were being introduced in IB regional conferences and in MYP workshops around the world. As a result, some examples of good practice are already emerging.

Following the recommendation of the MYP Projects guide, one school worked on clarifying the Personal Project assessment criteria with their MYP staff, paying special attention to defining the ATL skills which are a key part of the project. This collaborative work helped them come to agreements on working definitions of the value statements and define what 'excellent research skills', for example, looked like for year 5 MYP students in their institution. Once the expectations were clearly defined, teachers were able to use the clarification of the assessment criteria to internally standardise Personal Projects so strengthening their shared understanding of MYP assessment.

In another school, in order to make sure that teachers were focused on addressing the ATL skills in all subject groups, subject leaders (heads of department) worked collaboratively with their teachers to develop an assessment task bank, containing performance based tasks to address each of the four subject criteria. The ATL skills embedded in each subject were identified and unpacked, and tasks were designed to support the development of each skill. The plan is to develop as many tasks as possible, for each subject and of varying difficulty and complexity, in order to use them for formative assessment purposes throughout the five years of the MYP. This collaborative work has brought about enriching discussions on the importance of scaffolding ATL skills and formative tasks.

One MYP school has started exploring strategies to ensure the deepening of student understanding and the transfer of learning, embracing the 'Six Facets of Understanding' from the Understanding by Design framework (Wiggins and McTighe, 2005). The Six Facets of Understanding: the capacity to explain, interpret, apply, shift perspective, empathise and self-assess, can serve as indicators of understanding. The school uses these facets of understanding to develop assessment tasks, choosing the facets that would provide appropriate evidence of the targeted understanding that they were seeking.

In the US, many school districts and alternative schools have embraced the move towards assessment for understanding by joining organisations such as' the New York Performance Standards Consortium'. Some states in the US have incorporated performance-based tasks as additional measures into their annual assessments (The Maryland School Performance Assessment Program, Kentucky and Vermont). As Professor Chris Dede of the Harvard Graduate School of Education says: 'we need broader measures, multiple measures that look at the different kinds of things that students have learned and have mastered' (Darling-Hammond and Adamson, 2010).

Areas of opportunity

Greater use of performance-based tasks as summative assessments

If we want to gauge what students know and can do we need to provide opportunities for them to demonstrate their understanding. The MYP uses the term 'performances of understanding' in its broadest sense as: 'A particular kind of learning experience – one that encourages flexible thinking with knowledge in novel situations. They become "understanding performances" when students are asked to use information deliberately to advance a new understanding. Performances of understanding allow students both to build and demonstrate their understanding in and across subjects. They are based on the theory that understanding is not something we have – like a set of facts we possess – but rather is something we can do' (IB, 2014).

Even though the use of performance based tasks as an assessment strategy has been recommended by the IB since the publication of the MYP guide 'From Principles into Practice' in 2008, the influence of standardised testing in many countries has led to an undermining of the use of performance-based assessments as they demand more time and effort to design and carry out. Yet it is important that they become part of our classroom instruction if we expect students to apply and transfer the knowledge and skills they have learnt. Darling-Hammond and Adamson (2010) maintain that, 'Performance assessments can measure students' cognitive thinking and reasoning skills and their ability to apply knowledge to solve realistic, meaningful problems makes them a great tool to influence learning and support teachers' instruction.'

There is hope that as the implementation of the revised MYP gains pace, more schools will strengthen their understanding of these performance-based tasks, thereby fostering higher order thinking skills and preparing students with the skills, knowledge and understanding they will need for the future.

Assessment for and assessment of learning

Many schools have shared their concern about the lack of alignment between formative and summative assessment, in general. Assessment for learning (formative assessment) involves using evidence of students' knowledge, understanding and skills to inform teaching. The effectiveness of the assessment of learning (summative assessment) depends on the nature and quality of the feedback. It is important that students are involved in reviewing and reflecting on their learning and assessment process. As Black and Wiliam (1998) noted 'The awareness of learning and ability of learners to direct it for themselves is of increasing importance in the context of encouraging lifelong learning.'

The new MYP planner strengthens this relationship between formative and summative assessment. It ensures teachers determine the summative assessment in the first stage of the planner, choose the criteria that will assess it and identify the ATL skills that will be needed in order to be successful in achieving the task. Then in the second stage of the planner, teachers have to design learning experiences to develop those skills identified, and formatively assess them until mastery of those skills ensures success in the summative task. It is intended that the new planner will help teachers realise the importance of the interrelationship between formative assessment and the summative task and so lead to improvement in assessment practices.

Conclusion

Assessment in the MYP is moving forward and leading the world in some areas, particularly with the introduction of the concept-driven eAssessments. MYP assessment practices have been consolidated with the changes brought about by the revised programme. However, further steps could be taken by the IB in the near future to ensure that these changes in assessment can lead to a fundamental change in how education is approached. It has been suggested that if the curriculum is to improve, teachers must have the necessary insight, skills and attitudes for implementing change. They gain these by being educated or re-educated in their job (Doll, 1992). There is important evidence that links professional development, teacher capacity and student learning outcomes. One of the main reasons for investing in human capital is the return in terms of organisational effectiveness (Bredeson, 2005) or as it has been stated by Senge (1999), 'The key factor with 'profound change' (organizational changes that demand a shift in values, behaviours with external practices, strategies and systems) is that there is learning through capacity building.'

For these changes to be sustainable and implemented efficiently there should be a well thought out plan of sustained professional development for classroom instruction and assessment, a supportive learning community, pedagogical leadership that provides ongoing feedback on how the theory translates into the practice of the classroom, and a safe learning environment where experimenting with change is part of the learning experience for teachers.

The 21st century demands rigour and relevance in learning, and the changes proposed by the revised MYP point strongly in that direction. Schools now need to step up to the challenge. John Dewey said, 'If we teach today's students as we taught yesterday's, we rob them of tomorrow' (1944). The word 'teach' could readily be substituted by the word 'assess' to summarise the importance of the changes to assessment in the revised MYP: if we assess today's students as we assessed yesterday's, we rob them of tomorrow.

References

Bailey, K. M. (1998): Learning about language assessment: dilemmas, decisions, and directions. Heinle & Heinle: US.

Baker, E. L. (2008): *Measuring 21st century skills.* Invited paper presented at the Universidad Complutense de Madrid, Madrid, Spain.

Black, P.J. and Wiliam, D. (1998): *Assessment and Classroom Learning*, Assessment in Education, Volume 5, Issue 1,

Bredeson, P (2005): p 1-8 *Building Capacity in Schools: Some ethical considerations for authentic leadership and learning*, University of Wisconsin-Madison, USA, 2005 (VEEA VOL 4)

Brualdi, A. (1998): Implementing performance assessment in the classroom. Practical Assessment, Research &Evaluation, 6(2). Available online: http://ericae.net/pare/getvn.asp?v=6&n=2

Darling-Hammond and Adamson (2010): *Beyond basic skills: The role of performance assessment in achieving 21st century standards of learning.* Stanford, CA: Stanford University, USA, Stanford Center for Opportunity Policy in Education.

Denver Public Schools (2007): *'International Baccalaureate Prospectus'.* Denver, Colorado, USA.

Dewey, J (1944): *Democracy and Education,* New York: Macmillan Company, p167.

Doll R. (1992): *Curriculum Improvement: Decision Making and Process.* 8th ed. Needham Heights, MA, USA, Allyn and Bacon

Erickson, H L (2012): *Concept-based teaching and learning.* Cardiff, UK: IB Publishing.

IB (2008): *From Principles into Practice: Using assessment criteria.* Cardiff, UK: IB Publishing.

IB (2010): *The History of the MYP.* Cardiff, UK: IB Publishing.

IB (2014): *From Principles into Practice.* Cardiff, UK: IB Publishing.

IB (2015): Online workshop '*Managing assessment in the MYP*'.

Jackson D. (2006): "*The International Baccalaureate Middle Years Program: A Comparison of the Standards of Learning Achievement Levels by Total Group and Ethnicity*'. Dissertation submitted to the Faculty of the Virginia Polytechnic Institute and State University. Blacksburg, Virginia, USA.

Organization for Economic Cooperation and Development(OECD) (2005): *Definition and Selection of Key Competencies. Paris,* France.

Partnership for 21st Century Skills (2007) *21st Century Skills Assessment e-paper* Last revised 10.14.07.

Pink, D. (1995): *Drive.* New York, NY: Riverhead Books.

Senge, P., Kleiner, A., Roberts, C., Ross, R., Roth, G., & Smith, B. (1999): *The dance of change: The challenges of sustaining momentum in learning organizations.* New York, USA, Doubleday.

NFER (2012). *International Baccalaureate Middle Years Programme in the UK,* Slough, UK, National Foundation for Educational Research

Wiggins, G (1998): *Educative Assessment: Designing Assessments to Inform and Improve Student Performance.* San Francisco, Josey-Bass

Wiggins G. McTighe J. (2005): Understanding by Design. Alexandria, Virginia, USA, ASCD Publishing

Chapter 7

Assessing the MYP: eAssessing year 5 students

Gareth Hegarty

Introduction

As at November 2015, the development of the new eAssessment and Personal Project provision for the revised Middle Years Programme is complete; electronic examinations have been prepared for future examination sessions and numerous assessment trials have been completed. However, the assessment design is untested in the real world; it is yet to affect young people's lives or the way teachers teach. It remains still a vision, developed over years of research and planning. As such it is not possible to critique its success but only to report the aspirations of those who have shaped the assessment model, the challenges that have been faced in its implementation and how the assessment provision has evolved as result of these. This chapter aims to achieve this and to discuss how the assessments have been received so far.

A common feature of MYP eAssessment, as the name suggests, is that it all takes place in the digital domain. Access to IT equipment and its use to support the development of inquiry and investigation skills are intrinsically linked to a modern constructivist approach to teaching and learning. Schools have generally understood this and invested in technology but they have been held back by the assessment services offered by the IB and other organisations and awarding bodies. MYP schools, from 2015, will have an assessment system that is supportive of their efforts, appropriate for the modern classroom and for the development of the skills required in the MYP and for their lives thereafter.

For students at schools that choose to take part in eAssessment, the series of assessments in the final year of study (year 5 of the MYP) should provide a natural culmination of two to five years of MYP studies. Preparation for these assessments is supported through material released during the year which focuses discussion and inquiry around connected themes across the subject groups. Through this approach, the powerful influence of high stakes assessment, and in particular its oft quoted tendency to narrow curriculum (Mitchel, 2006), is used constructively to stimulate study, to model MYP interdisciplinary practice, and to inspire achievement. The assessments themselves will also be innovative, replacing the traditional imperative to memorise with a desire to understand, to apply concepts, to relate to global contexts, to practise transfer of knowledge and interdisciplinary exploration, and to inquire, communicate and reflect.

The new assessment provision for the MYP is undoubtedly ambitious and unique. In addition to making innovative use of digital technology, it aims to challenge established assessment paradigms and create an assessment provision which is authentic, supportive of best teaching practice, engaging for teachers and students alike and the best preparation for the IB Diploma Programme (DP) or any other further study.

Overview of MYP eAsessment

The main features of the new MYP assessment model are:

- Mandatory moderation of the Personal Project for all schools with candidates in year 5 of the programme. For the first time the MYP has its own mandatory assessment for all year 5 students. The Personal Project has long been a central part of MYP curriculum and assessment. This extended project allows students to explore an activity or a project of interest to them and provides a framework within which students can independently inquire, take action and reflect. The assessment of the project focuses on process rather than product and, in particular, the demonstration of Approaches to Learning (ATL) skills. By sampling the Personal Projects in all schools, the IB aims to learn from the range of activities undertaken in schools as well as supporting assessment literacy across the MYP community.

- On-screen examinations in Science, Individuals and Societies, Mathematics, Language and Literature and a new component designed to assess interdisciplinary learning. These innovative examinations use multimedia, animations and simulations to create engaging scenarios or express complex information in an easily digestible format. They require students to demonstrate inquiry, communication and reflective skills in addition to substantial subject knowledge, but they are conceptual in nature, not content-based.

- An ePortfolio to be submitted for Arts, Design and/or Physical and Health Education and another for Language Acquisition. For the ePortfolios some key aspects are prescribed, including the summative assessment tasks, and distributed in the form of a partially completed MYP unit planner. Teachers complete the plan, carry out assessment, record their assessment outcomes and submit a sample of student work for moderation to the IB. Prescription enables the IB to specify the breadth of work studied and the type and amount of work used for assessment which ensures fairness for students as well as manageability and reliability of marking.

In all, students aiming for the MYP Certificate will take eight assessments: five examinations, the completion of two ePortfolios and the Personal Project. Each assessment is graded on the usual IB grade scale of 1-7; students who achieve a minimum of 28 points with a grade 3 or more in each assessment will be awarded an MYP Certificate.

Challenges

The creation of concept-based examinations and improving the established MYP moderation process brings with it considerable academic and practical challenge. Furthermore, although IT is an enabler, building new IT solutions has produced many technological challenges for the IB in the first years of development.

Establishing parameters for student learning

The established MYP moderation method, in use up until 2015, provided schools with a good service in terms of supporting the delivery and assessment of the MYP in schools, but it lacked some of the mechanisms necessary to apply one universal assessment standard and lacked broad recognition. The model would have been extremely well rated in terms of validity, (Griffith University, 2015) but less so in terms of the other facets of good assessment design in particular the manageability for schools and examiners, and the reliability of student outcomes. The new model seeks to redress this balance and in order to do so, both the ePortfolio and on-screen examinations seek to contain the range of evidence to be assessed by establishing some parameters around what students learn.

The partially populated unit planners for the ePortfolio still allow a great deal of flexibility for the final unit of study but require the unit to be developed around the same themes, and describe what should be submitted for assessment. This allows teams of examiners to establish standards through a standardisation process once submissions are received, reasonably safe in the knowledge that decisions established in the process will apply to all work received.

Examinations take this further in that all students respond to the same questions, but establishing fair accessible and rigorous questions is challenging without an explicit syllabus. In order to meet the challenge a compromise to the 'content agnostic' nature of the MYP was necessary because we found that our authors brought with them assumptions about the kinds of topics that were typically taught in an MYP classroom for this age group. All questions, even when they target conceptual knowledge, require a context, and students who were familiar with a context would have an advantage over those who were not. There was, therefore, a need to make that expected knowledge explicit. Topic lists in each disciplinary subject were established. This could have resulted in the production of a long and detailed syllabus resulting in more traditional looking examinations, but instead our topic lists are brief and high level in nature. The lists do not express what students will be tested on, *per se*, but rather provide prior warning that concept, skill or knowledge questions in a subject may require a particular background in order to access them.

Furthermore, topic lists were deemed necessary as typically one quarter of MYP assessments reward students for 'knowledge and understanding' (or criterion A). These are often open in nature and allow students to bring to the exam the specific content of their classroom but will always be asked from within the safe ground of the topic lists. Typically exams also assess inquiry skills, communication skills and reflection. Again, though not specific in nature, these questions explore familiar concepts and aim to present them in non-familiar contexts. Students bring their skills of transfer of knowledge to bear on the given situation and communicate their new understandings. In order to ask questions like this, examiners need to have an understanding of what is expected knowledge and what is not.

Technology

In terms of manageability for all concerned, eAssessment takes advantage of technology to facilitate the secure upload of student work. The new approach to moderation known in the IB as 'dynamic sampling' requires schools to upload a sample of five, eight or 10 students' work using an interface that has already received praise from DP schools. The samples themselves are smaller, having been carefully defined by the unit planner and where agreement is found between examiners and the school in the first three student samples, all marking outcomes of the school are accepted without further analysis. This results in fewer small moderation adjustments and greater endorsement of school standards. The same approach of sampling is used for the Personal Project. Although going through any technology process for the first time is inevitably challenging for schools, it is anticipated that after the first submission, they will appreciate the reduced burden required to submit work for ePortfolio.

There was a decision early on in the development process to create an on-screen but not online examination system. At the time of writing the internet is less than 100% dependable, even in those countries where modern infrastructure exists. For large numbers of students online examinations would be prone to failure somewhere. It would also clearly limit the participation of schools in countries where the infrastructure is less robust or where poor data transfer speeds are experienced. Furthermore the examinations were planned to contain video and other data rich media. Enabling large numbers of students to stream the same content simultaneously would have been impossible in even the best equipped schools.

The decision to go on-screen but not online means that all schools can take part; an internet connection is required but the quality of that connection is not critical. This is because it is only needed as a delivery system; prior to the examination, schools download the exam in the form of an executable file and after the exam student responses are uploaded for marking. The criticality is eliminated as none of this needs to happen during or even on the day of the exam. Once downloaded no internet activity (or inactivity) can interfere with the smooth operation of the examination files. In addition to using the internet as a delivery system, for those schools who do have a reliable internet connection there are some functions that the examination system does make use of, these are automatic upload at the end of the examination and automatic backup of exams as they are taken. The former makes examination management easier for schools and the latter offers an additional layer of security in the event of computer failure. Schools that can't make use of these features are offered alternative support to ensure their examinations remain manageable and secure. The on-screen nature of the examinations does have work implications for schools; they have to download the files and load them on to each machine on which an examination is to be taken.

The benefits of assessment technology

The use of IT is a powerful enabler for a global organisation such as the IB and offers opportunities for efficiencies and scalability of the assessment process. In the electronic domain, documents are transferred between schools, the IB and examiners quickly and securely, eliminating one of the major complications that arise from the global distribution of IB schools. Working with files in the digital domain allows for elaborate business process mapping; files can be automatically transformed and transported between different environments and tools, each one tailored to its specific purpose in the assessment process. For example, for examinations, students' responses can be anonymised and broken into small sections for marking, and the marks generated for each section combined later in the process to find the student total. This breaking up of examination papers into small question item groups (QIGs) allows examiners to mark by question groups rather than entire scripts and research shows that this QIGing (question item grouping) approach reduces cognitive demand on examiners and significantly improves reliability (Wheadon and Pinot de Moira, 2013). Similarly, the digital domain allows for a robust quality assurance model which is employed during the marking process. After a standardisation process, the model requires examiners to demonstrate accuracy and reliability through first qualifying before marking begins, and then being closely monitored through seeding. Both processes involve examiners marking scripts which have previously been marked by the principal examiner and therefore have a 'known' mark. The application of these processes results in the elimination of possible sources of bias and ensures examiners maintain fair and accurate marking.

eAssessment in detail

The ePortfolio

Subjects that have a performative or coursework element are assessed using a submitted ePortfolio. An ePortfolio in the MYP context is a range of evidence that demonstrates and supports the level of achievement awarded to a student by their teacher. This body of evidence is uploaded to the IB for moderation. The nature of the evidence collected differs according to the subject or discipline being assessed and is communicated to schools via a partially completed unit planner. The unit planner for the Arts, Design and Physical and Health Education (PHE) have similarities and are slightly different in nature to that of Language Acquisition.

The assessment process begins with the release of the MYP Global Context and partially populated unit planners for ePortfolio subjects five months before the deadline for completion, marking and submission of samples in year 5 of the MYP. The release of materials allows teachers to consider the demands of the prescribed parts of the unit planner and the limitations of their own school context to be able to complete the development of the planner. Teaching the unit of study should take about 20 hours.

The unit planner is a central structure in MYP teaching and learning and should be used routinely to plan relevant, demanding units of study which are conceptual in nature and are supported by high quality well-resourced summative assessment. It also enables schools to integrate a range of topics or content which may be demanded at the national or district level into the MYP teaching and learning framework. For eAssessment unit planners are partially completed, that means that the following sections of the planner are completed by the IB:

- Key concepts: broad, organising, powerful, ideas that have relevance within and across subjects

- Related concepts: these provide a focus for inquiry into subject-specific content

- Global context: authentic world settings, events and circumstances, that provide concrete perspectives for teaching and learning

- Statement of inquiry: the key and related concepts and the global context expressed as a meaningful inquiry statement that students can understand

- Factual, conceptual and debatable enquiry questions: developments of the statement of inquiry that enable it to be explored in greater detail.

(IB, 2013)

Whilst related and key concepts differ between subjects and disciplines, all of the unit planners for a given assessment session share the same Global Context, as does at least one task in each of the disciplinary examinations and all of the interdisciplinary examinations. The release of the Global Context along with the partially completed unit planner therefore reveals key information about all of the assessment activities for the session.

The summative assessment details section is where the unit planners differ the most. For Arts, Design and PHE the assessment activities are largely defined by the subject and the way the assessment criteria are arranged; they all feature tasks which help capture evidence from each stage of their respective enquiry/ creative cycles. The Language Acquisition ePortfolio is offered at three levels which correspond to three of the six phases of MYP language study: emergent, capable and proficient. Assessment tasks are consistent between these levels and comprise: an aural comprehension, written comprehension an interactive oral and a writing task. Whereas for other ePortfolio subjects, the nature of the task is prescribed, for Language Acquisition the assessment activities themselves are much more exam like and set centrally. Each task uses a series of visual, written or spoken texts and along with the unit planner, the IB provides a range of material for this purpose. This approach is a compromise between establishing a fair assessment in terms of comparability between the assessment tasks used in different schools and the security risk of providing highly secure, prescribed assessment material 6 months before it is to be used in schools. It also preserves freedom for teachers to contribute to assessment design for their own students.

On-screen examinations

Four subject groups and a new assessment of interdisciplinary learning are assessed using concept based, on-screen examinations. These make use of multimedia and digital data to bring to life real world issues to which students respond and use an inquiry approach to offer solutions and to demonstrate a broad range of skills and understanding.

MYP on-screen examinations are designed to look and feel like other electronic environments with which students would be familiar. On opening the examination, students meet an 'overview page' which lists the questions available in the exam in question order, each question in its own blue box container. The questions are organised into three tasks and the first question in a task contains information about the task as a whole. Successive questions are represented as a brief summary only, enough to provide an indication of the question whilst ensuring that the overview page remains uncluttered, and an aid rather than an impediment to time management. Clicking on any of the question fields takes students directly to the question. A navigation bar to the right of the screen offers another way for students to navigate the exam. A configurable clock and a 'tag' facility highlights questions to which a student may wish to return to complete the basic functions of the system. Overall the design and functionality is simple and uncluttered, allowing students control without distracting them with excessive functionality.

Once selected, questions are presented as a series of stimulus, question and response 'objects' all within their own container on a scrollable page. Stimulus objects can be text, data tables, audio, video, a simulation or a combination of all or some of these. Question items are always text based with a consistent format whilst response objects can be in the form of text, data, tables, graph or a still image such as an infographic, poster, mind map, flowchart. The only limitation being that it must be able to be captured as a still image. This design is very flexible.

Whilst maintaining a number of programme wide presentational features, each subject group has its own structure or examination blueprint which dictates the number of marks available in each task, the nature of the task (investigation and communication or knowledge and understanding for example) and how this is related to the subject group assessment criteria. Overall each examination must address every possible strand of every criteria and maintain an even distribution of marks across the examination for each of the four MYP assessment criteria. In combination with the subject criteria and topic lists, the blueprint serves to ensure that although each examination will feel unique, students know what to expect. In other words, the examinations are engaging but there should be no surprises!

It is common for tasks to begin with a combination of media and some simpler questions in order to capture student's interest and engage them in the context of the question. Questions may then become more challenging but they tend to be open questions and therefore accessible to all. Each question, and the task as a whole, is constructed around presenting the stimulus required and asking the right question to provoke responses from students, responses that demonstrate achievement against the level descriptors for each criteria being assessed. The marks allocated to the question reflect the depth and demand of the question as specified in the subject's assessment criteria level descriptors. The deeper the question, the greater the achievement available to the candidate, so questions that allow students to demonstrate level eight understanding will be rewarded with more marks than questions that allow demonstration of level five or six achievement only. Consequently the marks awarded to each question usually reflect the length of time required for candidates to respond.

Language and Literature

The Language and Literature exam begins with a task built around the analysis and comparison of two texts, one of which is rich media in nature. MYP Language and Literature requires the analysis of visual communication in order to understand how language and images interact. Assessment of these skills would not have been possible in a paper based examination and this exemplifies how much the on-screen exam approach can contribute to assessment validity. The second and third tasks are based around extended response items which demonstrate the students' ability to produce literary and non-literary texts. The benefit of producing such text in an electronic format has been well demonstrated by feedback from students even from the first trials, indeed producing written text in any other way is becoming increasingly invalid.

Individuals and Societies

The three tasks for Individuals and Societies are written to assess students' ability to investigate, communicate and think critically. The former requires students to formulate and justify research questions, formulate action plans and to evaluate an investigation. The on-screen exam makes good use of sources to stimulate and contextualise these activities. In the communicating task, students are required to engage creatively with a topic and present ideas in an appropriate style. Examples could be blogs, posters, infographics or more formal written articles or reports. Again these activities are contextualised by rich media content. The third task develops ideas through shorter response questions but culminates in an extended piece of writing demonstrating the student's ability to discuss issues, arguments and perspectives.

Sciences

Whilst the criterion A requirement (knowledge and understanding) of Individuals and Societies is well integrated into the exam, and demonstrated through the use of examples and evidence to support arguments in writing tasks, in the Sciences, the first task is designed to assess this alone. Shorter questions are designed to sample the breadth and depth of the topic list but not to look for gaps or to explore remote aspects of the topic in question. Video or simulations are often used to present familiar ideas in non-familiar contexts and in doing so test students ability to transfer their scientific knowledge to novel situations. The second task is half of the mark allocation of the examination and tests the student's investigative skills; again, models and simulations or real video can be used to put students at the heart of an authentic investigation, using measurement, table and graphing tools to collect data, process data and draw conclusions. The final task explores how science is applied in the world, including the many ethical issues it raises, using longer response-style questions.

Mathematics

Mathematics examinations share some of the characteristics with the Sciences exam, as the titles of the three tasks demonstrate: knowing and understanding; applying mathematics in real life contexts; investigating patterns. In the first task, knowledge of the mathematics skills framework is explored and in the second task, longer responses are required in order for students to evaluate and justify the use of mathematical models in a range of contexts. The final task requires students to undertake a mathematical investigation; these questions are carefully designed to model a relationship or investigative approach and then allow students to demonstrate the methodology themselves. This final task is a real innovation in mathematics examination design.

Interdisciplinary learning

Interdisciplinary teaching and learning has been an important component of the MYP from its beginnings but, as a result of the review of the programme, it is now supported with a dedicated guide and assessment criteria. Along with the guide, the interdisciplinary examination has been developed to support the requirement of MYP schools to teach at least one interdisciplinary unit each year. The exam makes it possible for the IB to demonstrate interdisciplinary activities and the application of the interdisciplinary marking criteria. It also ensures this important part of the programme is given the consideration it requires in schools as it carries with it the same weighting as any single disciplinary exam. The interdisciplinary examination sets the standards in many ways for other disciplinary exams to follow, as in addition to assessing interdisciplinary understanding, it provides an excellent opportunity to examine knowledge transfer, conceptual understanding and the application of Global Contexts.

Unlike the other on-screen examinations there is no topic list for interdisciplinary learning. All on-screen examinations go beyond factual knowledge and lead directly to deeper conceptual questions by using sources and stimuli to provide a factual background or framework for students. The interdisciplinary exam takes this one step further by making use of pre-release material. Pre-release material (PRM) is published as an internet web page about six weeks before the exam takes place and consists of a series of articles, literature extracts, graphics, and charts or graphical data, all presented as a range of media types. It focuses on discussions that would have been stimulated by the release of the Global Context five months earlier, and establishes the theme around which the exam is based. Together with knowledge of the two subject groups which are to be explored (this is announced at the same time), with the PRM students are well armed to discuss with teachers how the two subjects relate to the rich stimulus material the PRM contains. However what is included in the PRM is selected with care. It should stimulate interest and discussion, but it should also provide plenty of opportunity for development so that predicting the examinations content is not a rewarding strategy!

The exam is made up of three tasks: disciplinary grounding; interdisciplinary synthesis and communication; and reflection. The first task explores the disciplinary nature of source material and/or the pre-release material, the emphasis here being on thinking like a mathematician or in a way expected in Language and Literature for example. We are not trying to produce the kind of questions that would already have been seen in the disciplinary exam; it's the ways of knowing that matter.

The second task requires students to consider examples of disciplinary and interdisciplinary material and to discuss the properties of the material; they are also asked to produce an interdisciplinary product themselves and comment on some of the choices they have made. The final task asks students to reflect on their experience of interdisciplinarity, either within the exam or throughout their studies. They may have used the ways of knowing of a mathematician, but do they understand that was what they were doing, what the ways of knowing used by a mathematician are, and what that brings to a situation? Have they thought about what other subject could be brought to bear on the issue at hand, and how that subject might interact with the two chosen? These are deeply metacognitive questions, and it remains to be seen whether we can capture genuine metacognition or will students simply learn the answers? Does it matter of they do? We will know after a few sessions how successful we have been in capturing and measuring interdisciplinary understanding.

Personal Project and Approaches to Learning

The Personal Project allows students to choose an area of their own interest and then independently undertake the inquiry and action required to produce the desired product or outcome. Students then complete the inquiry cycle with structured reflection. Students are assessed against criteria for investigating, planning, taking action and reflection.

While the investigating criterion requires a judgement to be made about the students research skills, the planning phase requires self-management skills. The action phase requires demonstration of thinking, communication and social skills and reflection itself forms one of the ATL categories. These are just the skills assessed directly; it's fair to say that all of the ATL skills are brought to bear in a good Personal Project and rewarded by the criteria when they are.

Outcomes of the pilot on-screen examination session: May 2015

Following a number of years of technological and academic development, with trials held in September 2013 and January 2014, the first complete on-screen examinations prepared for MYP year 5 students were piloted in May 2015. Sixty-three schools took part in the pilot with over 4,000 subject entries. There were between 700-750 candidates in the four disciplinary subjects offered (History, Biology, Language and Literature, and Mathematics) and over 1250 candidates for interdisciplinary learning.

Overall, the pilot was a positive experience for the IB and for schools. The examinations were well received by schools with some very encouraging feedback. The exams worked, candidate responses were captured successfully, and all the examining teams were able to mark candidates responses and they demonstrated acceptable levels of reliability or better. Delivery of the eAssessments to the schools took place very smoothly, with a relatively small number of technical glitches, each of which was resolved with good collaboration between the schools and the IB.

The results for Language and Literature were by far the strongest, showing the kind of distribution expected of a mature examination. Interdisciplinary learning and History also showed promising results but results in Mathematics and Biology were lower than for the other subjects.

These results, however, have to be considered in context. The students had never seen a complete MYP examination in Mathematics and Biology and so would not have been prepared for them. In these subjects MYP on-screen examinations are perhaps the least traditional in content and presentation with Mathematics, for example, requiring extended responses and an investigation. We therefore believe that exposure to these styles of questions through the release of specimen examinations will support teachers in their future preparation of students.

We have also learned from some of the limitations of students in the pilot and this will inform future task design. In particular we have reduced the time required to complete the exams, in most cases through simplifying the structure of questions. For Individuals and Societies and Language and Literature revised blueprints have been developed.

The pilot generated large quantities of qualitative and quantitative data and an opportunity to follow through an entire assessment cycle in preparation for 2016. The most satisfying result of the trial was the fact that so many head teachers, MYP coordinators, teachers and students supported the developments and kindly provided encouraging feedback even though carrying out the download and distribution, and some technical glitches, often made for a very busy and stressful week for them. The IB is extremely grateful to them for their commitment to making the pilot work and for sharing our vision. The work of these schools in this less structured, inaugural session has helped all schools who will take part in examinations in future as we have learned how best to support schools in the new processes.

Teachers and coordinators provided frank feedback about specific and practical aspects of the pilot, but they were highly supportive of our work in general, and praised the examinations. On the whole it's fair to say that the overwhelming response was positive, including feedback provided by students in their reflections taken directly after the examination.

Sample feedback from schools:

> *"The majority of our candidates had a wonderful experience in this well-designed, user-friendly examination package...We think that this experience has already given them a taste of what Onscreen examination is... And most importantly, it has also offered teachers a better picture about the new MYP assessment...We think this is a very successful trial. The backwash effect would be of great significance."*

> *"The students, by the way, are enjoying the experience"*

> *"The tasks themselves were rich and cool; much more interactive and pleasing than any written text can ever be."*

> *"This has been an interesting and highly valuable experience. We conducted the exams without real incident with highly committed students, which was truly a privilege to experience."*

Some reflective feedback from students:

> *"I would tell them that the experience challenges your knowledge, and is not based on memorising the content. it is highly conceptual and draws on your knowledge of your entire learning experience in the subject."*

> *"I really enjoyed the experience, as I found it to be mentally challenging and stimulating."*

"It was a good way of testing language abilities and the time stated for each activity was helpful."

"The most effective learning strategy was researching skills."

"MYP doesn't teach you to remember the years just to pass the test. MYP makes you think deeper and analyse historical events. It's not just telling what happened at what year or who did what, but it is also why and how it was done/ happened. This is why MYP history is not boring."

"It is a little complicated doing an exam on a computer application, but it is certainly faster than handwriting it. I think it is more effective because I type fast, and my handwriting is usually bad. This makes it better to read."

Conclusion

There is no question that the ways in which young people learn about the world have changed dramatically. The way that information is transferred has shifted from paper-based to electronic media, evident through the ubiquity of personal computers, tablets and mobile phones, and the rise of educational games and social media. This shift has had a dramatic impact on schools and good teaching practice.

Good MYP teaching will harness the opportunities information technology offers in the classroom and, with the resulting changes in the nature, methods, and organisation of education, must also come changes in assessment. The questions that those involved in assessment design should ask is how assessment can progress in order to remain relevant in this information rich world and, even more importantly, how it can effectively contribute to the educational achievement of every student? MYP eAssessment seeks to be relevant and support student learning and achievement by using the structures already present in a progressive academic programme and constructing a rigorous, valid means of assessment to support growth, recognition and high quality delivery of the programme.

Development of the eAssessment, including a live pilot, has been challenging but initial findings are very encouraging. The first steps have been taken. The model is adaptable so future iterations and the technology will be used to make continuous improvements. There are also other areas of the MYP, for example the Learner Profile and the skills of ATL, that could find creative uses for this assessment technology.

Better education and better assessment for the young people of today is out there for the taking. The revised MYP curriculum, combined with eAssessment, provides a glimpse of what is possible. Time will tell whether the many balances made in its design have been well judged and whether school communities are ready for a truly modern approach to assessment.

References

Griffith University(no date given) *Designing effective assessment:Assessment Matters.* Available URL http://app.griffith.edu.au/assessment-matters/docs/design-assessment/principles [accessed November 2015]

IB (2014): *MYP From principles into Practice.* Cardiff, UK: IB Publishing.

IB (2015): *MYP Guide to eAssessment.* Cardiff, UK: IB Publishing

Mitchel, R. (2006): High-stakes testing and effects on instruction: Research review. *Centre for Public Education.* Available URL http://www.centerforpubliceducation.org/Main-Menu/Instruction/High-stakes-testing-and-effects-on-instruction-At-a-glance/High-stakes-testing-and-effects-on-instruction-Research-review.html [accessed August 2015]

Wheadon, C. and Pinot de Moira, A. (2013) Gains in Marking Reliability from Item-Level Marking: Is the Sum of the Parts Better than the Whole? *Educational Research and Evaluation.* v19 n8 p665-679. 15 pp.

Part B
Practitioner perspectives

116

Chapter 8

Do we really reach all? Holism in the MYP

Hege Myhre

"Do not let kids go through the school not knowing what they are good at." (Sir Ken Robinson)

IB Middle Years Programme and holism

As the winds of change blow through the International Baccalaureate (IB) Middle Years Programme (MYP), one thing has remained intact from the earlier versions of the programme: the aim of the MYP being an inclusive and holistic programme. Ideas of holistic education have been expressed and shaped in many forms over time, and theorists including John Dewey, Jean Piaget, Ralph Waldo Emerson, Henry David Thoreau, Maria Montessori, Kurt Hahn, Rudolf Steiner and Noam Chomsky, among many others, have brought different perspectives to the concept. Ron Miller, founder of the journal *Holistic Education Review*, explains that 'The art of holistic education lies in its responsiveness to the diverse learning styles and needs of evolving human beings' (Miller, 2000). Holism is often seen as being opposed to reductionism, advocating recognition of diversity and the many-faceted layers of meaning and expression of human life, where the individuals' intelligence, skills and abilities are regarded as intrinsically complex. Rather than simply address the cognitive dimension of human beings through education, practitioners of holism aim at developing the whole person, including the moral, emotional, physical, psychological and spiritual dimensions. In defining holism, Miller states that 'Holistic education is based on the premise that each person finds identity, meaning, and purpose in life through connections to the community, to the natural world, and to spiritual values such as compassion and peace. Holistic education aims to call forth from people an intrinsic reverence for life and a passionate love of learning.' (Miller, 2000). Holistic education enforces the importance of active and engaged students who question ideas, theories and the world around them, and use reflection to aid their learning. Experience and interaction with the community are preferred to thick textbooks, and building relationships with different collaborators is of importance.

Without doubt, holism is at the very core of MYP philosophy. The previous model of MYP emphasised three fundamental concepts: Holistic Learning, Intercultural Awareness and Communication. Even though these are not explicitly stated as overarching concepts in the revised MYP, the concepts are implicitly expressed through the IB Learner Profile – a set of attributes of internationally-minded people which represent a broad range of human capacities. The IB states that 'Promoting open communication based on understanding and respect, the IB encourages students to become active, compassionate lifelong learners. An IB education is holistic in nature – it is concerned with the whole person. Along with cognitive development, IB programmes and qualifications address students' social, emotional and physical well-being.' (IB, 2014a, p9). The circular representation of the MYP model places the learner in the centre, and through extensive inquiry, action and reflection, students are expected to engage with authentic issues that are local, regional and global. Concepts are explored in contexts that are meaningful to the learner, and the programme is expected to be flexible enough to allow each individual to draw on their strengths and talents, in addition to their own learning preferences, in order to foster increased competence. Students are expected to develop a strong sense of personal identity at the same time as seeing themselves as a meaningful part of a bigger whole in the global society.

The eight subject groups of the MYP are given equal representation in the balanced programme model, representing the IB's expressed intention of a broad and balanced curriculum, and the blurring color shades among the subject groups reflect the IB's focus on interdisciplinary learning. The IB expects both students and teachers to benefit from interdisciplinary learning environments, which not only provide a holistic picture of complex ideas and issues to study, but through collaboration also deepen holistic understanding of disciplinary concepts and contexts when students and teachers synthesise relevant information from different disciplines (IB, 2014b). The entire MYP, culminating in either the Community Project or the Personal Project, promotes the importance of developing and demonstrating Approaches to Learning (ATL) skills, as these foster the development of independent, lifelong learners (IB, 2014a). Finally, the MYP is designed to be inclusive in terms of access whereby all students can thrive and benefit from the programme, and educational inclusion is viewed as an ongoing process which can ensure better engagement in learning for all. The practice of full inclusion is seen as putting aspects of the Learner Profile in action, and 'IB programme principles and practices call for schools to be organized in ways that value student diversity and respect individual learning differences. Valuing diversity and difference is a key aspect of becoming more internationally-minded and is an important goal of all IB programmes.' (IB, 2014a, p27)

Building on such a clear philosophical outline of the MYP's holistic aims, this chapter will consider how some of the changes in the revised programme (as described earlier in this book) might impact upon the practical achievement of holism in the MYP, for better or worse. Given constraints upon the length of this chapter I have chosen to focus on four particular dimensions: organisational structures, leadership, inclusion and standardisation.

Programme structure

Despite the equal value placed on all subject groups in the MYP curriculum model, this equal value is seldom reflected in practice. Quite typically some subjects are allocated considerably more teaching time than others, and in most cases 'academic' subjects such as Mathematics, Sciences, Languages and Individuals and Societies are given priority over 'less important' or 'less academic' subjects such as the Arts, Design and Physical & Health Education. This stigmatised perception has always puzzled me, as I don't see the subject group or discipline as being academic in itself; rather it is the way we look at an issue or choose to treat it that determines the extent of its academic rigour – which can be applied to any of the subjects, including Music and Dance. The problem with such a stigmatised preference for some of the subject groups is that students with interests, talents and skills in the subjects perceived as 'less important' are provided with less opportunity to develop to their fullest, and to celebrate their individuality. In some cases these students may even feel less inclined to attend an IB school. Schools' stigmatised perception of fair imbalance is shared by many parents worldwide, and is also reflected in state requirements or cultural expectations. For instance, through a decade serving as the Head and Coordinator of the MYP in an international school I have received numerous mails and phone calls from parents letting me know that their children are sick and would only come to school for the 'important' lessons, such as Science; we should excuse them due to illness before the PE classes in the afternoon. I have yet to encounter a parent wishing to send their child to a Visual Arts class but have them excused from Mathematics.

With the introduction of the subject group flexibility option, the MYP now allows students or even schools to opt out of some subject groups in the final two years of the programme – if the students are believed to be better served by studying fewer subjects (IB, 2014a). It might be imagined that, in a holistic system where balance and equal value are highlighted, the student or the school would be able to choose which subject groups to cut in such a situation. In reality however, it is Arts, Design and Physical & Health education that are the three optional subject groups from which students only have to study one of the three, while the five other groups remain compulsory. This hierarchical perspective of the MYP subject groups is further emphasized by the requirements for the validated certificate, as well as by the suggested teaching hours if subjects are to be validated. In practice, schools in some countries are under increasing pressure to opt for the subject flexibility option despite their best pedagogical intentions. This is the case in Norway, where the host country culture emphasises the importance of 'kids being kids' and having plenty of time for play; factors including public transport, school buses and early afternoon practice time for local sports clubs limit the possibility of long school days. In addition, national requirements include that all students in Norway, no matter which school they attend, should study at least three languages across the MYP age range. Furthermore, problems with aligning the IB models with the national system in terms of age and levels – a requirement if state funding is to be received – has led to most MYP schools in the country offering only the last four years of the MYP, rather than all five. With limitations on teaching time as described, there is growing speculation amongst some parents, educators and boards as to whether schools would be better off cutting down on the number of subjects and concentrating only on the "important" subjects. Yet other schools, with more teaching time available, might find themselves limiting the options due to human and financial resources. Small schools, for instance, that do not have enough students at each grade level to fill several options in subject choices – which would lead to running half-full classes – might limit choices in order to cut costs, with the choice of preferred subjects being potentially dominated by current staffing and expertise rather than by ideas about holism. The need for costly equipment, in offering for instance a proper Design programme, might also be a limitation, with a consequence being that some school leaders with limited resources might be tempted to avoid spreading those resources too thinly and to concentrate on fewer subject groups with greater resources for those that are offered.

To my mind, the institutionalised devaluation of some subjects threatens some of the aims I expect the IB to uphold in striving to promote holistic education. While the revised MYP acknowledges that Physical and Health Education may not be meaningful in all contexts or to all students, and that some will therefore prefer to opt out, those who do not see the value in Mathematics and Science are not offered the option of weighing their strengths, weaknesses, personalities and goals in the same manner. As the world is already overfilled with rhetoric about students needing more Mathematics and Science, when research actually bears out that the Arts, Humanities and Design are producing the creative thinking from which innovation is most likely to spring, I wonder how the IB expects to continue to hold the high ground and to be the change it purports to want to see in the world. Following Norway's admission as a member of Horizon 2020 – the largest EU Research and Innovation programme ever, aimed at stimulating economic growth and creating jobs – I was fortunate enough to participate in one of the first conferences discussing the needs of competence for the future. In a setting with 200 other participants, nearly all business leaders, the most vividly used terms in the room were creativity, innovation, ingenuity, adaptability and stamina. Indeed Sir Ken Robinson, one of the foremost advocates of fostering creativity in schools, has pointed out in a number of speeches, interviews and books that it is time to question the basis for upscaling some subjects at the cost of others. Robinson proposes that there is a gap between what schools are teaching and what modern economies actually need, arguing that the new jobs in current and future society need new skill sets. He argues 'The irony is that in many countries there's plenty of work to be done but despite the massive investment in education, too many people don't have the skills that are needed to do it' (Robinson and Aronica, 2015, p16). In calling for more support for vocational skills alongside academic skills,

Robinson argues that human intelligence goes further than academic ability, and that we need achievement in intelligence and skills developed through the arts, sports, technology, business, engineering, and so on.

As the world needs interdisciplinary thinking and creativity, the importance of teaching Arts, for example, should be obvious. Studying Arts fosters imagination and risk-taking, collaborative as well as individual work, and the ability to critique as well as the ability to make use of critique in one's own work. The processes of review, reflection and originating new ideas are all inherent in working with the arts. Creativity is of course much more than the Arts alone, but studying arts can be a meaningful way of developing creative abilities. Robinson states that being creative is about more than wild, random ideas that are seen as opposites of discipline and control; creativity involves a thorough process of refining, testing, focusing on improvement, critical judgement and original thinking (Robinson and Aronica, 2015). Studying Design, and Physical & Health Education as well as the Arts has value in itself, as they stimulate other aspects of the human capacity than Mathematics, Languages and so on. In my view, this value should be better protected in holistic education.

As much as the previous MYP unit planner was a great tool for ensuring inquiry-based learning, the new version is even better. Used wisely, the unit planner ensures rich opportunities for increased student input, including student design and ownership of their own learning process. The conceptual framework allows for tapping into content that is of interest and relevance for individuals, and cleverly conducting the planning process can make the learning personal and authentic to each student. Putting the unit planner into practice calls for continued inquiry, as both teachers and students can develop additional questions to explore throughout the unit. The increased emphasis on reflection prior to, during and after the unit further strengthens collaboration between the teacher and the students and, together with a strong ATL focus, should foster transformation of personal understanding as opposed to factual rote learning. The interdisciplinary units (IDUs) support holism further, providing both teachers and students with opportunities to deal with issues and problems as a whole. Some schools go off timetable for a set period of time and arrange the IDUs as full time study. This arrangement can allow students to choose between a number of IDUs based on particular interests and, instead of study groups being arranged by age, students study in mixed class groups. Such alternative organisation can be seen as a more authentic picture of what students are likely to encounter in their future working lives. Many schools are organised the way they are – with classes organised by age, timetables and bells – just because this is how it always has been, not because this is the way it necessarily should be, nor necessarily the way that promotes best learning. In fact, the enforced learning outcome requirements of service action and the introduction of the community project all promote students' learning by doing, and strengthen the students' learning about themselves and others, and how they can develop as responsible citizens of a global world.

Already touched upon briefly above, time constraints deserve their own paragraph here. Ask any IB practitioner, whether teacher or MYP Coordinator, what they regard as the greatest challenge in their work, and almost without exception they will include amongst their first answers "too little time to accomplish the given tasks". The MYP is a rigorous programme and some teachers, if not all, will argue that the aims and the objectives of the subject groups are so rigorous that the allocated teaching time is not nearly sufficient. The new IDU framework, with separate unit planner and separate assessment, leads to even less time for teaching towards the summative discipline-based assessment. Add to that the required time for eAssessment preparations that some schools have implemented, and the feeling of being overwhelmed is not unusual. The feeling of being stretched and not having enough time is unfortunate, and can lead to unwanted practice in the classroom. It takes time to design personalised teaching and learning, and time to allow students to shape their competence by inquiry. Feeling too stretched and not being able to "cover enough" might tempt teachers to change teaching practices, including focusing more on transmission of knowledge rather than on the development of competence.

Leadership

The flexibility of the IB allows schools to organise their administration in several ways. In my experience, this leads to great variety in successful leadership for implementation of the MYP. Louis and Miles make a distinction between managers and leaders in proposing that 'leaders set the course for the organization; managers make sure the course is followed. Leaders make strategic plans; managers design operational systems for carrying out the plans. Leaders stimulate and inspire; managers use their interpersonal influence and authority to translate that energy into productive work' (in Hayden and Thompson, 2008). The need for both dimensions is inherent in any programme, yet the new *MYP: From Principles into Practice* publication calls explicitly for a shift from a management model to pedagogical leadership. The role and importance of the MYP Coordinator is continually emphasised in the documentation, and is even further strengthened with the suggestion of creating an MYP Educational Team, or steering committee, to assist the Coordinator. Not only does a steering committee allow for broader perspectives and a higher degree of involvement of the leadership team; by including more people in the leadership structure, schools are less vulnerable when key individuals move on. I will return to the notion of stability shortly.

Even though the IB places most importance on the role of the Coordinator, Heads or Principals and Boards are still at the top of the school's organisational chart. Who are these leaders? And what profile do they have? The fact is that even though the IB calls for pedagogical leadership and this is seen as a stamp of quality, there is no official requirement for a Head or Principal in an IB school to have broad pedagogical insight. In many situations the Head/ Principal/CEO has a business-oriented profile, and some schools have even made use of hired consultants. The combination of business orientation and pedagogical leadership might be a great success if the different leaders have a shared vision and acknowledge each other's responsibilities in working towards a common achievement. However, a more business oriented leader with less insight into the philosophical grounding of the pedagogical principles might be under greater influence from external stakeholders who press for change, whether they be Boards or parents, or from the results of national or PISA tests, state laws and so on. Such leaders might even initiate action within the school that threatens the notion of holism, forcing the Coordinator to comply. I have witnessed leaders who advocate the MYP as such a rigorous academic programme that they claim the "MYP is not for all", and thus counsel students and parents away from the programme, believing they are being helpful on the basis of what they perceive to be justifiable assumptions. I have also witnessed leaders who have been more concerned about their own career and personal development than about the holistic development of the institution they have been directing.

On the other hand, I have also had the sincere pleasure of meeting very many highly competent and inspirational leaders throughout my years of IB experience. It is not necessarily poor leaders who are the main problem in schools, so much as a lack of stability in the leadership. Very often Heads are recruited for only a short-term commitment, typically two to three years, with Coordinators tending to stay a little longer. In the 12 years since my current school was founded, we have had six Principals. In addition, the IB Primary Years Programme (PYP) has had seven different Coordinators and has shifted between shared or split Coordinator and Head of PYP in the same position. Fortunately, the MYP department has had stable leadership for most of these years. The Board has changed its Chair six times, while other Board members are appointed by their companies for short term service on the Board – typically two years maximum. This situation is not unique, and indeed seems to be typical for many schools, especially smaller schools in smaller cities. In effect this frequent change of leadership can be somewhat detrimental to the development of the schools in question. Two years is hardly enough time to see the fruits of the work initiated, and typically every new leader introduces their own ideas and changes. Too many changes in the leadership makes it nearly impossible to foster strategic planning, and the lack of long term commitment from leaders might challenge the sense of a shared vision and mission among all staff. Short term committed leaders might also have less insight into holism in a school, being familiar only with fragments of the learning environment's individuality. Hayden and Thompson note that 'it would be an unwise head who took no interest in policy-making and an unusual board who took no interest in the implementation of that policy' (Hayden and Thompson, 2008, p66). Yet the IB recognises through the programme standards that there is a need for evaluating leadership commitment, strategic planning and implementation of the mission statement. The IB states that full adoption of the MYP approach will lead to change not only in the classroom but also throughout the whole school (IB, 2014a). A shared vision and a living mission statement throughout the school, supported by the entire leadership and combined with a strong focus on professional development, will empower teachers and students to develop their individual strengths and foster their holistic growth. In a holistic environment the leaders are not expected to have all the best ideas themselves and to control staff and students by regulations and force. Holistic leaders foster an environment where everyone may make brilliant contributions, and ensure that collaboration is respectful, tolerant and stimulating for all, irrespective of role and preferences.

When considering relationships between schools and the IB, many questions arise as to who should be in control of what. As the IB has grown, the need for a flexible framework has deepened. A flexible framework is easier to adapt to different cultures and different needs in different schools worldwide. It is reasonable to question, though, whether one framework really can fit all, or whether the flexibility of the framework forces through a need for the exercise of control through other measures. As Tarc points out, greater accessibility also increases the risks, and this is a fact also among the different MYP schools (Tarc, 2013). A shared framework does not necessarily ensure shared quality, and in striving for global recognition of the reliability and validity of the programme, the IB has enforced more prescriptive guidelines to ensure that schools implement the programmes as intended. The move towards increased prescription has been received with mixed feelings by school leaders. On one hand, the detailed requirements and increased prescription in the support material can be of enormous help for Coordinators and teachers struggling to understand how to put the principles into practice. On the other hand, if the IB becomes too prescriptive this might hinder the growth that comes out of creativity from individual schools and individual teachers. As holistic education is very much reliant on individualised and personalised learning environments, too much standardised prescription will eventually threaten the holistic nature of the programmes.

Inclusion

A section in the new *MYP: From Principles into Practice* document highlights the need for inclusion in holistic education and states that it is the school's responsibility to ensure that no matter what their learning preferences, learning needs and/or language capacities, all students must receive positive and differentiated support in their individual learning progress. The IB recognises the trend away from separating students with learning needs from others in class, under the supervision of a specialist teacher, to the more modern practice of differentiation being a collective responsibility where all relevant teachers ensure the provision of differentiated support through collaborative planning (IB, 2014a). In terms of the solid philosophical basis of personalised, holistic education, it might be seen as slightly redundant to include such detailed descriptions of inclusion. If the programme is as holistic as stated in the philosophy, is there any need to emphasise the responsibility for inclusion? Wouldn't differentiation come naturally through individualised learning? Yet, as the IB also points out, teachers are learners too, and differentiation in class as well as student-focused contextual learning might be challenging to teachers who have not been previously trained in or familiarised with such an approach. The idea of individualised inquiry is brilliant, but how does the teacher cater for the 25 different individuals in the classroom at the same time? In practice, such situations can call for unfamiliar classroom management skills. Again, it is of utmost importance that visionary leadership supports and guides the teachers, and ensures that they feel empowered to implement the intended teaching strategies.

A range of practices are implemented with respect to inclusion in different settings. Admissions policies, admissions interviews and state regulations are all factors that impact the complexity of the student body. In some countries including Norway, students of all abilities are ensured admission through state regulations. Over the past four years, one of our MYP classes has included a student with Down's Syndrome, a situation that has challenged but enriched both staff and other students in terms of providing an optimal learning environment for all. In some MYP schools in other countries, students cannot be admitted unless they have lived abroad for three years or more. This regulation places limits on those who are able to apply to the MYP school, and such schools seem to have student bodies from more limited backgrounds than if admission was open for all. Having a particular interest in special educational needs, my experience from several countries suggests that successful inclusion is based on a number of common features. These are a personalised approach, a broad and varied curriculum with close links to students' interests, the use of several working sites (ie ensuring that students are working not only on school premises but also in other environments and facilities – outdoors, or in other organisations for instance), collaboration with the community, the use of alternative groupings and alternative hours (making use also, for instance, of evenings and weekends rather than only following the regular school day timetable), a range of teaching and learning strategies, addressing social and emotional dimensions as well as the academic, and even fostering vocational skills. It is my belief, however, that this does not work only for special educational needs, but rather works for all, and is in fact the means by which holistic education is truly described and fostered.

On a final note, it is my view that the design and implementation of optional MYP eAssessments are not in line with an inclusive approach, but rather favours students who are strong writers and who are able to pull together all their resources in a very limited time, thus disregarding the diversity in learning preferences. I will return to this point more fully in the next section.

Standardisation

In describing a pilot project designed to enhance the building of a quality curriculum, the IB stated that parts of the service offered in this pilot would be mandatory for all schools when monitoring of assessment was replaced by monitoring of unit planning from January 2016 (IB, 2015). Personally I believe this to be a very good move, and a powerful tool to support schools in effective programme implementation. To my mind it is more difficult, however, to see how the introduction of eAssessment is fostering holistic education. The devaluation of some subjects has already been noted above, as has the time involved for schools in preparing for the test. Furthermore, high-stake tests might lead to a reduction in the types of assessment that are in use the rest of the year, training towards the exam, and at worst the use of the tests to define a standard curriculum and to focus instruction. As eAssessment in the MYP is discussed more fully in another chapter of this book I will limit myself to mentioning some aspects that relate directly to the issue of holism.

First, I wonder how a two hour examination can provide a better and fairer assessment of a student's achievement than the assessment a trained teacher can make after a year of close collaboration. A holistic approach is reliant on personalisation of the education process and close collaboration between teacher and student. How can high-stake tests match this? If students fail on one test, are they then less able? How do we ensure that all students, with all their diversity, have the same opportunity to demonstrate their fullest potential in one, standardised format of an e-exam? Ironically, the subjects of the least value for the IB validated certificate have the most authentic form of moderated assessment, allowing students to submit ePortfolios developed over an entire unit. Furthermore, open-ended questions call for individual judgements by moderators; how do we ensure standardisation and reliability between moderators and thus fair assessment of all students?

Secondly, I wonder why – if standardisation is supposed to promote better learning as well as more valid and reliable results – we standardise eAssessment results of students instead of standardising professional development or testing the didactic level of the teachers – or even leadership skills of the leaders. Teachers' subject expertise is one thing, but the skills needed to inspire and motivate each individual student are another. The call for monitoring unit planning is one step in this direction, and yet the eAssessment is alone dictating the results presented on the IB validated certificate. If it is the case that we cannot trust internal assessment to be reliable and valid, then why are we focusing the standardisation tool on the students, and not on the staff? This top-down control from the IB does not necessarily empower schools, or increase learning, but there is a risk that such emphasis on a very limited form of assessment will increase pressure and anxiety for both students and educators. If alignment of the MYP to the IB Diploma Programme is a goal, why not call for a change in the Diploma Programme assessment model instead of in that of the MYP? Even universities are opening up to a wider range of assessment modes these days.

"The fundamental work of schools is not to increase test results but to facilitate learning" (Robinson and Aronica, 2015, p 70). Personally, I do not believe in standardised tests as a successful tool for increasing learning. My experience with the Norwegian national tests and with PISA suggests that what might be convenient to test is not necessarily the most important achievement worth testing as the content is adjusted to the format of the test and the need for digitalisation. Politicians as well as the media speculate as to why Norwegian schools scores are only mediocre on the tests when a fair amount of money is spent on education, and the pressure for short term changes to boost scores steals the focus from long term improvement for a holistic environment. This poses the questions of who is demanding and enforcing changes, and how, for what purpose? I do not doubt the intentions of the IB, and from what I have seen of the eAssessment so far the test designs seem advanced: probably the best of the standardised high-stake tests I've seen. Yet they can never be authentic. For example, no matter how much thought and consideration is put into science exams to incorporate questions that simulate and replicate a practical science component, it is simply not the same. And they will never be holistic, in the sense of providing a fair judgement of all the skills, knowledge, competence and abilities the students have. They serve as a snapshot, and if the students blink when the snapshot is taken, the moment is gone.

Conclusion

Noting that the IB is a story of success, McKenzie is still asking (in relation to IB and its development) how big is big enough, and when is it too big? And how does development change the ideology? He claims that 'it is imperative that the giants of the future are nurtured and that their voices are heard and acted upon. The sense of vibrance and novelty that was such an obvious part of the early IB community has to be recaptured.' (McKenzie, 2011, p171). Some ask whether the IB mission is more of a slogan these days, and whether IB is establishing a globally recognised product, akin to a brand such as Burger King. I would claim, however, that even though the school I have been working in for the past decade or so was founded for partly pragmatic reasons, the school aims to fulfill the ideology outlined in the mission to its best. I believe this to be the case in most of the schools I have encountered. This aligns well with the observation that 'International schools, then, are diverse and growing rapidly in response to both pragmatic demands (of globally-mobile expatriate families) and ideological motivators concerned with offering education focused on encouraging young people to become "global citizens" with a concern for world peace, environmental responsibility and sustainable development.' (Hayden and Thompson, 2008 p27).

The aims of the original IB philosophy are still intact in the current MYP, and there should be enough room and quality support from the IB to allow schools to develop holistic education that caters for all. I would argue, however, that in order to succeed with holism, schools require strong, visionary and pedagogical leaders as well as well-informed and trained teachers to protect the intended programme. Different stakeholders or interest groups may consciously or subconsciously try to impact the shaping of education (Robinson and Aronica, 2015): politicians, media, parents, employers, boards, students, educators, commercial organisations and publishers, as well as national laws and regulations, all have opinions about how to prioritise and organise education. The challenge is that they don't always see the holistic picture of education, or value holism as an aim. As an IB educator and a lifelong learner, with a commitment to fulfil the aims of the IB mission statement to the full, I think it is time to challenge my own chapter title. Rather than asking "Do we really reach all with the MYP?" I should ask myself "How can I use all my resources to ensure that we do really reach all?" Through conscious inquiry into our local setting, reflection around resources and needs, and making informed choices and seeing them through, I should be able to foster holism – and that's exactly what I want within my own school!

References

IB (2014a) *Middle Years Programme: From Principles Into Practice*, Cardiff: International Baccalaureate Organization

IB (2014b) *Fostering interdisciplinary teaching and learning in the MYP*, Cardiff: International Baccalaureate Organization

Hayden, M and Thompson, J (2008) *International schools: growth and influence*, Paris: UNESCO: International Institute for Educational Planning.

McKenzie, M (2011) *Faces for our Changing Future*, in G Walker (ed) The Changing Face of International Education: Challenges for the IB, Cardiff: International Baccalaureate

Miller, R (2000) 'A brief introduction to holistic education', the encyclopaedia of informal education. [http://infed.org/mobi/a-brief-introduction-to-holistic-education/. Retrieved: 2 August 2015]

Robinson, K and Aronica, L (2015) *Creative Schools, The Grassroots Revolution That's Transforming Education*. New York: Viking Penguin

Tarc, P (2013) *International Education in Global Times, Engaging the Pedagogic*, New York: Peter Lang Publishing

Chapter 9

Let's leave the church in the village: a concept-based approach to learning languages

Michael Huber

Introduction

Languages are funny. They are funny because they are so different from each other, and when we learn a new language we might find ourselves confronted with a phrase that just does not quite make sense if it's translated word by word into our own language. 'Let's leave the church in the village!' is one of those. As may be clear, this is not an English phrase. It is the direct translation of the German '*Wir sollten die Kirche im Dorf lassen*'. Now, as an English speaker one might think: 'Well, why shouldn't we?' or 'Where else should we put it?' or 'Germans are funny'. A possible though not confirmed explanation of how this phrase came into being has its roots in medieval times. Catholic processions through little villages often grew to be bigger than the village centre location of the church could accommodate. The procession was therefore held outside the village. This did not always meet with the approval of the villagers, who believed that church-focused activities should take place within the village, even if this meant that the procession would need to be smaller. So, metaphorically, the meaning of the phrase is that we should not exaggerate or overdo something; we should stick with the facts.

Language tends to be metaphoric. Littlemore (2009) argues that 'our ability to engage in higher-order reasoning and deal with abstract concepts is related to our more direct physical interactions with the world by means of a number of conceptual metaphors' (p95). These conceptual metaphors, which are 'deeply embedded in the collective subconscious of a speech community' (*ibid*, p98), and the less deeply-embedded linguistic metaphors such as 'leaving the church in the village', often pose great difficulty for second language learners. Another area of language learning that is difficult for many students is grammar. Here too students face grammatical structures and phenomena that might not exist or might be different in their first language. The question that arises is how to best teach the language?

Many different styles are used in language teaching and learning, including the academic style that emphasises the importance of grammar and translation in language learning, and the audio-lingual style which views language learning as a behavioural process and aims to create the habitual use of language by drill exercises (Cook, 2008).

The International Baccalaureate (IB) Middle Years Programme (MYP), as already noted in earlier chapters of this book, is a concept-based curriculum. Instead of prescribing content it sets a framework for concepts to be discovered, explored and built upon in and across eight subject disciplines. One question that arises is how well this concept-based approach to teaching and learning fits with the teaching and learning of a foreign language. Do the students, for instance, gain a better understanding of phrases such as 'leaving the church in the village' or does the IB approach actually take the church out of the village?

The MYP and concept-based instruction and learning

The world is changing. This is not new, but the pace of change is accelerating and it seems that we are still far from reaching the maximum speed. In what is now commonly referred to as the information age or digital age, information develops and changes so quickly that curriculum content is sometimes obsolete before it is even agreed upon. Giddens (2007) sees a problem of this nature in nursing education in the United States. Competencies and knowledge are expanding and the attempt to meet these expansions has led to 'content saturation' (p65) of the curriculum. Giddens (2007) therefore suggests a concept-based curriculum. In their updating of *Bloom's Taxonomy*, Anderson and Krathwohl (2001) distinguish between factual knowledge and conceptual knowledge. They use the latter term to describe 'complex organized knowledge forms' and highlight 'the need for educators to teach for deep understanding of conceptual knowledge, not just for remembering isolated and small bits of factual knowledge' (p42).

The MYP was designed to be a curriculum framework that could be adjusted to suit schools around the world. The concept-based approach to teaching and learning was already inherent in the previous MYP framework but has been made more explicit in the current version. Changes in the curriculum framework are heavily based on Erickson's (2012) model of a concept-based curriculum. Erickson suggests that such a model 'focus[es] on concepts, principles and generalizations, using related facts and skills as tools to gain deeper understanding of disciplinary content, transdisciplinary themes and interdisciplinary issues, and to facilitate conceptual transfer through time, across cultures and across situations' (p4). Instead of placing transmission of 'facts' in the foreground, factual knowledge 'provide[s] the foundation and support for deeper, conceptual thinking and understanding' (*ibid*, p4). The student can no longer be seen as a vessel that needs to be filled with information; rather, teachers need to create tasks that build on students' preconceptions of the subject matter (Bransford, 2000). Erickson (2012) points out that: 'Concept-based models encourage collaborative group work to enhance thinking and problem-solving. Different minds working together scaffold each other and generate new ideas and solutions. The social construction of meaning and collaborative group work is a significant aspect of all IB programmes. School days filled with teacher-dominated lectures to passive students, locked into parallel rows of desks, are hopefully a relic of past pedagogies' (p9).

All this makes perfect sense. In modern teacher education a student-centred approach to teaching and learning is not regarded as a Waldorfian eccentricity. It is part of the professional practice of many teachers and has been part of the philosophy of MYP teaching since the programme originated. One question that arises, however, is how well a unit planning process such as that in the MYP, which organizes all its content around the delivery of concepts, fits the needs of the subject Language Acquisition.

Language Acquisition in the MYP

Unit Planning

Language Acquisition is one of eight subject disciplines within the MYP curriculum framework. Language Acquisition follows the same MYP unit planning process as any other process (see Figure 1).

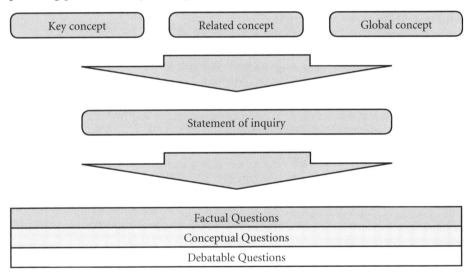

Figure 1: Visualization of the MYP unit planning process (Adapted from IB 2014a, p52)

In planning a unit, a teacher chooses a key concept, related concept(s) and a global context, which act as the basis for a statement of inquiry and lead to factual, conceptual and debatable unit questions that drive teaching and learning in the unit. The teacher then decides on the assessments and Approaches to Learning (ATL) skills before determining the content of the unit. This approach to a concept-based curriculum is grounded mainly in the work of Erickson, who also authored a position paper for the IB (Erickson, 2012) explaining the make-up of the concept-based curriculum in the IB

Primary Years Programme and Diploma Programme, as well as the MYP. This chapter will mainly focus on the first two parts of the unit planning process (key concepts and related concepts) and will discuss related opportunities and challenges in the classroom.

Key and related concepts

The key concepts are what Erickson (2012) would call the 'macro concepts'. They 'transfer knowledge through time, across cultures and across situations' (p6). They are the big ideas and they require the student to look beyond the subject discipline in order to understand them. The IBO (2014a) describes them as 'broad, organizing, powerful ideas that have relevance within and across subjects and disciplines, providing connections that can transfer across time and culture' (p15). There are 16 MYP key concepts. Four of these are relevant and to be used in Language Acquisition. These are *communication, connections, creativity* and *culture*. Teachers can also use other key concepts if they feel that those provide a better framework for their unit planning (IB, 2014b). Teachers need to choose one key concept per unit.

The related concepts are grounded in the subject discipline itself and promote 'deep learning' (IB, 2014a). Erickson (2014) highlights their importance in terms of in-depth learning within the disciplines, and calls them the 'micro concepts' (p42). In the Language Acquisition guide (IB, 2014b) the IB suggests 36 related concepts (see Table 1) that are relevant to language learning. These are organised into three groups: Phases 1 and 2, Phases 3 and 4, and Phases 5 and 6. The phases are levels of language proficiency. Beginners are in Phase 1 and the most advanced foreign language students in Phase 6. This suggests that students need to explore and understand different concepts at different phases of language proficiency. The related concepts build on the fundamentals of language research. There are linguistic concepts such as 'pattern', semantic concepts such as 'meaning', and pragmatic concepts including, for instance, 'audience'. Teachers can also choose related concepts from other phases or other subject groups if they feel that those are relevant to the unit (IB, 2014b).

Phases 1-2					
Audience	Context	Purpose	Conventions	Message	Word choice
Meaning	Function	Structure	Patterns	Form	Accent
Phases 3-4					
Audience	Context	Purpose	Conventions	Message	Word choice
Meaning	Function	Structure	Idiom	Empathy	Point of view
Phases 5-6					
Audience	Context	Purpose	Stylistic choices	Voice	Inference
Bias	Theme	Argument	Idiom	Empathy	Point of view

Table 1: Related concepts in Language Acquisition (IB, 2014b, p38)

The conceptual approach to teaching and learning is not new to the MYP and was inherent in the previous MYP framework in the significant concepts which were similar to the related concepts. The idea of a key concept that is not solely rooted in the heart of a discipline is, however, a new addition.

Rationale for a concept-based curriculum in Language Acquisition

Concept-based teaching in the Language Acquisition classroom draws on Vygotsky's Sociocultural Theory which 'highlights unity of social, cultural, and psychological processes through understanding that human language is the fundamental tool for communication, cultural representation, and conceptualization' (Williams *et al*, 2013). Concept-based teaching puts the learner in the centre and emphasizes the importance of meaning-making of cultural and linguistic phenomena. The teacher functions as the mediator who supports the student through the learning process. The emphasis lies here on the making of meaning rather than on the teaching and memorising of morphological rules (*ibid*). The idea of student-centred learning goes hand in hand with the MYP programme model which pictures the student at the centre of all learning.

A common complaint among language teachers – and I have to admit I have often been one of them – is that a concept-based curriculum in Language Acquisition makes much more sense at later stages of the learning process. Once students have some factual knowledge in terms of grammar, vocabulary and cultural knowledge they can draw from this knowledge to discuss more complex conceptual ideas. Erickson (2012) argues that facts provide the foundation of deeper, conceptual thinking and understanding. One might argue that at the beginning stages of Language Acquisition there is just not enough factual knowledge upon which to build this foundation. There are, however, flaws in such an argument. Firstly, it assumes that students do not have any conception of how the use of language might work. Vygotsky argued that the development of a second language relies heavily on the conceptual understandings of one's first language (Eun and Lim, 2009), while Hill (2007) argues that with second language (L2) learners the 'conceptual development has already taken place and so the L2 morphology used to express a temporal relation may be very opaque conceptually. There may also be conflicts of a cultural nature in conceptual development' (p4). If that is the case then a conceptual approach to teaching and learning language is even more important. For instance, a simple sentence in English that could be taught within the first few hours of language learning is *I see him*. With only these three words students encounter a very important linguistic concept: the subject–verb–object sentence structure. Now, to a student who is familiar with the concept (a native speaker of German, for instance, will use the same sentence structure), this linguistic concept will be easy to grasp. For speakers of languages that follow a subject–object–verb order (for example Japanese) a conceptual understanding of this sentence, which looks so simple to us, might be more difficult. Teachers need to help students to work with their preconceptions and to build new conceptual understandings for the language to be learned. A second flaw in the argument that concepts cannot be taught in the early phase of language learning lies in the idea that conceptual understanding of language learning becomes more important as students progress. This presumes that students automatically learn and understand the concepts that are important in the early phases, for instance simple structural concepts such as the subject-verb-object sentence order in English. We cannot assume that the teaching of facts (such as vocabulary and grammar) alone will form the basis for a later conceptual understanding of what underpins the language and the culture. We need to ask which concepts we should focus on and if a unit planning process can be the same for a beginning class as for an advanced class in language learning. I will discuss this point later in the chapter.

In the MYP unit planning process the related concepts allow for conceptual learning to start at a very basic level. A particular strength is that teachers may choose from the given concepts relevant to the phase they are teaching. This ensures that there is a logical progression of language-specific concepts which students should develop. Teachers are also free to choose a related concept of another phase if they feel it is relevant to their teaching. Another strength is that the related concepts place heavy emphasis on the teaching and learning of grammar and vocabulary. A preconception of many teachers I have worked with is that concept-based teaching in language learning is solely about the concepts of the culture and disregards the importance of the language and its rules. Conceptual understanding of language – and of course of culture, too – is essentially what we are aiming for. Bransford (2000) argues that conceptual understanding allows students to transfer what they have learned to new situations. It is this conceptual framework that students need to build in Language Acquisition. This does not happen by teaching isolated items of grammar as they appear in a text book. But how best to achieve conceptual understanding? Grammatical phenomena cannot be taught in isolation. There is a pattern. Azar (2007) interestingly refers to grammar not as rules but as patterns (also a related concept) that need to be explored. When language learners of German understand the concept of a subject, a verb and an object, they are likely to understand what function cases have and hence are able to appreciate adjective endings. A common problem is that these conceptual understandings can seem a lot harder to teach than the key concepts. Well, they have to be! They are the concepts that provide each discipline with the subject depth. As Erickson (2012) points out, it is the understanding of related concepts that prepares the students for the academic rigor of the IB Diploma Programme, implying that the conceptual teaching of grammar needs to take place in the MYP.

A concept-based curriculum can also aid vocabulary learning. The meaning of words is often metaphoric and a conceptual approach to teaching and learning words can make it easier for students to understand them (Littlemore, 2006). A study carried out by Benjamin White (2012) advocates a conceptual approach to teaching phrasal verbs in English. By drawing a metaphorical sketch of the meaning of phrasal verbs, students gain a conceptual understanding of the combinations of verbs and prepositions, for instance 'to pick up a hobby'. A student might for example draw a picture of a person picking up a tennis racket to represent the metaphoric meaning of the phrasal verb. White furthermore argues that this happens most effectively using an inductive approach, giving students the freedom to figure out the metaphoric meaning of language rather than trying to present them with a rule for all possible phrasal verbs. This highlights the importance of student creation and creativity.

A related concept that teachers could choose if they wanted to place the emphasis on vocabulary learning could be 'word choice' and / or 'meaning'. If a new grammar phenomenon is introduced which structurally builds on an already known phenomenon then 'pattern' would be a good related concept. Teachers being required to consciously choose concepts in their unit planning process makes them actively consider how best to achieve this conceptual understanding in students.

Teachers new to the MYP are often startled by the fact that grammar or vocabulary cannot be summatively assessed in its own right, in the sense of students being able to get a grade 'that counts'. A major fear is that, as a result, students will believe the study of grammar or vocabulary is not important. Teachers therefore feel that grammar only plays a subordinate role. Especially in the previous MYP where unit plans were mainly driven by the Area of Interaction, putting heavy emphasis on the contextual setting into which a unit fits, this fear was evident. The introduction of the related concept should provide a strong counter-argument to the position that teaching of language is secondary, as it highlights the importance of language making its teaching and learning an essential part of any unit.

Challenges

A challenge faced by many Language Acquisition teachers is how to integrate the key concept meaningfully into the unit planning process. As noted above there are four main key concepts for students in Language Acquisition: *communication, connections, creativity* and *culture*. At first sight they may seem more easily accessible than some of the related concepts. In learning a language we also learn its culture. It is difficult, however, to discuss matters of culture in depth when the language at hand is limited (Bransford, 2000). As noted above, Erickson (2012) argues that knowledge of facts is the basis for conceptual understanding. Now if we argue that for both the language and cultural component of the Language Acquisition class we can make use of the first language (L1) and culture of the student, the question arises as to what role the actual use of language plays in the classroom. A concept-based approach to teaching and learning essentially questions the notion of monolingual instruction in the classroom (Eun and Lim, 2009). If students need to make use of their L1 concepts in order to understand concepts in a second language (L2) that implies a reflective discussion on how these concepts are similar or different. Only at an advanced stage of language learning would this be possible. If we assume that the understanding of key concepts in a beginner class can build on concepts with which the students are familiar in their L1, we would also welcome the use of L1 in the language learning classroom. This raises the question of how much L1 we allow in the classroom and to what extent it should be driven by the use of the L2. With a limited amount of time available for language instruction, teachers try to make use of the target language as much as possible, but if conceptual understanding is building on conceptual and factual knowledge of the L1 of the students and we allow students to use their L1, then this takes away time that students can speak and listen to the language.

One of the examples provided in the Language Acquisition Guide (IB, 2014b) for a possible unit planner is shown in Table 2.

Key concept	Culture
Related concepts	Idiom, Pattern, Meaning
Global context	Orientation in space and time
Statement of inquiry	The language spoken in the street reflects the dynamic social environments in which people make themselves understood.
Factual questions	How much slang is there in my language, and how acceptable is its usage?
Conceptual questions	How does street language evolve?
Debatable questions	What place does street language have in society?

Table 2 Language skills focus unit (IB, 2014b, p39ff)

If the statement of inquiry, articulated through the combination of key concept, related concepts and global context, should 'frame classroom inquiry and direct purposeful learning' (IB, 2014b, p39), then the question arises as to how much purposeful learning can occur within the use of the L2, especially in the beginning phases. If the statement of inquiry is as complex as the one in the example above, how can a student with limited language skills in the L2 be able to engage in activities and discussion that test the statement of inquiry? And if the assessments should show evidence that the students have inquired into the statement, what kind of assessment would that entail? The examples for questions guiding the teaching and learning furthermore heavily lean towards the cultural aspect of language teaching: acceptance of slang, evolving of street language and the place of street language in society. Where does this leave the teaching and learning of grammar and vocabulary? With the introduction of the related concept, the MYP stresses the importance of in-depth, discipline-specific conceptual knowledge. Language, therefore, cannot only be a means to an end, answering the broader questions posed by cultural concepts. Essentially the topics language teachers teach are the means to the end of learning the language and the culture. A topic such as 'school life' does not claim to introduce students to the idea of what a school is. We are clear that the topic itself should function as an easy entrance into the understanding of language concepts and the use of language, which will be much more of a challenge for the students. Therefore a topic on street language in Language Acquisition, such as in the example from the Language Acquisition guide, does not necessarily need to lead to an understanding of the evolution of slang. It should, however, provide students with the possibility of using and understanding the language which is necessary to communicate within this topic. For beginners that might mean different ways of saying 'hello', and understanding the contexts in which each way is acceptable. A more advanced course might allow comparison of sentence structure in street language with the standard language.

Treatment of the cultural aspect of language evolution and its importance for individual and group identity would be an interesting concept for a Language and Literature class, but goes beyond what the Language Acquisition classroom can offer. If we approach Language Acquisition as I propose, then the key concept is not so much one to be explored or understood as an area of knowledge that the students already have, thus creating a context of personal relevance for the topic content much like the global context. With this approach I would argue that the related concept is the more important one and should be in the forefront when planning a unit. Erickson (2014) also argues that 'to ensure conceptual depth, most of the unit generalizations should be written to represent more micro ideas' (p42). From my own experience I can say that the key concepts and their dominance in the inquiry statement inspire great unit ideas, but the actual inquiry into those ideas can be minimal within the language classroom. It is not that language teachers would not like to explore those big ideas in more detail with students, but they often feel pressed for time in their teaching of language and find it difficult to provide students with time where they can actually use the target language.

So, how much culture needs to be explored at the beginning phases of language learning? A rationale for the key concept and the global context is to locate subject content in a real world context, thus making it more accessible for the students. Eun and Lim (2009), however, argue that at the beginning level of language learning 'language instruction should be aimed toward fulfilling the students' basic interpersonal communication needs' (p22). A conceptual outreach to the wider world might therefore actually hinder the intrinsic motivation to communicate. Furthermore, unless we allow students to use their L1 to explore the key concepts and global contexts within the topic, the treatment of that topic will be more superficial than what the student is intellectually capable of, hence the motivation for inquiring into the topic might not be as high as expected. It is likely that every language teacher has come across the following scenario: There is a classroom discussion on a cultural topic, dinner etiquette for instance. Students use the imperative form to formulate rules on how to behave at the dinner table. Two students find they cannot agree on a rule. One is adamant that one needs to ask one's parents for permission when wanting to leave the table; the other student has never heard of such a rule. Initially the teacher tries to keep the conversation in the target language, maybe reminding the students of the use of modal verbs to phrase their ideas. But the discussion gets more heated, and finally the teacher gives in and discusses the issue in the L1 or the language of instruction of the school. After class the teacher might even talk to other teachers and tell them about the great discussion that has just taken place. These are exactly the discussions that form the basis of the inquiry into statements such as the example above on street language. How much discussion such as this should we as language teachers allow without jeopardizing the progression in language that students will eventually need to be successful in their IB Diploma Programme examinations?

Implementation

One question that needs to be addressed is how a conceptual approach to teaching language will look in the classroom. It is beyond the scope of this chapter to delve into pedagogical implications for the language classroom. However, some sources (*eg* White, 2012; Littlemore, 2006) suggest good ideas on how to facilitate a concept-based curriculum in the Language Acquisition classroom, a topic which could also be a focus for professional development. It cannot be assumed that all teachers have a solid knowledge of what concept-based teaching looks like in practice. Williams *et al* (2013) conducted a case study with expert and novice language teachers of Spanish, who were given an introduction into how to teach the preterite and the imperfect – two past tenses in Spanish – using a concept-based approach. One conclusion of the study was that teachers, whether novice or expert, tend to prefer teaching materials which are more familiar to them. The researchers also argued that contextual factors such as assessment practices have an influence on the success of the approach. This suggests that the provision of concepts does not necessarily imply that teachers know what they mean and what to do with them. How, for example, is the grammar and vocabulary content of the first years linked to twelve related concepts as indicated for Phases 1 and 2? As a first step there needs to be a platform where teachers can discuss the meaning of concepts. Teachers need to share a common understanding of the definitions of the concepts, and need to be consistent in applying them (Giddens, 2007). What does 'pattern' really refer to, for example? What patterns are to be understood at beginners level? How can we best teach these patterns? How can we make use of the L1 concepts that students bring into the classroom? What implications are there for our classroom techniques? These questions will not be answered only by presenting and practising the use of the unit planner as a whole. It is essential that teachers also have the opportunity to learn about, and share, concept-based teaching practices.

Professional development is especially important for teachers new to teaching languages in an international context. A concept-based approach to teaching languages needs to take conceptions of the L1 of the students into consideration or at least acknowledge that they will influence the conceptual understanding of the L2. Teachers coming from a background where, for example, they taught Spanish to only English students might find the teaching of concepts more difficult. As language classrooms in international schools are frequently very heterogeneous in terms of the language background of the students, teachers are often confronted with students who have different conceptual assumptions about a grammatical phenomenon. Teachers need to learn strategies and techniques for making use of the international diversity of language conceptions or for helping students to access these for their own development.

To my mind a concept-based approach to teaching and learning languages is the right way to go. Not only does it address the needs of the students; it also emphasises the importance of discipline-specific knowledge. However, a revision of the MYP unit planner and its feasibility for Language Acquisition would be beneficial. The overall planning process often appears to steer away from what would be helpful for students' language development. The culmination of concepts and global context in an inquiry statement often creates very interesting topics of high social relevance. The treatment of these topics, however, remains superficial due to restricted language possibilities in the L2. I do not argue that the key concepts are irrelevant; they allow the students to connect to bigger and more accessible concepts with which they might be more familiar. They are, furthermore, very important concepts to explore. The key concept *culture* for example does, of course, transcend the disciplinary borders, while also being deeply rooted within the subject. Learning a language also means learning about the cultural context in which it is used. A question that arises here is how much time we want to invest in the language classroom in order to build understanding of these broad concepts, especially at the beginning stages of language learning. A possible response to this question might be to adjust the unit planning process in language learning. Maybe the rather minimal key-conceptual understanding that is necessary for the subject in the first phases could be taught through the global context, which would imply a planning process very similar to the one in the previous MYP framework. Or perhaps teachers simply need more professional development on how to make better use of the unit planner. One way of facilitating this would also be to incorporate more useful examples for all phases. A table in the Language Acquisition guide is not sufficient. Teachers need to see examples of unit planners for different phases as well as advice about how to apply them in practice.

Conclusion

I believe the concept-based curriculum is a good basis for students to develop their language skills and to be able to understand the conceptual nature of phrases such as 'Let's leave the church in the village'. It is a powerful curriculum that enables students to make better use of and transfer their language knowledge, thus becoming more independent learners. It is therefore worth investing in the development of language teachers' understanding of concept-based instruction. But let's also leave the church in the village! Let's make sure we don't lose track of the fundamental practices in the language classroom. The need to unify a planning process for subjects that might be very different in nature is perhaps exaggerated. We have to look at the strengths of a concept-based curriculum and make the best out of it for each discipline, while leaving room for interdisciplinary connections. This might not be achieved with a generic plan. The use of different key and related concepts in different subjects has certainly been a step in the right direction. Now we have to have a look at the planning process itself.

References

Anderson, L. W. and Krathwohl, D. R. (eds.) (2001) *A Taxonomy for Learning, Teaching, and Assessing: A Revision of Bloom's Taxonomy of Educational Objectives.* New York: Longman.

Azar, B. (2007) Grammar-Based Teaching: A Practitioner's Perspective. TESL-EJ: *Teaching English as a Second or Foreign Language* [Online] 11 (2) Available at http://www.tesl-ej.org/wordpress/issues/volume11/ej42/ Last accessed: 19.02.2016

Bransford, J. D., Brown, A. L. and Cocking R. R (eds.) (2000). *How people learn – Brain, Mind, Experience and School.* Washington: National Academy Press.

Cook, V (2008). *Second Language Learning and Language Teaching.* London: Hodder Education.

Erickson, H. L. (2012) Concept-based teaching and learning. *IB position paper.* Cardiff: International Baccalaureate

Erickson, H. L. (2014) *Stirring the Head, Heart and Soul.* 3rd ed. Thousand Oaks: Corwin Press.

Eun, B. and Lim, H.-S. (2009) A Sociocultural View of Language Learning: The Importance of Meaning-Based Instruction. *TESL Canada Journal.* 27, 1, 13–26.

Giddens, J. F. and Brady, D. P. (2007) Rescuing Nursing Education from Content Saturation: The Case for a Concept-Based Curriculum. *Journal of Nursing Education.* 46, 2, 65–69.

Hill, K. (2007) Concept-Based Grammar Teaching: An Academic Responds to Azar. *Teaching English as a Second or Foreign Language* [Online] 11 (2) Available at http://www.tesl-ej.org/wordpress/issues/volume11/ej42/ Last accessed: 19.02.2016

International Baccalaureate. (2014a) *MYP: From principles into practice. For use from September 2014/January 2015.* Cardiff: International Baccalaureate

International Baccalaureate. (2014b) *MYP: Language Acquisition guide. For use from September 2014/January 2015.* Cardiff: International Baccalaureate

Littlemore, J. (2009) *Applying cognitive linguistics to second language learning and teaching.* Basingstoke: Palgrave.

White, B. J. (2012) A Conceptual Approach to the Instruction of Phrasal Verbs. *The Modern Language Journal.* 96, 3, 419–438.

Williams, L., Abraham, L. B. and Negueruela-Azarola, E. (2013) Using concept-based instruction in the L2 classroom: Perspectives from current and future language teachers. *Language Teaching Research.* 17, 3, 363–381.

Chapter 10

Offering the MYP in conjunction with IGCSE: A case study in Geography

Oyndrilla Mukherjee

Introduction

In the last decade, growing numbers of schools describing themselves as 'international schools' have been established in urban areas of the developing world, reflecting the growing demand for international education among affluent urban populations. As noted by Hayden (2006), a universally accepted definition of the term 'international school' is not available because of the diverse nature of such schools. What they tend to have in common, however, is that they offer a curriculum not of the 'host country'. This chapter will focus on schools that offer two different international programmes in conjunction with each other in order to teach specific subjects at the secondary age range. The two programmes to be discussed are the International Baccalaureate (IB) Middle Years Programme (MYP) and the Cambridge International Examinations (CIE) International General Certificate of Secondary Education (IGCSE), with Geography being highlighted for particular consideration. The chapter will begin with a description of the requirements of IBMYP Geography and IGCSE Geography, before going on to explain how these two programmes are combined to teach Geography at my school.

Located in Mumbai and owned by a group of Indian nationals, the school offers three IB programmes – Primary Years Programme (PYP), Middle Years Programme (MYP) and Diploma Programme (DP). It should be noted that in referring to the IBMYP I am referring to the recently revised version of the programme. The student body comprises mainly Indian nationals. In addition, the school is attended by some students of other nationalities, as well as by a number of Indian students whose parents are professionals who have lived and worked abroad. The teacher population is a mix of Indian and expatriate teachers. The administrators – Principal and Heads of Primary and Secondary schools – are experienced expatriate educators. I teach Geography to middle and senior school students.

The requirements of MYP Geography

Geography is included in MYP Individuals and Societies (I&S), the aims of which include the following (IB, 2014b):

- Appreciate environmental and human commonalities and diversity.

- Understand how environmental and human systems operate and evolve.

- Act as responsible citizens of local and global communities.

MYP Geography therefore shares the same aims. History and Integrated Humanities can also be offered as part of MYP Individuals and Societies.

The objectives of MYP Individuals and Societies are as follows:

a)   knowing and understanding;

b)   investigating;

c)   communicating; and

d)   thinking critically.

In an objectives-driven curriculum, objectives are made explicit and content is not prescribed. Similarly in the MYP Individuals and Societies curriculum, teachers select content and create opportunities through teaching and learning for the students to meet the stated objectives. In Geography, we select content and design opportunities for our students to display their knowledge, skills of investigation and skills of critical thinking, as well as to communicate their knowledge and skills effectively. The students are assessed in terms of whether they have been able to meet the objectives of Individuals and Societies according to specified assessment criteria.

Another aspect of MYP is engaging the students in concept-driven, contextual and inquiry-based learning. In MYP, there are two types of concepts: the key concept and the related concept. The key concepts of MYP Individuals and Societies are:

i)   time, place and space;

ii)   global interaction;

iii)   system;

iv)   change.

Being included in I&S, MYP Geography also needs to explore these concepts through its subject-specific content. Related concepts differ, according to the subject, stemming as they do from the content or the topic. Thus History has a different set of related concepts from Geography, some of which are (IB, 2014b): causality, scale, patterns and trends, processes, management and intervention.

The teaching and learning of MYP needs to be contextual – the global contexts provide context for the teaching and learning of a topic. Teachers identify a global context for teaching and learning, and help students to inquire through that context. As a teacher, I find some contexts more relevant to topics in Geography than others. However, we try to explore all the global contexts through the selection of diverse topics. The Geography units also need a statement of inquiry to drive the inquiry, while three different types of questions engage the students to inquire.

A significant aspect of MYP is Approaches to Learning (ATL); skills that help students to understand how they learn, as well as to improve the way in which they learn: thinking skills, social skills, communication skills, self-management and research skills (IB, 2014a). Some of these skills could be linked to the objectives of Individuals and Societies; for example the ATL skill of communication matches with the objective of communicating. In my Geography lessons, I need to provide opportunities for my students to identify, understand and develop these skills.

Assessment in MYP is criterion-based. Four objectives (A, B, C, D) are assessed by four criteria respectively, namely:

- Criterion A: Knowing and Understanding
- Criterion B: Investigating
- Criterion C: Communicating
- Criterion D: Thinking Critically

During one school semester, we ensure that students are assessed at least twice against each criterion. In an academic year comprising two semesters therefore, each student will be assessed against each criterion on a minimum of four occasions.

Another important aspect of MYP is service in action. In this aspect, students through their process of inquiry and conceptual understanding may be able to identify an issue faced in real life by people within or outside their own community. After understanding the issue, students try to engage with it in their own ways, thus bringing about change in their community or in their own behaviour. Students often engage in developing understanding of local and global challenges in physical and human geography. They also work with economic and social issues according to their geographic context.

The requirements of IGCSE Geography

Cambridge International Examinations (CIE) runs international education programmes for students aged five to nineteen (CIE 2015), including the internationally recognised International General Certificate of Secondary Education (IGCSE). The educational demands of this qualification are equivalent to the GCSE (General Certificate of Secondary Education) in England.

IGCSE qualifications are offered in a range of subjects including Geography, which is part of Group 2 – Humanities and Social Sciences. Cambridge IGCSE Geography has a prescribed syllabus (content) and related aims and assessment objectives. Students who wish to obtain this qualification study the prescribed syllabus and prepare for the IGCSE Geography examination, taken at the age of 16-plus.

Among the aims of the IGCSE Geography syllabus are helping students to develop the following: (CIE 2015)

- an understanding of scale (local, national, global *etc*);

- an understanding of processes in the physical and human environment;

- an appreciation and concern for our environment; and

- an understanding of opportunities and constraints provided by different environments.

Content is divided into three themes: population and settlement, natural environment and economic development, maintaining a mix of physical and human geography. Some of the topics studied under these themes (CIE, 2015) are population dynamics, problems faced by settlements, landforms created by rivers, causes and consequences of earthquake and volcanic eruptions, tourism, agriculture and some causes and impacts of the process of globalization. Case studies need to be developed for all topics. Clear guidance is provided in the syllabus on the type of case studies of which the students need to be aware.

Assessment of IGCSE Geography includes answering two compulsory papers: Paper 1 and Paper 2. The third assessment component may be coursework or, alternatively, answering a third paper. There are three objectives of the assessment, as follows:

1. Knowledge and understanding;

2. Skills and analysis; and

3. Judgement and decision-making.

Students' understanding of geographical aspects (for instance, processes, scales, interaction, places) is assessed by the first assessment objective. The skills of interpreting and analyzing geographical data including maps, photographs, diagrams and numerical data are assessed by the second objective. Skills of observing, collecting, organizing and presenting data are also assessed by this objective. The third objective assesses the students' skill of arriving at conclusions appropriate to the geographical context, and evaluating the data within the same context. The examination papers have varying weightings of assessment objectives. For example, the dominant assessment objective of Paper 2 is skills and analysis, while the 'knowledge and understanding' assessment objective is assessed primarily by Paper 1.

Students complete their study of the content of the Geography syllabus within a period of two years – in grades 9 and 10, at the end of which they take the IGCSE Geography examination.

Combining the two programmes: A case study of Geography

The subject of Geography is taught in my school by combining the requirements of MYP Individuals and Societies and, for students who wish to take the IGCSE Geography examination, of IGCSE Geography. A preference among some students to take the IGCSE examination in some subjects as well as following the MYP has its roots in historical reasons. Prior to 2014, the MYP was not recognised by universities in India. Students who did not wish to continue to the IB Diploma Programme left the school to study in one of the Indian colleges, which accept IGCSE certification as the basis for student enrolment. The school had to offer IGCSE certification for these students, with Geography being one of the subjects in which students would choose to take the IGCSE examination.

Over the years, some parents who wanted their children to progress from the MYP to studying the IB Diploma also started to opt for IGCSE examinations in some subjects. Their rationale was that as MYP did not have an externally set and marked examination, their children missed the opportunity of taking such an examination at the end of grade 10. It also needs to be understood that most parents in India have themselves taken an externally set and marked public examination when they were 16 years old, and many believed in the rigour of an externally set and marked examination over the MYP model of continuous internal assessment. From 2016, however, MYP students have the option of taking an externally set and marked examination, known as the onscreen MYP eAssessment. When the pilot of this examination was conducted in May 2015, a few parents from my school who were not keen on IGCSE examinations enrolled their children to take the eAssessment pilot examination.

Geography is one of the subjects at my school in which teaching of the MYP and IGCSE is combined. As noted above, MYP Geography is an objectives-driven curriculum, with four objectives described in the Subject Guide (IB, 2014b). Content is not prescribed. In the classes where students intend to take the IGCSE Geography examination, the content stated in the IGCSE Geography syllabus is used, while teachers design opportunities, arising from the syllabus content, for students to meet the MYP Individuals and Societies objectives. The content prescribed in the IGCSE Geography syllabus is used in combination with the objectives of MYP Individuals and Societies.

IGCSE Geography does not have subject objectives and assessment criteria but has three assessment objectives, which have some similarities and differences with the MYP Individuals and Societies objectives. There are similarities for instance between MYP Objective A and IGCSE Assessment Objective (AO) 1. Also, IGCSE AO2 and AO3 match with some of the MYP objectives B and D. When students answer IGCSE examination-style questions, they meet the AOs and some similar MYP objectives. Some assessment tasks are designed to enable the students to meet the MYP Geography objectives, especially Objectives B and C. For example, a strand of Objective B is that students should be able to formulate a research question for the investigation and formulate an action plan to complete the investigation. The Paper 4 examination questions of IGCSE Geography do not provide such opportunities for students. Students are often asked to take up an independent geographical investigation to meet these strands of Objective B. However, the strand about evaluating data in Objective B can be met by answering the IGCSE examination questions. So, some strands of MYP objectives are met by IGCSE examination-style questions, while the other strands are met by teacher-designed assessment tasks. A geographic investigation helps the students to meet all the objectives of investigating, with the assignment then being assessed against criterion B.

Students are provided with two scores when their assignment is based on answering an IGCSE examination-style question. The first score is out of 8, based on MYP assessment criteria. The other score is the marks achieved by the student out of the total marks allotted to the IGCSE examination-style question in the mark scheme. Task-specific clarifications help to unpack assessment criteria for the students. Providing task-specific clarification can be a challenge when applied to an IGCSE examination-style question. These clarifications are provided when students work on other assessment tasks.

MYP Objective C: communicating has several strands which are assessed against criterion C. This objective does not match explicitly with any IGCSE AOs. It deals with structuring and communicating information in an appropriate manner. Answering examination-style questions could to some extent meet this objective. However, the strand on documenting sources of information by using a recognized convention (IB, 2014b) is only met by research-based tasks on themes of the IGCSE Geography syllabus. As a teacher, I know it takes effort to plan and design tasks that will help students to complete the IGCSE examinations successfully as well as to meet all the objectives of MYP Individuals and Societies.

Other fundamental aspects of MYP are the 'key concepts', 'related concepts' and 'global contexts'. The global contexts provide a framework for inquiring about a topic. Each topic or unit needs to be underpinned by one key concept and two or more related concepts in order to bring about a conceptual understanding. In order to cover all the key concepts and related concepts through the five years of the MYP, mapping of the concepts across the years is recommended. Teachers decide the purpose of a unit and plan, keeping in mind mapping of context and concepts. The mapping helps in selection of specific topics of inquiry. However, in the IGCSE Geography syllabus, the purpose of the topic is already defined for the teachers and students. Two separate topics could have similar key concepts and global contexts, but the related concepts will differ. As a result, some key concepts and global contexts may be used more frequently than others while following the IGCSE Geography syllabus. An interesting point for noting here is that the aims of IGCSE Geography and some strands of the assessment objectives mention the key concepts of change, place and global interaction. The global contexts of 'Fairness and Development', 'Globalization' and 'Sustainability' are found too. Reference to related concepts of scale and processes is also evident. In my experience the essence of the subject of Geography is not different in the two programmes, but the approach to delivering it is.

Service in action is an important aspect of MYP. Students engage in service activities, which could arise out of inquiring about a particular topic. In the course of inquiry, students could come across an issue that they would like to understand in more depth and address in their own way. Incorporating service within their community and curriculum in this way helps the students to engage in service-learning. Since the content has been prescribed, as a teacher I need to guide the class discussions and activities towards issues that may provide opportunities for the students to understand and think of ways to handle them. For example, the topic of food shortage was part of IGCSE prescribed content. Students were encouraged to inquire about the reasons behind the urban poor facing food shortages in their own city. This inquiry led them to look for solutions that are available in the city. Soon, the students were visiting or volunteering with the organizations that work towards alleviating hunger and food shortages. The students' understanding of this issue has been enriched by incorporating service learning within the curriculum, although the need to complete all the topics within the academic year may reduce the number of hours that could be spent on engaging in service learning in class. Nevertheless, students sometimes continue volunteering to help these organizations on their own, at weekends and during holidays.

Interdisciplinary learning helps students to understand the interconnectedness of subjects across the MYP. Students transfer their skills and understanding of one subject to another in order to develop a holistic understanding of a topic. They come to understand that subjects do not exist in isolation. Engaging in such a unit requires teachers to collaborate on a topic and to plan activities that help students to understand the interconnected nature of the world, by transferring their skills and knowledge across subjects. The MYP requirement of providing one collaboratively designed interdisciplinary unit is usually met in an academic year. Nevertheless, the delivering of IGCSE syllabus content within a specified time often restricts us from engaging in more such units. Also, some content may not naturally lead to exploring the interlinking of subjects in greater depth. Independent content – that is, content determined by the teacher – could help here.

ATL skills do not feature explicitly in the aims, syllabus content or assessment objectives of IGCSE Geography. However, the MYP ATL skills: thinking, communication, self-management, social and research, are a part of all MYP subject groups. In a stand-alone IGCSE Geography class, I would be working towards helping my students develop these skills without being explicit about them. In MYP Geography we discuss these skills, track their development and ask students (as well as teachers) to reflect on them. ATL skills help students to understand and develop their process of learning.

One interesting observation is that in grade 9, students and teachers engage in all aspects of the MYP. The intensity of such engagement changes towards the end of grade 10. As the mock examination approaches, the focus shifts to revising the topics and practising examination-style questions in class. In the last couple of months of grade 10, the spotlight is on IGCSE assessment objectives.

Conclusion

The onscreen MYP eAssessment examinations are offered for the first time in 2016. Topics that will be assessed in the eAssessment of Geography are made available to teachers through the IB's Online Curriculum Centre (online support portal for IB teachers). As noted above, the essence of Geography is the same across both MYP and IGCSE. For example, population, settlement and tourism are included in the topics for MYP eAssessment in Geography. It appears the MYP has started to prescribe content for the eAssessment similar to other externally set examinations taken by students. Clearly, independent teacher-selected content would make it difficult to design such examinations. Some teachers argue that prescribing content deviates from the objectives-driven curriculum and gradually moves towards a focus on a content-driven curriculum, while others believe that students cannot prepare for eAssessment in the same way that they prepare for the IGCSE examination as implementing the concept-based MYP well in school will ensure successful performance in eAssessments. It seems to me that there exists some ambiguity here. Before the pilot eAssessment in May 2015, several teachers delivering the MYP argued that the popularity of externally set examinations such as IGCSE might decline in IB MYP schools as a result of the introduction of MYP eAssessment. Indeed, the pilot eAssessment generated a certain degree of confidence in both parents and teachers. The academic demands of onscreen eAssessment need, however, to be made more explicit to the teachers and students. Most externally set and marked examinations have a detailed syllabus and assessment weightings. Specimen examination papers help teachers to guide their students effectively. At present, without specimen papers and other meaningful resources, not all teachers and students are confident about the onscreen eAssessment, feeling more comfortable with the tried and tested IGCSE examinations.

If the MYP eAssessments are successful, parents may well be encouraged to choose eAssessment instead of IGCSE examinations. Teachers in schools such as mine will not then have to combine two separate programmes to deliver specific subjects. It would, however, make greater sense to reserve comments on this point until after students have taken the first MYP onscreen eAssessments.

In summary, it can be concluded that the two programmes, MYP and IGCSE Geography, have commonalities and differences. The essence of Geography stays the same in both programmes, while the approaches to delivering the subject are different. Consequently, educators have to invest considerable effort if they are to meet the requirements of both. They need to innovate in order to maintain the principles of both programmes, since it is arguably less challenging to teach to the examination than it is to encourage concept-based learning. It remains to be seen whether the days of combining the MYP and IGCSE in subject teaching will soon be over.

References

Cambridge International Examinations (2015) *Cambridge IGCSE Geography Syllabus.* Cambridge: Cambridge International Examinations.

Hayden, M C (2006) *Introduction to International Education.* London: Sage.

International Baccalaureate (2014a) *MYP: From principles into practice.* Cardiff: International Baccalaureate.

International Baccalaureate (2014b) *MYP Individuals and Societies Guide.* Cardiff: International Baccalaureate.

Chapter 11

MYP to DP: Development and transitions

Anthony Hemmens

None of us requires scientific verification to know the monumental development undertaken by young people between the ages of 11 and 18; it is immense. There is the obvious physical change of growing up and filling out, puberty and the development of secondary sexual characteristics, growth in mental capacity and cognitive competencies, social and political awakening, cultural and economic engagement, the maturing of character, beginning formation of personal identity and the experiential encounter with the initiating acts that mark the rite of passage into adulthood. All this played out to a cacophony of affective turmoil. What a time! At the age of 18 there are still many more years of maturing ahead (indeed it is an ongoing, lifelong journey) but by this age the process of maturation has come a long way from the mewling and puking of infanthood and the whining of school-children with satchels and shining morning faces. All aspects of development during adolescence need to be carefully nurtured, with the two primary sources of support in most cultural contexts, parents in the home and teachers at school, fulfilling distinct yet complementary roles in the supportive process. The idiosyncratic nature of personal development may, at times, feel like the slow creep of a snail, yet it is punctured with points of sudden transition and change along its way, some that occur in the natural and social scheme of growing up, others unforeseen and unexpected.

Transitions as points of change are usually charged with a subtle blend of excitement and trepidation. Schools have a responsibility to the students in their care to manage, oversee and support all transitions – particularly those, I would argue, that exist due to the construction of education itself; between educational stages, educational programmes, school buildings and sets of educational practitioners. Adjustment stresses can result in physical and behavioural manifestations, with younger children – reluctant to leave mum or dad – crying at the school gate, while older students may become withdrawn or uncooperative. New surroundings, new people, a more serious atmosphere, new expectations of behaviour and social engagement, the sudden demand for greater maturity, possibly out of sync with the individual student's natural position of maturation, can result in an affective response marked by anxiety, resentment and confusion. It is usual that schools are aware of this, alert to the signs, and have in place systems of pastoral care that include tutors, advisors, mentors and counselors. But the affective domain is not the only area of well-being and development affected by these points of educational transition.

How aware are schools, how prepared and effective are they – and indeed educational systems at large – at supporting students at points of transition when it comes to effects on their learning experience, which is, after all, the central role of schools and education?

Both developmental and transformative, the education provided by the International Baccalaureate (IB) is about bridging points of transition and overcoming borders, boundaries and barriers. Its consistent philosophy is twofold; to develop the whole child, focusing on intellectual, personal, emotional and social growth; and to develop international mindedness (IB, 2008). Through its mission of developing intercultural understanding and respect, the IB aims to develop, in the students engaging in its programmes, an understanding of the world that transcends national borders. The IB takes a holistic view of knowledge and learning in which all knowledge is inter-related (IB, 2009), with curriculum design in the programmes of the IB continuum emphasizing transdisciplinary and interdisciplinary connectivity to enhance learning and transcend the compartmentalization of subject boundaries. Completed in 1997 with the introduction of the Primary Years Programme (PYP), for ages 3-12, the IB continuum for general education consists of the PYP, the Middle Years Programme (MYP) and the Diploma Programme (DP). Schools are not required to offer more than one of the programmes (each stands independently and is self-contained); however, when offered consecutively they are intended to form a coherent and meaningful learning sequence (IB, 2008). In this way the IB seeks to support the process of overcoming the barriers of transition between educational programmes.

Transitions and transformation

The establishment of the DP, first offered by the IB in 1968 for students aged 16-19, came as a pragmatic response to the needs of the growing socio-educational phenomenon represented by international schools serving the children of a globally mobile population. The practical aim was to provide an internationally-recognized university entrance qualification for students seeking tertiary placements all over the world, while the pedagogical aim was to develop the powers of the mind and encourage understanding rather than general knowledge acquisition (Peterson, 2011), a process-driven constructivist curriculum approach (IB, 2010). Twenty-six years later, this same mix of pragmatism and pedagogy would, after approximately 15 years of development (IB, 2010), lead to the first offering by the IB of the MYP in 1994, for students aged 11-16. If the DP was born from the International School of Geneva (Ecole Internationale de Genève, or Ecolint), Switzerland, then the birthplace of the MYP was the International School Moshi, Tanzania which, in 1980, hosted an International Schools Association (ISA) conference entitled 'The Needs of the Child in the Middle Years of Schooling (ages 11-16)' (Bunnell, 2011). Concern over the school's middle years educational provision had grown from the disjunction of philosophic and pedagogic approach of using programmes such as England's O-level (replaced with the GCSE in 1988) as the course of pre-DP preparation, leading the then headmaster, Lister Hannah, to suggest the development of a two year pre-DP curriculum 'which would align much more comfortably with the Diploma Programme' (IB, 2010: p2). Thus, MYP-DP programme alignment has been a central consideration of the MYP from its inception, with the intention that the MYP would prepare students for success in the DP (IB, 2014).

Preceded by the PYP with the DP as successor, the MYP faces in two directions and needs to accommodate students in transition both into and out of their middle years educational experience; for K-12 IB World Schools (schools that offer one or more of the IB programmes) the question of how to engineer the most productive school-wide learning environment emerged as a challenge for policy and practice (Hallinger *et al*, 2011). Responding to survey findings and anecdotal evidence from schools regarding IB programme alignment and issues of MYP implementation, in late 2010 the IB initiated a review, and ultimately re-design, of the MYP (IB, 2012). As a result, the IB published new documentation in 2014 (including eight subject guides, a Personal Project guide, a guide to interdisciplinary teaching and learning and a new *MYP: From principles into practice*) detailing significant changes to its programme for middle year students. These changes are not revolutionary; it is still discernably the same MYP with a continued commitment to Holistic Learning, Intercultural Awareness and Communication (IB, 2014). Rather they represent an evolution of the programme and its further development as part of the IB continuum of international education (IB, 2013), including alignment with the DP to prepare students for success in that programme (IB, 2014).

MYP-DP alignment: old concerns

The IB defines programme alignment as the agreement in both principle and practice of values and aspirations of learning, teaching and the demonstration of learning: the written, taught and assessed curriculum (IB, 2014). Commonality through structural design between the MYP and DP is an essential beginning to programme alignment. Both programmes have had, and continue to have, breadth and balance of study, the MYP consisting of eight subject groups across the disciplinary spectrum with the DP having six; an emphasis on language development and second Language Acquisition; a commitment to learning to learn and experiential learning, (Service and Action in the MYP; Creativity, Activity, Service (CAS) in the DP); a developmental focus on personal attributes, as outlined in the IB Learner Profile, and international mindedness, as expressed in the IB mission statement; a concluding culminating experience, an individual research project that synthesizes learning (the Personal Project in the MYP, the extended essay in the DP); pedagogic emphasis on enquiry-based Holistic Learning, a constructivist approach to teaching and learning: development of cognitive competencies and the encouragement of interdisciplinary understanding. What then of the differences?

Requirements imposed from stakeholders external to the school setting necessitate compromise and expediency in curriculum design for both the MYP and DP. Both programmes are discipline-orientated curriculum models, with subjects less connected and subject boundaries more defined in the DP. In large part due to university expectations, with the programme leading to high-stake formal assessment providing accreditation and a qualification for university entrance, curriculum content in the DP is detailed and prescribed. In contrast, the IB acknowledges that, due to legislative requirements at local and national level (IB, 2012), many schools will not be in a position to exercise autonomy in deciding subject content (IB, 2014). The MYP, therefore, does not consist of a prescribed curriculum at subject content level, but provides greater flexibility so that schools can accommodate external requirements. School circumstances, therefore, determine subject content and organization in the MYP, the IB providing a curriculum framework which is filled in with content details by the school according to its specific context and needs.

Findings from the IB global survey of IB programme coordinators, undertaken in 2008 to better understand the extent and nature of transitional issues between IB programmes, suggested that the most significant factor for MYP-DP transition was this difference in the fundamental nature of the two programmes; prescribed curriculum and external formal assessment in the DP, no prescribed curriculum content or external assessment in the MYP (Hallinger *et al*, 2011). A prescribed MYP content curriculum was one area recommended by IB coordinators for change to facilitate better MYP-DP transition (Hallinger *et al*, 2011). Research findings from Stobie (2005) had also identified differences in curriculum design and assessment models as a source of transitional tension between the two programmes. His research indicated that developing relevant and sufficient subject knowledge, between the MYP and the DP, was less coherent than other elements of the programmes, and varied according to subject; some teachers – particularly in languages, the arts and social studies – seeing a natural progression from the MYP to the DP, with other teachers – most commonly of Mathematics and Science – expressing the desire for more direction to help structure student learning in the MYP with DP requirements in mind.

Responsibility for MYP-DP alignment and the development of the written curriculum continues to reside at the school level (IB, 2014). With the publication of the 2014 MYP documentation, concerns over structural differences between the MYP and DP have been addressed and more direction provided.

MYP-DP alignment: New configuration

There are both changes and shifts of emphasis in the new MYP. The Areas of

Interaction have been replaced; approaches to learning (ATL) and community and service still remain (ATL with a greater emphasis), but the other component parts – health and social education, environments and human ingenuity – have been combined into 'global contexts' (IB, 2012). Global contexts have been developed from, and extend, the transdisciplinary themes of the PYP (thus providing greater coherence between the PYP and MYP) (IB, 2014). The contextualization of learning encourages learning which is more meaningful and directly relevant for the learner, increasing the likelihood of greater social and affective engagement in classroom activity and cognitive engagement with subject content and concepts. Contextualizing learning in issues and themes which have global scope and significance make the developmental intentions of the IB mission, of encouraging intercultural understanding and international mindedness, more explicit and central to the new MYP than in its pre-2014 form.

There is a greater emphasis in the new MYP on conceptual learning, simultaneously grounded in specific disciplines, to encourage deeper levels of understanding, and providing the MYP's structural approach to interdisciplinary learning, where organizing ideas transcend subject boundaries and facilitate evaluation from multiple disciplinary perspectives (IB, 2014). Interdisciplinary learning, therefore, is grounded in the disciplines rather than in alternative interdisciplinary approaches, such as problem-solving. The MYP emphasis on school-based assessment, with teachers providing formative feedback on assessment tasks to inform and promote the learning function and improve the teaching process, remains unchanged. The IB has, however, introduced optional end-of-programme formal assessment, facilitated via online technology, providing students with an opportunity to demonstrate learning and be awarded IB validated grades (IB, 2014). In this way, the IB has modified the MYP for greater alignment with the DP, with its end of programme formal assessment, addressing the perceived MYP-DP transitional tension that existed pre-2014. An educational programme which adopts a framework approach, as with the MYP, is dependent on the agents of implementation to a greater degree than a programme with detailed content prescription. It is difficult to navigate learning pathways in the absence of an ultimate destination, or when that destination point may be obscured from view – as when it is the end point of a succeeding programme. It may therefore be the case that inclusion of external assessment provides a necessary level of support and guidance to those schools and teachers uncomfortable with an open stretch of un-signposted learning highway, while having that assessment as an optional choice allows schools that are confident in what they are presently doing to stay on their present course. Whether a school decides to enter its students, in their final year of the MYP (MYP year 5), for external assessment or not, it is the assessment criteria, rather than the assessment itself, which act in a guiding capacity to direct curriculum construction as written by the school; backwash from MYP assessment, rather than backwash from DP assessment, directing the MYP written curriculum. Where MYP assessment objectives and instruments are aligned with those of the DP, then programme alignment through their respective assessment models will be enhanced, providing incremental learning development through points of external assessment first at the end of the MYP (age 16), then again at the end of the DP (age 18/19). The IB claims that subject examinations in the MYP are aligned with understanding and skills that prepare students for high levels of achievement in DP subjects (IB, 2014).

New IB subject group guides for the MYP set out the scope of learning in each subject with objectives encompassing the 'factual, conceptual, procedural and metacognitive dimensions of knowledge' (IB, 2013: p8). Subjects are structured through sets of aims and objectives listed through the new assessment criteria categories with an emphasis on essential subject knowledge, understanding, skills and attitudes, where subject knowledge acquisition is for transfer and application to novel contexts rather than the short-term superficial purpose of memorization and recall. In this way, academic rigour, traditionally seen as a strength of the DP rather than the MYP (Stobie, 2005), is explicitly embedded in the MYP. The task of the schools, therefore, as they plan and write MYP subject curriculum, is to identify the essential subject content, knowledge and skills to enable conceptual understanding, with meaningful interdisciplinary links, presented in a real-world global context. For MYP-DP continuum schools, through alignment under each subject group's final objectives, MYP curriculum content needs to provide continuity and progression from the MYP year 5 into the two-year DP (IB, 2014).

MYP-DP alignment: Curriculum planning

Curriculum, as a fundamental component of the quality of student learning, needs to be understood as a central concern of any school (Ashworth, 2013). The IB describes the MYP written curriculum as the 'formal, comprehensive school-wide set of documents ... that describe what will be taught in each subject to each age group' (2014, p42). MYP curriculum documentation consists of unit plans, subject-group overviews and ATL planning, with the process of unit planning helping to develop the written, taught and assessed curriculum (IB, 2013). Curriculum construction on this scale, with vertical and horizontal planning, will require a collaborative approach involving teachers, programme coordinators, curriculum leaders, departmental heads and managerial administrators in both the MYP and DP. MYP horizontal planning is the planning of curriculum for coherence and cohesion across the programme and the disciplinary subjects, incorporating its component parts and identifying interdisciplinary conceptual links and global contexts. Vertical planning for programme alignment entails construction of longitudinal coherence and cohesion across the combined seven years of the MYP-DP continuum, providing developmentally appropriate learning experiences year-on-year. Within the MYP this is structurally enabled by the IB through the use of subject objectives for years 1 to 5 which outline a progression of learning and provide continuity (IB, 2014). To enhance MYP-DP cohesion when developing MYP subject curriculum content, schools should consult the relevant DP subject guides (IB, 2014).

Ashworth argues that the construction of written MYP curriculum, and articulation of learning across the programme and into the DP, requires not insignificant skills in curriculum-building and teachers with sufficiently wide-ranging subject experience for its effective accomplishment. She suggests that 'it is perhaps a mistake to assume that all teachers are in a position to be curriculum-builders in the manner needed' (Ashworth, 2013: 210). That curriculum unit planning is teacher dependent should be expected of an educational programme which itself developed from excellent classroom practice and committed practitioners reflecting on and responding to the immediate needs of their students. This is the essential role of the teacher. It is a challenge that teachers need not only to embrace as a professional obligation, but also to welcome as a professional opportunity and insist upon as a professional right; the alternative, of highly prescribed content that must be taught and tested, as with a national curriculum or common core, does not strike me as an appealing prospect. Flexibility, a quality identified as one of the greatest strengths of the MYP (Stobie, 2005), brings with it professional freedom and also responsibility. An essential initial step, therefore, is twofold: professional empowerment that enables teachers to use their creativity and professionalism to develop units of work that engage students in learning the essence of their disciplines (IB, 2014), together with professional support extended to each teacher in accordance with his/her position of competence and understanding and the school-wide development of supporting structures, professional development opportunities and practices that support the creation of a professional learning community (Stobie, 2009: cited by IB, 2010: p24). Much will depend on the culture of the school, where professional freedom is respected and professional collaboration flows from collegiality. Creative teacher professionalism is relevant to both the MYP and DP, but in the absence of prescribed curriculum content the MYP represents a high challenge (Ashworth, 2013) that will require teacher professionalism of the highest order (Stobie, 2009: cited by IB, 2010).

Curriculum planning – the central importance of experience

The starting point for effective collaborative curriculum planning is not a scheduled meeting slot and a blank unit plan sheet set in the middle of a table with a selection of coloured pens with which to fill it in. It is a dialogue between educational practitioners expert in pedagogy and their chosen academic disciplines, with a shared understanding of the common agenda and common goal, and a thorough understanding of MYP documentation including the programme's requirements, structure and philosophy. It will require time to read, process and understand MYP documentation, a large undertaking in itself. Vertical planning for MYP-DP alignment will further require a thorough understanding of the DP and the complementary nature of these two programmes. Research by Hallinger *et al* (2010, in Hallinger *et al*, 2011) identified strategies and practices employed in IB schools in the Asia-Pacific region that address issues of programme transition; these included cross-programme teaching, student cross-programme interaction, curriculum backward mapping and staff position switching.

For the purpose of effective MYP-DP alignment and vertical planning of the MYP that facilitates effective learner transition into the DP, it is imperative that teachers, as classroom practitioners and curriculum planners, have direct multi-grade cross-programme experience as the most effective means of acquiring a thorough understanding of both the MYP and DP; where the students 'are coming from' and where they 'are going to' (Currer, 2011). Structural continuity provided by the IB becomes a school reality, with effective programme alignment and MYP-DP transitional support to students, when teachers have direct experiential engagement in both programmes. In research conducted by Stobie (2005) teachers, almost unanimously, indicated that their teaching in the DP significantly impacted on how they taught the last two years of the MYP, with that time being utilized to prepare students for the demands of the DP. Conversely, the same teachers reported that their MYP experience did not influence their approach to teaching in the DP. Cross-programme teaching, therefore, either concurrently or in alternate years, has the benefit of informing MYP-DP alignment in unit planning and curriculum writing as well as in the practical delivery of learning in the classroom. To my mind the division of teaching faculty between the MYP and the DP is not, therefore, necessarily the best practical strategy.

Currer (2011) argues there is a tendency among teachers to prioritize and favour students studying in the DP programme, so that younger non-examination classes can take 'second place'. It can often be the practice in subject departments for teachers more senior in position and longevity to monopolize the more 'glamorous' examination courses. It is the responsibility of the school to address this culture where it exists and to timetable a balanced spread of grades across the teaching schedules of all teachers, particularly those relatively new to the profession who will benefit greatly from this professional exposure and experience.

Finally, both vertical and horizontal planning can be enhanced through professional understanding gleaned through a system of lesson observation – not for the purpose of appraisal, but for familiarization of pedagogical approach, learning emphasis and content focus, including learning objectives and assessment procedures, across subjects and years. This necessitates a school-wide 'open-door' culture. Explanations from colleagues regarding learning in the various subjects and differing year groups is no substitute for direct experience of that learning, either observational or practical.

From MYP to DP: Students in transition

Students, as they complete the MYP at the age of 16, have developmentally come a long way in their five years of MYP participation. It has always been my experience that the transition they make from the MYP into the DP is different to other points of transition they experience at earlier stages of their education. Without much of a backward glance and little by way of outward display of any trepidation they may feel, students exit the MYP and embrace the full challenge of the DP, many already eyeing the glittering prize awaiting them at the end of the experience.

It is highly advantageous, although not essential, to a successful DP experience that students in their first year of the DP begin those studies from a solid foundational position of knowledge, understanding, skills and attitudes, so that the teaching and learning in the DP can focus on the content of the programme itself. The demands of the DP, both as a whole programme and within each individual subject, are so great that there is often insufficient time to cover all content at the desired depth of engagement and to facilitate sufficient student developmental progress within its two-year duration; this is exacerbated when a student's starting position is low. In the DP, time is at a premium. An essential role of the MYP is to prepare students with the requisite skills, attitudes, attributes, epistemological understanding, subject knowledge and expectations of learning that provide a significant boost to DP performance when understanding and skills, at the core of both MYP and DP subject objectives, have been maximized at the point of DP entry (Ashworth, 2013).

An essential outcome of any middle years programme, as it relates to the DP, is the development of learner identity and learning to learn skills, so that students have both an effective attitude to learning and an understanding of what learning in the DP entails. Research by Stobie (2005) found that teachers and administrators considered the development of approaches to learning and critical thinking skills as the MYP's main contributing points in preparation for the DP, and furthermore that these were the most important ways in which the MYP could prepare students for the DP. The complexity of facilitating effective learning is diminished when a student is an effective learner. Student expectations of the learning experience prior to beginning the DP need to be aligned with the learning reality. Where expectation is misaligned, affective tension can result, leading to resistance; it is imperative to learning success that the student have faith in the learning provision of the programme and the teacher. If a student does not believe they are learning, or can learn within a given educational context, then their learning can be impaired. Much of the DP is familiar to students on beginning the programme when they transit to it from the MYP, the only component entirely novel being the Theory of Knowledge (ToK). Students from other middle years backgrounds, however, can often require longer to settle in the DP, particularly when they have come from an educational context where more traditional didactic approaches formed their learning experience. The switch from being taught through 'teacher-telling' to being expected to understand through independent construction, in accordance with a constructivist approach – the teacher as learning facilitator rather than source of answer, is a leap in learning approach welcomed by some students but resisted by others who cannot perceive it as learning. An essential part of the preparation of students in the year preceding the start of their DP studies, therefore, will be to convey to them an understanding of what the DP entails, what they can expect from the programme and what will be expected of them as DP students.

Conclusion

In addition to the transitional points between IB programmes, PYP-MYP-DP, a further transition occurs within the MYP itself, between MYP years 1, 2, 3 and MYP years 4 and 5; both sets of years facing in the direction of their closer neighbouring programme. Currer (2011) questions if the curriculum programme most suitable for students in the opening years of their middle years experience will also be the most appropriate for pre-DP students needing skills and content-heavy preparation for that programme and its formal assessment. Clearly a student's experience of learning in MYP year 5 will not, and can not, be the same as their experience in MYP year 1. This is attested to by reports from teachers on how they approach teaching and learning in MYP years 4 and 5, and evidenced in the attitudes of students in those two years as they increasingly become focused on future plans and the future challenge represented by the DP, university placement and ultimately career choice and life beyond education. The IB states that schools are required to assist students in their subject choices in the MYP years 4 and 5 so that those choices reflect further study plans and ensure appropriate preparation for DP studies (IB, 2014). Furthermore, subject-group flexibility in the MYP years 4 and 5 allows students, if they are better served in doing so, to study six subject groups rather than the full MYP breadth of eight subjects, this allowance reflecting the subject spread of the DP (IB, 2014). The MYP is about supporting the developmental progress of adolescents between the ages of 11 and 16. Passage through the MYP, sandwiched as it is between two adjacent programmes, will inevitably necessitate the process of re-orientation of the learner to face in a different direction. It seems, therefore, quite natural that there should be a transitional period within the MYP itself.

Consideration of a student's future is an essential responsibility of educators and schools, the preparatory foundations needing to be carefully and thoughtfully laid through backward planning. Effective MYP-DP alignment will mean that, as a result of completing their MYP studies, students are well-prepared for the challenge of the DP and examination success, and additionally that throughout the two-year duration of the DP students are able to build on their MYP achievements. The central concern of MYP-DP transition needs to focus on the learning function of the programmes, ensuring that learning is not detrimentally affected and that no loss of learning occurs. Differences between the MYP and DP, where they adversely impact on a school's capacity to deliver coherency in learning content and culture for students as they transition between programmes, need to be addressed. With a modified MYP, the IB took a significant step towards this with the 2014 publication of new MYP documentation, schools being required to translate this into a learning reality.

While the MYP will, and does, function to prepare students for the DP, it should also be conceived as a programme in its own right providing the development appropriate for the age range it serves. Ultimately, the preparation for final formal assessment in the DP is provided by the DP itself. The role of the MYP should not solely be perceived as a preparation for the DP, which is itself most often seen as a preparation for university, but as a partner programme to the DP in the development of young people aged 11-18, the MYP rolling into the DP with a common educational philosophy, approach to teaching and learning, and learning objectives. Differences between the MYP and DP are what make them distinctive, and each of them is valued accordingly (Hallinger *et al*, 2011). While the programmes need to support each other, they also need to serve the students, with their different developmental needs, for whom they are intended (Ashworth, 2013: p215).

Research by Stobie (2005) found that, in the DP, preparing students for the IB external examinations was perceived to require a more traditional focus and preparation than that encouraged by the MYP's looser framework. For many teachers and students this was seen as a natural progression, while for others it was viewed as a big leap. The research suggested that important learning objectives, clearly identified in DP documentation, are considered less important, or not even recognized, by a number of teachers because of the pressure they are under to get students through a tough and traditional academic examination. Many teachers and administrators felt that the 'holistic' elements of the Diploma were only bolted onto the programme through courses such as ToK and CAS, and were not their responsibility. Perhaps now the challenge lies with the DP. What is its responsibility to programme alignment in the IB continuum? Can it also evolve to become a more holistic programme with core elements integrated, to a greater degree than is presently the case, into its subject groups? Perhaps we shall see with the revised programme.

References

Ashworth, G. (2013) 'Articulating the Gap: The IB MYP and DP'. in *Exploring Issues of Continuity: The International Baccalaureate in a Wider Context.* Ed. Hayden, M and Thompson, J. Woodbridge: John Catt Educational, pp195-218.

Bunnell, T. (2011) 'The International Baccalaureate Middle Years Programme after 30 Years: A Critical Inquiry.' *Journal of Research in International Education* 10, 3, 261-74.

Currer, D. (2011) 'The MYP: A Wider Stakeholder Context.' in *Taking the MYP Forward.* Ed.

Hayden, M and Thompson, J. Woodbridge: John Catt Educational, pp 161-69

Hallinger, P., Lee, M., and Walker, A. (2011) 'Program Transition Challenges in International Baccalaureate Schools.' *Journal of Research in International Education* 10, 2, 123-36

IB (2010) *History of the Middle Years Programme.* Cardiff: International Baccalaureate.

IB (2014) *MYP: From principles into practice.* Cardiff: International Baccalaureate.

IB (2012) *MYP: Next chapter development report (October 2012).* Cardiff: International Baccalaureate.

IB (2012) *MYP: Next chapter development report (August 2013).* Cardiff: International Baccalaureate.

IB (2009) *The Middle Years Programme: A basis for practice.* Cardiff: International Baccalaureate.

IB (2008) *Towards a Continuum of International Education.* Cardiff: International Baccalaureate.

Peterson, A. D. C. (2011) *Schools across Frontiers: The Story of the International Baccalaureate and the United World Colleges.* Chicago, IL: Open Court

Stobie, T. D. (2005) To What Extent Do the Middle Years Programme and Diploma Programme of the International Baccalaureate Organisation Provide a Coherent and Consistent Educational Continuum? *International Schools Journal,* 25, 1, 30-40.

Part C
Leading the change

Chapter 12

MYP leadership in five concepts

Gillian Ashworth

Establishing the purpose

Much has been said about the International Baccalaureate's Middle Years Programme (MYP), though not always as succinctly as in a comment from one MYP teacher: "If it's done badly (which is common) then it's an absolute train wreck. If it's done well then it's amazing...." (ISR, 2015).

The task of determining which option is ultimately embraced by an MYP school falls to that school's 'leadership', not infrequently a complex organogram intertwined with roles of complex responsibilities, among which lies the job of navigating teachers through a sea of concepts, global contexts, Statements of Inquiry and the like to a land of meaningful student learning of all of the kinds which the programme encompasses. The most direct form of 'leadership' in the case of any International Baccalaureate (IB) programme is carried out by the programme coordinator; a role mandated by the IB, and under whose auspices responsibility for the practical implementation of an individual programme falls. The coordinator may be accompanied by separate satellite roles also with direct leadership and implementation responsibilities for elements such as approaches to learning, service as action and the Personal Project, or as subject leaders. More senior leadership may encompass principals, vice-principals, curriculum coordinators, academic/pastoral directors and so on. As Sperandio notes, however, and as the IB's public website (IB, 2015c) demonstrates, 'The program is clearly attractive to many different types of school in many different educational and geographical contexts' (Sperandio, 2010, p142). What such leadership may look like in nature and structure may thus vary enormously in the wildly differing contexts in which the MYP is found across the globe, from the smaller school in which the programme coordinator is also the section principal – and indeed the entire leadership of the MYP in him- or herself, to highly complex structures and position descriptions.

Whatever the immediate context of a school, however, significant responsibilities fall in the same way to its leadership for the quality of the implementation of its MYP, a programme which encompasses a range of common requirements, the implementation of which can be materially affected by the nature of the leadership understandings and practices present. The importance of such leadership and its impact on programme implementation quality has been increasingly recognized by the IB itself over recent years, which have seen the gradual introduction of firstly a requirement from 2008 for the 'school head or designée' in a school implementing each programme to participate in a dedicated workshop for 'Heads' for that programme; followed later by opportunities to become certified in IB leadership (IB, 2015d), including as part of Masters degree studies in educational leadership and management courses, schools not infrequently require of their would-be principals and heads these days (Hayden, 2006). Meanwhile the recent introduction of changes to the MYP as the culmination of the 'Next Chapter' project was accompanied by newly-developed Heads and Coordinators' programme workshops at both category 1 and 2 levels, and 2015-16 has seen and will see the roll-out of category 3 leadership-focused workshops covering topics such as pedagogical leadership, 'understanding leadership', vision and strategy, culture and context, leading for effective teaching and learning, and professional learning communities; as well as leadership webinars (IB, 2015e).

All of these are aimed at producing 'a better-informed administrator workforce (with the hope that being better informed will feed into the improvement of practice)' (Hayden, 2006, pp110-11) – the remarks being directed more generally at administrators obtaining postgraduate qualifications, but having equal resonance in the context of a programme whose workshop leaders would attest, in not insignificant number, to frustrations of participants at insufficient leadership understanding of the programme within their schools, and consequent insufficient support for its effective implementation. School leaders, however, ask equally in workshops both how MYP might be implemented in a way which is preferably 'amazing', but certainly avoids being a 'train wreck', and how to deal with doubts expressed at times by their own teachers at various points on the scale of acceptability, but which tend to reflect the sentiment – whether in more or less polite terms – 'The MYP is difficult to implement, not because it hasn't been thought through, but because it requires a lot of work, more than in just your subject' (Robertson, 2011, p137).

Such questions have, meanwhile, arisen with increasing frequency as the number of MYP schools has risen to over 1,149 schools in 101 different countries at a recent count (IB, 2015f). Yet, as noted by Lee *et al*, there exists despite the growth rate a relative paucity of empirical evidence relating to leadership in the context of IB schools (2012, pp291-2). Where such studies do exist, meanwhile, the MYP can be a notable absentee – 'strong leadership from principals and IB programme coordinators played a key role in successful DP implementation'; 'strong leadership was a key factor that facilitated successful PYP implementation' (Lee *et al*, 2012, p292) being one example. One is thus left having to surmise in the case of the MYP that 'strong leadership' might be useful for effective implementation there also.

The absence of substantial empirical evidence leaves the field open to – appropriately enough in the context of an inquiry-based programme – the possibility of conducting something of an inquiry into what 'strong leadership' might comprise in practice, within the context of the MYP. In this we might take something of a journey into the programme and put some of its tools in the shape of key concepts to productive use, identifying particular spheres of leadership which may play a role in keeping an MYP implementation process on the rails, and on the right track. Of the 16 key concepts which form the basis for unit planning in the MYP, five might be particularly appropriate here, as indicated in upper case and italic.

Aesthetics	*CHANGE*	*COMMUNICATION*	*COMMUNITIES*
Connections	Creativity	*CULTURE*	Development
Form	Global interactions	Identity	Logic
Perspective	*RELATIONSHIPS*	Systems	Time, space and place

Always underlying an MYP implementation process is the need to facilitate change, and in doing so to navigate the 'multiple realities of people, who are the main participants in it' (Fullan, 2007, p96). Some of the more pertinent of those realities in the context of MYP implementation lie in the nature of communities formed, cultures created, and relationships developed within them; along with the communication which impacts on all. These will therefore represent the five concepts to be considered here.

A need for change

> Change is a conversion, transformation or movement from one form, state or value to another. Inquiry into the concept of change involves understanding and evaluating causes, processes and consequences. (IB 2014a, p56)

Change is an immutable element of educational dynamics, and none more so in the case of those dynamics which reside in the MYP. Schools taking on the programme are advised that '…school-wide adoption of the MYP approach will require change not only in the classroom but throughout the school' (IB, 2014a, p29), and while a decision to adopt any new programme means inevitable commitment to substantial change, quite possibly involving 'all elements of a school's operating environment', including 'all grade levels, all students, and all elements of school practice' (Keltner, 1998, pp1-2), the MYP in particular has rarely been perceived as residing in the basket marked 'easy' when identified as the programme of choice. Hence the warning that 'school-wide adoption of the MYP approach… is likely to be slow and challenging' (IB, 2014a, p29), while the muted anguish of observations such as those of Codrington in the tartly-titled article 'The pain of curriculum change' – 'In contrast to the very positive experiences of introducing the Diploma Programme (DP) and the Primary Years Programme (PYP) at Prince Alfred College in Adelaide, Australia, implementation of the Middle Years Programme (MYP) has been problematic' (Codrington, 2002) – serve as first-hand testimony to that.

As is not infrequently pointed out, the MYP is a programme which 'does not comprise an actual curriculum' (Hallinger and Lee, 2012, p480), while the IB itself specifies the 'three main strands [which] initiate and drive school change' as being the curricular-centric elements of unit planning, collaborative planning, and assessment (IB, 2014a, p29). All of this necessitates that teachers 'populate their [MYP] programmes themselves with all of the complexity such curriculum-building involves' (Ashworth, 2013, p167), with such complexity often comprising in practice the seeking out of suitable content to form the basis for exploration of concepts and contexts, and for the development of 'procedural knowledge', or skills – most notably, critical thinking skills – within each individual subject area. This must then be fed into 'The concept-driven curriculum frameworks of the MYP' (IB, 2014a, p14), which may in themselves represent uncertain curricular territory for teachers in the programme, along with their related elements such as global contexts, inquiry statements and questions, and interdisciplinary teaching and learning. The task for schools and teachers with all of this is to 'organize and plan this effectively to address all of the learning objectives in a subject, and articulate learning across the programme – and then [possibly] across to the DP' (Ashworth, 2013, p174). The task is not a minor one, and neither is the subsequent need to deliver it all meaningfully in the classroom, quite possibly via pedagogical approaches which may also not be the most familiar of acquaintances to all teachers.

Understanding of, and an ability to execute, change are thus critical elements of an MYP leadership armoury, whether in a candidate or authorized school; change motivated both by something of an initial curricular void when the programme is adopted, and by the nature of a number of the programme features which must be engaged with in order to fill it. Worthy of some note in regard to the latter may be a study of reasons for adopting the MYP cited on school application forms, in which 'innovative program features' appeared most popularly, these referring to aspects such as interdisciplinary initiatives, the Personal Project, and the now superseded Areas of Interaction (Sperandio, 2010, pp143-4). The 'creativity offered to teachers' is further cited by the IB itself (IB, 2010) as a reason for the MYP proving popular with schools, while Watts has spoken of 'one of the strengths of the MYP' being that 'it liberat[es] teachers from prescriptive curricular and summative assessment, thus allowing them to create challenging curriculums and new teaching methodologies' (Watts, 2002, p16). Innovation is thus at the heart of what the MYP is perceived to offer, and it may be from this that perceptions of a programme which could be 'amazing' are formed.

Within 'innovation' lurks unfamiliarity and 'newness', however, and a probable concomitant need for development of and changes to existing knowledge, understandings and practices on the parts of those charged with its implementation. Fullan indeed talks of 'implementation' as 'consist[ing] of the process of putting into practice an idea, program, or set of activities and structures new to the people attempting or expected to change' (2007, p69), but there is an ominous note too in the warning that 'The history of implementation research is not pleasant. It shows that planned change attempts rarely succeed as intended' (Fullan, 2007, p10). Other experts in the area of change concur: 'Few organizational change efforts tend to be ... entirely successful ... Most efforts encounter problems; they often take longer than expected and desired, they sometimes kill morale, and they often cost a great deal in terms of managerial time or emotional upheaval' (Kotter and Schlesinger, 2008, p132). Others directly involved in programme implementation reference a daunting challenge: '[MYP coordinators] felt that much resistance to the MYP constructivist approach from high school teachers was about 'being uncomfortable without a prescribed curriculum'' (Robertson, 2011, pp136-7); ''finding one's way' with the constructivist elements of this curriculum was a constant source of anxiety to many teachers' (Robertson, 2011, p140).

The pressing need for leadership within a context of MYP implementation to 'understand and evaluate change and its causes, processes and consequences' (IB 2014a, p56) is thus clear, though no better is its inherent challenges illustrated than by Machiavelli's moment of insight: '...it ought to be remembered that there is nothing more difficult to take in hand, more perilous to conduct, more uncertain in its success, nor more dangerous to handle, than to take the lead in the introduction of a new order of things' (2006, p83) Not least among the navigation issues is the fundamental fact that schools are 'reliant on teachers to produce the majority of the work' (Robertson, 2011, p142), and the reality is, as Kotter and Schlesinger point out, that 'for a number of different reasons, individuals or groups can react very differently to change – from passively resisting it, to aggressively trying to undermine it, to sincerely embracing it' (2008, p131). Hence 'educational change is a process of coming to grips with the multiple realities of people, who are the main participants in it' (Fullan, 2007, p96).

Creating communities

Communities are groups that exist in proximity defined by space, time or relationship. Communities include, for example, groups of people sharing particular characteristics, beliefs or values as well as groups of interdependent organisms living together in a specific habitat. (IB 2014a, p57)

Gathering together 'multiple realities' and the people who go with them, in order to create the MYP team which will implement the programme, is very much an exercise in creating communities through bringing together groups of 'interdependent organisms' in the forms of leadership and faculty, and endeavouring to develop within those the particular 'characteristics, beliefs and values' analogous with successful MYP practice. In creating these, organizational structures both formal and informal represent a critical element, with 'Successful implementation of the MYP', according to the IB, being dependent in part on 'the support and practical involvement of the school's leadership (including its governing body, administrators and pedagogical leaders), particularly in setting up an organizational infrastructure.' (IB, 2014a, p29). Allied to that structural vision is a wider one of creating in the school a learning community which 'encourage[s] school leaders, teachers, students, parents and local community members to value learning as an essential and integral part of their everyday lives' (IB, 2014a, p10). The route to realizing these respective practical and philosophical dimensions of community-building is often perceived to lie in the implementation of strategies relating to appointment practices, distributed leadership, and professional learning communities.

Reviewing appointment practices

The most immediate task in forming an MYP community lies in populating it, a process at its minimum level involving the appointment of an MYP coordinator, 'The pedagogical leader of the MYP in the school who oversees the effective development of the programme' (IB, 2014a, p112); other mandated leadership roles, and those teachers to whom it will fall 'to produce the majority of the work' (Robertson, 2011, p142). External hiring for MYP positions, as in the case of recruitment for IB programmes generally, often places some premium on experience and whether, how much, and what type of this might be needed: 'Most leaders in the case study schools preferred to hire teachers with previous IB teaching experience, though this was not a prerequisite. Hiring teachers with IB experience enabled a smoother transition. The new staff would be more familiar with the substantial IB jargon and also possess requisite knowledge of the IB philosophy and related learning and teaching practices' (Lee *et al*, 2012, pp301-2). Greater speed of implementation might also be an anticipated consequence of appointing a greater degree of experience, perhaps along with a degree of attitudinal filtering where any antipathy towards the programme spawned in one past MYP experience might act as a deterrent to some teachers against seeking further employment in another.

The above reflects something of Collins' comments in his exposition of organizational movement from 'good to great' that: 'To decide where to drive the bus before you have the right people on the bus, and the wrong people off the bus, is absolutely the wrong approach' (Collins, 2001). This is certainly a key consideration, though factors such as overall programme growth and candidate availability, as well as at times undercooked programme knowledge and expectations of those charged with appointing, can impact on both coordination and teacher recruitment, and the reality in a school may thus lie in a continuum of experience being represented.

Distributing leadership

Mandated leadership by the IB for the MYP comprises appointment of an MYP coordinator, assignation of leadership for curriculum development in subject groups, and an organizational arrangement which will provide support for the implementation of approaches to learning, service as action, and the personal and/or community projects (IB, 2014a, p32). Beyond this, the precise nature of an MYP leadership structure can 'vary widely according to local requirements and context' (IB, 2014a, p30), and may, as noted earlier, range from single individual leadership to a highly complex network, possibly extending beyond individuals to committees and teams of various kinds (Lee *et al*, 2012, p301), and which may interweave a range of school-wide responsibilities with equally complex possible MYP-related involvement, bringing with it a need for careful consideration of role delineation.

Two of the more frequently-considered options for carrying out additional leadership functions for the programme are those of a curriculum specialist, and an MYP steering committee or leadership team. Given the pressing need for 'direct accountability for the quality of curriculum' which is, as has been seen, such a foundational aspect of MYP implementation; and for 'overseeing the process and monitoring and reviewing the various aspects of it properly' (Ashworth, 2013, p176), thought is given in schools at times as to whether and how a curriculum specialist may add to existing capacity in this area, if it is felt an MYP coordinator in tandem with subject leaders may not have the necessary time and / or experience to take on the substantial accountabilities it brings.

An MYP steering committee may, meanwhile, 'assist the MYP coordinator and ensure involvement of the school leadership' (IB, 2014a, p31); and offer increased knowledge of and involvement in the programme for members of leadership teams. Several sources attest to the value of school leadership being seen to be 'walking the walk and not just talking the talk', or 'in the trenches being the model' (Porter, 2011, p226); while Robertson relates in his review of MYP coordination challenges how interviewees reported on the relative ineffectiveness of 'senior managers who were not sufficiently involved in MYP implementation' (2011, p142). Membership of a steering committee offers a potentially manageable option for the hard-pressed administrator to keep abreast of implementation progress, grow their programme knowledge, and (not to underestimate the importance of symbolic leadership) be seen to be involved and interested.

This MYP leadership model, outlined within *MYP: From Principles into Practice*, represents even in its most minimal mandated form one of distributed leadership, defined by Spillane as leadership which is 'distributed over an interactive web of people and situations' (2005, p144), and where responsibilities and initiatives are shared across varied positions, thus offering greater autonomy and scope for decision-making for individual role-holders within the overall organizational structure. Its applicability to the varied elements and complexities of MYP implementation and associated leadership practices are clear, while it represents too part of a leadership philosophy predicated on a theory of 'people work[ing] together in such a way that they pool their initiative and expertise,' with the outcome being 'a product or energy which is greater than the sum of their individual actions' (Woods *et al*, 2004, p441). It thus offers considerable potential benefits for capacity-building, both for those within the distributed leadership network, and for those they lead in turn; which renders success in change processes more likely.

Relatively thin empirical evidence continues to cast some doubt ultimately on the actual impact of distributed leadership in practice, however (Bennett *et al*, 2003; Spillane, 2005; Mayrowetz, 2008), and the nature, scope and potential consequences (for instance role confusion and micropolitical behaviours) of any strategic deployment of distributed leadership practices are worthy of some forethought. On the positive side are findings by Hallinger and Lee in research considering MYP – DP cross-programme transition that 'leadership practices strategically aiming to deploy instructional leadership responsibilities were positively associated with successful program transition' (2012, p489), though Lee *et al* conversely report elsewhere that 'Leadership responsibilities were ... widely distributed both formally and informally' in certain case study IB schools, where 'elaborate leadership teams ... represented a coordination challenge' (2012, p301). Also noted was the impact of supplementing 'formal administrative and curriculum leadership roles' with 'special committees (*eg* articulation committees) and teams (*eg* pastoral support teams, project teams)' – addenda very commonly found with leadership networks within MYP schools, which served in the case study schools to render 'not an easy task' the efforts of IB school leaders to 'establish the necessary 'connective tissue' in such multilayered organizational structures' (Lee *et al*, 2012, p301).

The IB advises that 'Implementing the MYP requires schools to focus on the development of leadership and structures that support teaching and learning' (IB, 2014a, p30). Beyond the somewhat limited IB-mandated roles, the task falls to schools to determine their own organizational structures, and the use of the distributed leadership approach inherent there, with its potential for expansion within a school, is worthy of careful consideration in terms of needs, roles – and ultimate efficacy. 'Support[ing] teaching and learning' ought to represent the key phrase in terms of purpose, and 'strategically aiming to deploy instructional leadership responsibilities' the best way to go about 'getting the right people on the bus' and in the 'right places'.

Developing a collaborative culture and professional learning communities

Developing an MYP community which can foster in reality the 'characteristics, values and beliefs' which underpin successful MYP implementation requires something more than people on the bus and attending carefully to their seating arrangements, however. Further structures are needed which facilitate meaningful collaboration between the passengers, which will motivate in turn the development of programme understandings – of the nature of its 'innovative features', and the philosophy and intended learning benefits which lie behind those; and of the knowledge, understandings and skills which will be needed on the parts of educators to enable the intended learning to take place in turn on the parts of students.

Structures to consider in this respect include 'meeting time, course timetabling, funding' (Robertson, 2011, p142). The three are not mutually exclusive, however, since sufficient of the latter two are needed to facilitate the former; this being necessary in turn for addressing the substantial strategic, action, horizontal (disciplinary and interdisciplinary) and vertical (intra- and cross-programme) planning requirements of the MYP, and for providing scope for the collaboration which will allow those to be addressed with understanding.

The notion of collaboration forms a cornerstone of MYP philosophy and practice, being one of its six pedagogical principles (IB, 2014a, pp66-7), and an unequivocal requirement across all IB programmes – Standard C1 of the *Programme Standards and Practices* is entirely devoted to 'Collaborative planning', with the phrase 'Collaborative planning and reflection' forming the opening of each practice there. Its further citing by the IB as one of the three strands which 'drive and initiate school change' (IB, 2014a, p29) is, meanwhile, validated by Fullan's observation that 'Numerous studies document the fact that professional learning communities or collaborative work cultures at the school... are critical for the implementation of attempted reforms' (2007, p96). The significance of collaboration, however, needs to lie in its focus and purpose, which need in turn to be rooted not in '*administrivia*' (Garmston, 2007, p55) as meetings of other types may be, but in 'ensur[ing] common understandings and common approaches to teaching and learning in the school, leading to a coherent learning experience for students' (IB, 2014a, p29). From understandings can then emerge purposeful planning through further collaboration of more complex learning initiatives, such as those for interdisciplinary learning which will demonstrate to students 'the need to use concepts, knowledge and skills from different disciplines in order to solve problems' (IB, 2014a, p29).

The IB's philosophical notion of collaboration, as expounded in its documentation, has much in common with the concept of the 'professional learning community', which has over recent years become an increasing feature of the general educational landscape, and the preferred collaborative model for adoption by many IB schools. Professional learning communities may take the forms of 'every imaginable combination of individuals with an interest in education – a grade-level teaching team, a school committee, a high school department, an entire school district, a state department of education, a national professional organization, and so on' (DuFour, 2004b), thus comfortably accommodating the notion of MYP teams in the forms of subject departments, grade level teacher groups of different kinds, perhaps an MYP steering committee, and so on within an MYP context. Meanwhile as with the stated IB aim for collaborative time to 'provide a coherent learning experience for students" (IB, 2014a, p29), the concept of the professional learning community is also firmly predicated on student learning outcomes: 'As the school moves forward, every professional in the building must engage with colleagues in the ongoing exploration of three crucial questions that drive

173

the work of those within a professional learning community:

- What do we want each student to learn?

- How will we know when each student has learned it?

- How will we respond when a student experiences difficulty in learning?' (DuFour, 2004b).

The focus must therefore be on student learning.

The championing of collaborative planning is meanwhile borne out of its perceived benefits, in terms of teacher working practices and outcomes, which are similar to those ideas espoused by Woods *et al*, and others, in relation to distributed leadership: 'Where people work together in such a way that they pool their initiative and expertise, the outcome is a product or energy which is greater than the sum of their individual actions' (2004, p441). DuFour suggests 'products' which may emerge may take forms such as student learning-based 'lists of essential outcomes, different kinds of assessment, analyses of student achievement, and strategies for improving results' (DuFour, 2004b). Similar 'products' anticipated in an MYP context take the forms of various required curricular elements such as meaningful unit plans and subject overviews, along with the 'common understandings' cited by the IB as an intended outcome of collaborative time, and which are required in the first place to generate these.

A further sought after 'product' of the process is often perceived as attitudinal, however – an important consideration within substantial change processes, and for the MYP: 'When teachers are regular participants in decisions that affect their students and have many opportunities to collaborate with colleagues, their energy levels, capacity for creative thinking, efficiency, and goodwill increase. At the same time, the cynicism, foot dragging, and defensiveness that hamper change efforts decrease' (Kohm and Nance, 2007, p207). Within IB contexts themselves, Lee *et al* and Robertson respectively record findings that 'the complex web of teacher interactions involved in IB PYP implementation contributed significantly to a culture of shared responsibility for student learning' (Lee *et al*, 2012b, p293), and that '[MYP] coordinators' contributions were better received when emerging within a genuinely collaborative process' (Robertson, 2011, p140).

Comments such as the above indicate the potential value of collaborative time, and illustrate why educational trends, including those seen within IB programmes, place such store by it. Caveats nonetheless exist in regard to the management of this within schools – anecdotal evidence from school visits and workshops, where the issue of meeting time is recurrently expressed as a concern, suggests that distinctions between 'collaborative time' and other meeting time is not always recognized by MYP schools, which may assign such time without sufficient clarity as to its purpose and organizational needs. 'Collaboration' can thus be interspersed with '*administrivia*', with a resultant confusion serving to impede the collaborative planning needs of an MYP school and the intended outcomes of those; as well as to frustrate those present. Loose planning and structures, meanwhile, along with a focus on the 'collaboration' rather than on what it is supposed to produce, can compound perceptions of teachers that they are being asked to 'collaborate' as something of an externally-directed educational 'fad', and that value in relation to time and resources spent make the exchange less than worthwhile.

The underlying need is thus for the development of a 'collaborative *culture*' within a school, in which 'learned and shared beliefs, values, interests, attitudes' may lead to a productive process and outcomes as a norm. Establishing any cultural norm is far from a straightforward matter, however, with strategizing needed to accomplish this, and to negotiate various challenges which may present themselves along the way.

Cultural norms

> Culture encompasses a range of learned and shared beliefs, values, interests, attitudes, products, ways of knowing and patterns of behaviour created by human communities. The concept of culture is dynamic and organic. (IB 2014a, p57)

Culture is also ubiquitously described as 'the way we do things around here', and involves school leadership in 'shap[ing] the norms of behavior (and thus the culture) of their organizations in a number of ways' (DuFour, 2004a). Robertson suggests that 'changing cultural norms' (2011, p138) represents an integral part of MYP implementation, necessary because, as Kohm and Nance in turn suggest, '… how plans are implemented and their ultimate success still depends on the behavior of teachers in classrooms. And that behavior is strongly affected by school culture' (2007, p206). Hence the need in MYP schools for 'leaders who can create a fundamental transformation in the learning cultures of schools' (Fullan, 2002); and for 'Principals who … are interested in school reform' to 'work with their faculties to build cultural norms that support their instructional efforts' (Kohm and Nance, 2007, p206). One cultural norm highly applicable to MYP implementation is, as seen above, that of collaboration, with a culture of adult learning and inquiry also being a necessary factor of success there.

Nurturing a culture of collaboration

While collaboration may begin with provision of the material means to collaborate – time, space, flipcharts, pens, associated costs – and perhaps designation of some 'professional learning communities', a collaborative culture itself is not an automatic outcome. DuFour warns that 'Perhaps there are schools that have made the transition to a professional learning community without conflict or anxiety, but I am unaware of any. Disagreements and tension are to be expected'; further recounting from his own experience how '... in the early stages of implementing the changes that helped the school become a professional learning community, each principal faced challenges from one or more staff members who either aggressively or passively resisted the school's new direction' (DuFour, 2004a, p64).

Taking a horse to an MYP professional learning community without being able to compel it to drink there is not an uncommon feature of an MYP school. Reasons for resistance may vary, though several sources allude to teachers holding on to self-perceptions of themselves as 'autonomous professionals' (Robertson, 2011, p141) with comments such as "I am struggling with some of my teachers who believe that working collaboratively will hinder their individuality" not unknown in MYP administrator workshops.

Developing a collaborative culture may thus be a time-laden process for schools, which are not generally time-rich. However, 'The problem in schools is that teams almost never start out as great teams' (DuFour, 2004a, p64), while 'Intuitive working relations are the common understandings and shared approaches to working that may emerge from close interdependency among staff *over a period of time* [my italics]' (Gronn, 2008, p434). Kohm and Nance, whose breathlessness-inducing comment that 'Collaborative cultures take the brakes off, release new energy, and accelerate a staff's capacity to improve instruction' (2007) may suggest a speedier journey, recount a rather more measured process in practice: '... we built trust and helped teachers develop a broader view by working on these decisions together. At first our conversations were inefficient, cautious, and sometimes fractious. However, in time, we became increasingly skilled at stating our opinions clearly and succinctly, respecting one another's viewpoints, and keeping our focus on mutually agreed-on goals' (Kohm and Nance, 2007, p214).

Also of note in relation to maintaining a learning-focused discussion at the centre of such collaboration is DuFour's reference to 'ensur[ing] that each member of the group [has] sufficient knowledge to make good decisions' (2003). Consideration must be given in an MYP context to levels of knowledge needed in order to 'generate products' such as meaningful discussion, and equally meaningful consequent unit plans, curriculum overviews, and so on; and thus to how such knowledge may be acquired by those charged with producing those. Such products and outcomes, anecdotal evidence suggests, may not always be so frequent a byproduct of a school's collaborative processes as they perhaps should be.

Acknowledging adult learning culture

Hence when Kohm and Nance talk of the need for leadership to 'work with their faculties to build cultural norms that support their instructional efforts' (Kohm and Nance, 2007, p206), a collaborative culture on its own is not sufficient to generate such 'products' if knowledge – and relevant understandings and skills also – is not at the level needed for these to be of the desired quality and meaning. Amidst the collaboration, therefore, need also to be nurtured 'sustainable cultures of adult learning' (Fahey, 2013, p66), and a 'culture of inquiry' (Garmston, 2007, p55) which will facilitate genuine learning on the parts of faculty, and lead to knowledge acquisition which may in turn give rise to the outcomes sought.

'Innovative program features' do, as seen from evidence of MYP application forms, represent one of the more common reasons for schools to choose to adopt the programme. They carry with them also, however, implications of new learning and understandings for those charged with their effective delivery in the classroom. Such learning is not always found easy. Alternatives can appear much more appealing; 'staff could easily retreat to what was safe, predictable and stable – and their subject-based habitats', and thus a frequent reality schools face is that reflected in Robertson's reporting that 'It was evident … that all [MYP coordinator] interviewees struggled in trying to change mind-sets' (Robertson, 2011, p138).

A role may be played also by perceptions of 'de-skilling' which entry into the world of MYP may bring with it. Hayden describes, in a context of physical relocation of international teachers, the 'very common cause of stress to experienced … teachers [of] feeling unexpectedly 'de-skilled'' (2006, p85), but the phenomenon has clear applicability for the MYP also, where teachers may similarly encounter unfamiliar elements and expectations, without certain and immediate prospects of coming fully to terms with those. Where, as Kohm and Nance point out, schools 'are filled with intelligent and experienced teachers' (2007), who may well 'have done well under the old conditions' (Machiavelli, 2006, p83) they previously worked within, clear scope exists for feelings of uncertainty about new learning needed – both in nature and quantity, and implicit questioning in that of the worth of previous experience. Not all teachers relish either the prospect of taking on the effective status of 'newbie' once again; while having to continue in the midst of new educational explorations exhibiting certain levels of knowledge and competence on a constant basis in front of some demanding audiences forms an ongoing challenge.

These represent compelling considerations unlikely to be sufficiently mitigated only by provision of meetings, space and agendas, however detailed and results-oriented – though these represent foundational elements of creating an environment for learning to take place. Also of importance amid the collaborative structures, however, is developing a culture of learning and inquiry, and pedagogical leadership which can address that, along with potential socio-emotional undercurrents which may manifest themselves in resistance of different kinds.

As with students, meanwhile, acquisition of the different types of learning needs different approaches. As Fahey points out, instrumental learning 'is particularly useful … where clear answers, expert knowledge, or technical support are needed' (2013, p67) – there is an initial need to know, for instance, that there are six global contexts and what those are, before one can delve more deeply into what to actually do with them. At this level there is certainly a place for the direct presentation format, which evidence of both heads and coordinator, and pedagogical leadership workshops has suggested may be the default approach to 'MYP professional development' in-school sessions in a number of schools; and indeed assumed to be the most appropriate one for the 'adult learners' present. That will allow teachers to recite but not integrate, however, and the reality is that a 'culture of inquiry' is needed for developing understandings, and active learning is needed in the case of skills; and that this applies as much to adult learners as to young adult ones.

Developing cultural norms through pedagogical leadership

Fullan's statement that 'Unclear and unspecified changes can cause great anxiety and frustration to those sincerely trying to implement them' (2007, p77) underlines the need for those implementing the MYP to be clear about what they are being asked to do, and why they are being asked to do it. There is thus a need for developing understandings of the purposes and value of the programme's components in relation to student learning and what teachers will do in the classroom in practical terms; and for developing a personal investment in that process also.

Developing a culture of inquiry and learning among MYP teachers is a process requiring pedagogical leadership; hence the requirement for all IB schools that: 'The head of school/school principal and programme coordinator demonstrate pedagogical leadership' (IB, 2014b, p3); while *MYP: From principles into practice* talks too of the need to establish within an MYP school 'a leadership structure that is ... more focused on pedagogical leadership' (IB, 2014a, p30). Little further pedagogical guidance is given on how this might be put into practice, however, although a section on pedagogical leadership on the DP 'Approaches to Teaching and Learning' (ATL) website suggests that an 'effective way of embedding ATL in the school culture is to ensure that in-school professional development (PD) activities not only focus on, but also model, the approaches to teaching and learning being discussed' (IB, 2015a).

Fahey, in an echo of such advice, describes how two principals in a non-MYP context responded to perceived learning needs of their teachers by 'turn[ing] every faculty meeting for a year into a class, complete with essential questions, goals, presentations, group activities, and homework' (2013, p67). This presents something of a visual insight into what 'pedagogical leadership' of the type alluded to in IB documentation may look like in practice. It echoes too what should happen in an IB workshop, a key tool in a process of creating an adult learning culture, and which should take the form of an inquiry-based collaborative learning environment in which various strategies are modelled and linked to different kinds of learning, thus providing insight into how such strategies are implemented in practice. It should offer too, of course, 'instrumental learning' about the programme, along with facilitating – and demonstrating how that may be achieved – learning at levels of understanding and skill strategies; workshop elements often especially valued by participants, whose own-school contexts may not have been so example-rich with demonstrations of what 'inquiry-based' or 'concept-based' learning may look like in practice.

The IB workshop leader him- or herself, too, should model a pedagogical leader in action, demonstrating and addressing learning of different kinds, and thus forming one source of information on what pedagogical leadership, and creating a culture of adult learning, actually entails. It may represent an especially valuable aspect of heads' and coordinators' workshops to note by participants (and as has been noted, attendance at a heads' and coordinators' workshop is mandated for all MYP school heads (or a designée) and programme coordinators). Meanwhile workshops explicitly addressing pedagogical leadership for the programme are also available.

IB workshops for teachers are also important components of creating a culture of adult learning, although the formal requirements for participation, which extend to just one member of each subject group (hence a school for instance offering Music, Visual Arts, Dance and Drama in its Arts subject group needs only to send one teacher from across all four subjects to fulfill the formal IB requirement), need careful consideration by schools in order to maximize the learning value provided by such workshops to the school overall. Other factors to consider include the options for workshops to be either online or face-to-face. All of these factors have implications as to how the learning potential of workshops may be managed within a school.

In view of this the choice of who participates in individual training, and how, represent pertinent strategic considerations, given the need to ensure in circumstances in which a minimal proportion of teachers may participate in IB workshops themselves that 'any professional development undertaken by individual teachers is subsequently made use of more widely within the school', with 'processes for ensuring this becom[ing] of greater significance' (Ashworth, 2013, p176). In terms of transferring such learnings, instrumental learning should be relatively straightforward, but strategies may be less so.

This is where online workshops – which have proliferated over recent years – may be considered, as while strategies may not be demonstrated first hand in that particular workshop environment, availability of relevant video content ensures that participants may still see these being demonstrated. Indeed the workshop experience as a whole may – informally at least – be shared to a greater or lesser degree along the way by colleagues, with substantial material being available and accessible during that period and for some time afterwards, and providing much stimulus for dialogue within professional learning communities. Other potential advantages of online workshops lie in the greater flexibility they provide in how a professional development budget might be dispersed, and provide scope for a greater number of teachers to participate directly. They may offer too a more extended and reflective journey through implementation material; both through the global perspectives, resource-sharing and discussion which takes place in what are non-region specific workshops; and through discussion which is often more thoughtfully produced, as – barring an extremely short window – what has been written and posted by participants cannot be retracted later. All of this provides greater scope for familiarization with the programme and its various aspects, in greater depth – a characteristic of these workshops which may render them potentially especially helpful to teachers new to the MYP. On the converse side, lack of face to face (and synchronous) discussion and the ability to view practical classroom strategies firsthand in action are the main negatives.

Further cost-effective options which school leadership can sometimes be surprisingly unaware of can be found in the range of in-school workshops available, which offer an opportunity for a wide range of faculty within an individual school to receive at the same time training in generic areas such as assessment or approaches to learning, without (as in the case of online workshops) having to leave the school.

One further professional development opportunity perhaps worthy of note, finally, lies in the ever-expanding International Baccalaureate Educator Network (IBEN), comprised of the IB's workshop leaders and school visitors, recruited from school personnel. Experienced and competent practitioners applicants must be to begin with, but the professional development experience offered which builds further on that practice, and perhaps particularly in a context of pedagogical leadership, marks this training out as a potentially powerful capacity-builder for those trainees who take part, and for the colleagues back in school with whom they may work, putting newly-developed knowledge and pedagogical leadership skills designed to be at a level needed for IB workshops and participants whose schools have paid substantial fees to be there to valuable use immediately within their own schools.

IBEN is increasingly a route taken by those in leadership positions for the MYP, and represents, where the possibility exists, substantial potential training leaders may receive in pedagogical leadership knowledge, understandings, and strategies, beyond those which can be gained through attending workshops as a participant. Pedagogical leadership in itself is a crucial factor in the development of an adult learning culture within a school, in facilitating opportunities for learning to take place, and in the successful implementation of collaborative structures and the nurturing of an effective and purposeful collaborative culture within a school.

Supovitz and Christman comment that 'the theory of action underlying the development of teacher communities is that the fostering of these kinds of teacher communities will instigate improvements in the quality of instruction, which will lead to enhanced student learning' (2003, pii). Facilitating communities which will work in such a way extends beyond provision of time, space, personnel, and any assumptions of guaranteed success, however; and indeed beyond the other necessary intrastructural elements of collaborative work. It depends too on being able to provide the support and sense and clarity of purpose, without which a danger exists that 'initial enthusiasm gives way to confusion about the fundamental concepts driving the initiative, followed by inevitable implementation problems' (DuFour, 2004b). Such support may lie in provision of necessary knowledge, or in pedagogical approaches to professional development sessions. It must also lie, however, in a crucial ingredient of pedagogical leadership, an understanding of and engagement with relationships of different kinds.

Relationships matter

> Relationships are the connections and associations between properties, objects, people and ideas – including the human community's connections with the world in which we live. Any change in relationship brings consequences – some of which may occur on a small scale, while others may be far-reaching, affecting large networks and systems such as human societies and the planetary ecosystem. (IB 2014a, p57)

A collaborative culture necessarily involves relationships and all of the accompanying complexities of these – a further significant factor in the nature of the collaborative and learning cultures a school may hope to develop. As one head participating in an MYP heads' workshop once remarked: 'Getting a diverse community to work together requires a constant nurturing of relationships.'

Amid the many possible relationships which may be formed and found within an MYP community, one particular relational triangle is perhaps particularly worthy of consideration. At one point lies the MYP coordinator role, with his or her relations with implementing teachers and relevant senior leadership members respectively underpinning the implementation process, and impacting too on the nature of the relationship between those two parties. All three relationships can significantly influence the cultures and practices, and thus the nature of the MYP implementation experience.

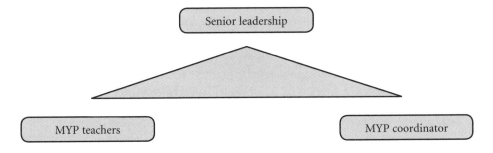

Robertson, in his investigation into issues of MYP coordination (2011), appears to envisage a slightly different model, talking of the coordinator as 'the '[wo]man in the middle'', who is 'situated in between the senior management and the teaching faculty', thus providing a 'bridge' between 'the two distinctive viewpoints' (Robertson, 2011, p143):

While this relational structure certainly exists, and may possibly explain some of the relational difficulties which can emerge between a coordinator and senior leadership, it appears to diminish or possibly preclude the direct relationship which does – and perhaps needs to – exist between teachers and senior leadership also in regard to MYP implementation.

The MYP coordinator and MYP teachers

Robertson defines the role of an MYP coordinator in terms of three functions, the 'guide alongside', 'administrator' and 'orchestrator'. The first two of these are discussed very much in terms of relational considerations, and their resulting impact on MYP implementation.

The 'guide alongside' function is one which takes into consideration the potential socio-emotional effects on teachers of programme implementation efforts, as well as the pragmatic and cognitive needs of this, which often represent the limit to which implementation needs are considered. The MYP is a programme which 'requires a lot of work'; in which 'Progress, according to several interviewees, occurred by experimenting, and sometimes by learning from failures'; and with which 'teachers sometimes struggled' (Robertson, 2011, pp138-9).

It is within such a landscape that the 'guide alongside' function is suggested as a valuable tool in programme implementation, founded in a belief that the 'most important responsibility was for supporting teachers' (Robertson, 2011, p139), and predicated on a collaborative approach which places a coordinator firmly alongside teachers as 'co-constructors' and "one of the gang' in partnership and solidarity with the teaching staff' (2011, pp139-40). Since coordinators are often teachers themselves, in such a role they could establish credibility with teachers by showing 'the value and 'do-ability' of the MYP approach' (2011, p139).

The coordinator in the 'guide alongside' role is thus placed hierarchically alongside teachers, a positioning which 'helped to establish trust and foster risk-taking in teachers' (Robertson, 2011, p140). The need for trust in change processes is well-documented (Lee *et al*, 2012; Kotter and Schlesinger, 2008; Nonaka and Takeuchi, 1995; Fullan, 2001, Goleman, 1999), and teacher perceptions of alignment between the role of the MYP coordinator and themselves, and the accompanying suggestions of support and co-constructivism were felt to provide conditions under which trust might develop further: 'coordinators were able to establish respect and build trust with staff', which led in turn to 'Requests for ... extra work, trying new things, and fulfilling the accompanying accountability measures' being 'then received more constructively' (2011, p140). Providing 'avenues for ongoing communication, support and collaboration', along with scope to teachers for "finding one's way" with the constructivist elements of this curriculum' – 'a constant source of anxiety to many teachers, and even coordinators' reflects assertions such as that of Kohm and Nance that 'Reform should be something that's done with teachers, not to them' (2007, p207), and is deemed in Robertson's study as 'essential to meaningful change' (2011, p140).

Implied in all of this is the notion of a 'guide alongside' function, founded on an aim of influencing the 'emotional exchange' which 'constitutes an interpersonal economy, part of every human interaction' (Goleman, 1999, p164), and which can engage productively with socio-emotional concerns such as lack of trust, or fear of not being able to 'to develop the new skills and behavior that will be required of them' (Kotter and Schlesinger, 2008, p134) – factors which may otherwise give rise to resistance to change. Inferred at the same time, meanwhile, is a relative lack of efficacy which may be anticipated where more coercive approaches are adopted which fail to take into account socio-emotional considerations. This is indeed indicated in research findings into change management, such as those from Fullan who reports that a coercive leadership style 'negatively affected climate, and in turn, performance', as 'people resent and resist' (2001, p35). Kotter and Schlesinger comment that 'using coercion is a risky process because inevitably people resent forced change' (2008, p137), while Kohm and Nance explain that 'When top-down edicts identify problems and dictate solutions, teachers see these problems as somebody else's fault and solutions as somebody else's responsibility' (2007, p206). Robertson's investigation further found that 'coordinators' contributions were less well-received when they were presented as a prescribed set of ingredients of a 'change recipe" (2011, p140), while where teachers perceived themselves as 'forced to be [collaborative] curriculum developers themselves [interviewee no. 4]', this led to 'much resistance to the MYP constructivist approach' (Robertson, 2011, pp136-7). The implications of all of this for coercive approaches within an MYP implementation context are clear.

While the 'guide alongside' function of an MYP coordinator's role clearly has significant value within an MYP implementation process, however, and caution in the use of coercion may be judicious, there may well – as Robertson's study accepts – exist a need for strategic deployment of more coercive approaches at times. Specific requirements of MYP implementation, such as attending meetings and producing documentation, are suggested potential catalysts, while 'in situations where speed is essential and where the changes will not be popular, regardless of how they are introduced, coercion may be the manager's only option' (Kotter and Schlesinger, 2008, p137). Additional attention is drawn to shortcomings of 'the participation process ... Not only can it lead to a poor solution if the process is not carefully managed, but also it can be enormously time consuming' (2008, p135). Kotter and Schlesinger further point out that 'All human beings are limited in their ability to change, with some people much more limited than others' (2008, p135), suggesting that coercion may always be needed in certain cases, whatever the circumstances.

A need exists for coercive approaches at times, therefore, but these where they arise may not sit comfortably with a 'guide alongside' function of MYP coordination which is perceived as 'more closely aligned with the teaching staff than with senior management' (Robertson, 2011, p139). The key concept definition of 'relationships' states that 'any change in relationship brings consequences', and such may occur where coordinators are called upon to play an 'administrator' role, involving 'asking teaching colleagues to attend meetings and produce curriculum documents'; 'calling teachers to account', and 'ensur[ing] compliance' – tasks in general which could involve them in "play[ing] the heavy" with teachers. Given too that coordinators have "little formal authority to ensure compliance", and tend to be in a position of having '... the main responsibility for this complex undertaking [MYP implementation] ... without direct ... authority over personnel' (Robertson, 2011, p142), the coordinator can easily find him- or herself in the 'bind' described by Kotter and Schlesinger, in which 'a manager has a weak position vis-à-vis the people whom he thinks need a change and yet is faced with serious consequences if the change is not implemented immediately' (2008, p139). Unsurprisingly in view of the potentially conflictual nature of these dimensions of an MYP coordinator's role, a strong sense pervades the study that coordinators saw 'acting as the 'authority figure'' (Robertson, 2011, p142) as a major function of senior leadership in MYP implementation.

The MYP coordinator and senior leadership

The presence of a coordinator between senior leadership and teachers in an MYP school removes the former further from direct leadership and management of teachers than may be the case in non-MYP schools, where such a coordination role with explicit pedagogical leadership responsibilities does not exist. Robertson presents the pivotal role of a coordinator, 'sometimes advocating for teachers to the senior manager (*eg* for time or other resources) and at other times trying to persuade senior management to demand more of teachers (*eg*, documentation submission, incorporating MYP expectations into teacher evaluations)' (2011, p143), as a relational picture which, while hierarchical in terms of a material power structure, has the coordinator at the centre, and both teachers and senior management dependent in different ways on that role for meaningful engagement with MYP implementation. As such it has quite significant potential to impact on scenarios such as that described by Fahey, in which principals play out direct leadership roles with faculty, such as in professional development sessions (2013, p67). As roles of this nature might more often be assumed by the programme coordinator in an MYP school, this represents a structure with potential implications for how roles, and power, may be perceived within a school.

In terms of the former, IB documentation states that 'The specific responsibilities of the MYP coordinator will vary depending on the number of students and teachers, the type of school and its management structure' (IB, 2014a, p31). Role specifics are thus left up to individual schools. Without clarification of these, however, the organizational structure created for the MYP within a school, possibly supplemented by an MYP educational team or steering committee, is one with potential for role confusion or misunderstandings, unclear accountabilities, or indeed micropolitical behaviours. Distributed leadership structures of this kind, for all their potential strengths, have the capacity also to, as McCarthy comments, 'turn into distributed anarchy and chaos' (McCarthy, 2010) where insufficient clarity of roles exists.

A pragmatic approach is thus needed towards clarifying roles, parameters of these, expectations and accountabilities; and in collaborating in designing, reviewing, editing, and arriving at common understandings of the specifics of job descriptions among an MYP coordinator and senior leadership. Role confusion between the coordinator and one or more members of a senior leadership team represents a common area of difficulty arising with MYP implementation, and a common topic raised in the course of workshops and school visits.

Beyond pragmatic role considerations, however, may lie issues of more socio-emotional origin. The presence of an MYP coordinator in the leadership structure can mean a relative lack of 'hands on' involvement, and of the symbolic leadership which direct leadership of meetings, professional development sessions and the like bring with them; along with possible perceptions of diluted power and control, for more senior leadership. The coordinator role may have some impact in such respects also, and cognizance of this, and of possible 'emotional undercurrents' (Goleman, 1999, p166) which may emanate in consequence, may be a judicious component of an MYP coordinator's toolbox. Trust and transparency which allow for discussion of such issues in the course of professional dialogue are valuable commodities, where these may be possible in a coordinator–senior leadership relationship. Whatever form conversations may take between the two sides, however, Robertson's observation that 'effective coordination involved a sensitive political framing of the role' (2011, p139) is an astute one.

Amidst the role parameters of a coordinator and senior leadership respectively, meanwhile, arises, as has been seen, the question of assignation of collaborative and coercive approaches to needs arising within the MYP. Concerns raised within Robertson's study about the impact which adopting an 'administrator' role, and engaging in coercive approaches, may have on the 'guide alongside' function of the coordinator, are legitimate ones; and in the absence of any functional power to discipline teachers in any formal manner, it is undoubtedly the case that coordinators are 'ultimately reliant on their senior managers to call ... teachers to account' (2011, pp141-2). In the distribution of role responsibilities, therefore, recognition is needed of occasions on which some intervention of this kind may most appropriately come from more senior leadership.

Abdication of all responsibility for coercive functioning on the part of the coordinator may, however, lie at odds with the coordinator's own position within a senior leadership team (the IB-mandated senior pedagogical leadership team) in the school, and the ultimate accountability the coordinator does have for programme quality and implementation. It may be at odds too with wider leadership aspirations often held by those who take on this role; and with Fullan's view of leadership in general as necessarily involving 'combining elements that do not easily and comfortably go together', such as having to balance 'the authoritative element' with a need 'to build good relationships' (2001, p42) – rarely is such a good opportunity offered to practise that particular balancing act as when coordinating the MYP. DuFour articulates a similar view of leadership, commenting (in relation to principals, but with equal relevance to MYP coordinators) in terms evocative of the 'guide alongside' and 'administrator' functions of a coordinator, that: 'A critical element in creating these powerful school cultures is the principal's leadership. Each is clearly committed to empowering staff, delegating authority, and developing collaborative decision-making processes, but none is unwilling to confront a staff member who violates the fundamental concepts of the school's culture' (DuFour, 2004a, p64). Goleman too talks of 'The most effective people in organizations' who rather than relying on any default position 'use their emotional radar to sense how others are reacting, and then fine-tune their own response to push the interaction in the best direction' (1999, p167). All see combining such aspects as an expected part of leadership, rather than as fatally conflicting.

Nonetheless, responsibilities for addressing collaborative and coercive needs arising within an MYP implementation process do represent an area for negotiation and common understandings between the MYP coordinator and senior leadership, given the practicalities of the power differential on each side. Who does what when a need arises – and as DuFour points out, the question is one of when 'we are immersed in the conflict that accompanies significant change', rather than of being able to prevent such conflict (DuFour, 2004a, p64) – is important to determine. Of greatest efficacy, however, may be the working relationship encompassing joint analysis and strategizing, and mutual support.

Ongoing collaboration within the MYP coordinator–senior leader relationship is thus key to the nature and quality of an implementation process, with a need for negotiation on both sides as to how they may most productively interact at any given time and in response to particular scenarios which may arise. Such interaction should encompass thorough analysis of aspects of the implementation process as might be needed, and in a manner allowing for informed decisions as to who might act and how, within different scenarios which arise. No less importantly, perhaps, it may play a role too in mitigating political or socio-emotional concerns on either side in relation to perceptions of power. Many aspects of the roles played by each, and associated accountabilities, may and should be formalized within job descriptions in endeavours to avoid the type of 'coordination challenge' (Lee *et al*, 2012, p301) presented where roles may be unclear and potential overlap may occur in some respects. Such formalized role parameters are not in themselves cognizant of other relational undercurrents, however, which a transparent and collaborative relationship may be able to address to a greater degree. In such a way, therefore, in overall MYP leadership terms, might a school not only get the right people on the bus and in the right seats, but also have them remaining seated, working together, doing what is needed, and trampling as little as possible over any fellow passengers.

Senior leadership and MYP teachers

Given the position of the MYP coordinator in the leadership structure of an MYP school, the relationship of more senior leaders with teachers may, as has been seen, be more indirect than may be the case elsewhere, certainly in relation to programme implementation. Robertson's study does nonetheless outline the importance of senior leadership, and not only in demanding unpopular paperwork on behalf of the coordinator, and being 'perceived unfavourably' (Robertson, 2011, p141) as a result. Senior managers are presented 'who were well respected by staff', and who, in exercising 'the art of persuasive dialogue' rather than applying 'coercive tactics', and offering ample support – resource and moral – for implementing teachers, are clearly substantially involved in MYP implementation processes.

Nonetheless, the role of 'playing the 'bad cop' in enforcing compliance by resistors' (Robertson, 2011, p142), and engaging in difficult conversations is one in which, as has been seen, senior leadership may need to engage, and which was often perceived in Robertson's study as the 'support' most readily looked for by coordinators taking part there. DuFour outlines the considered and process-based nature of the approach which may be taken in such a context, which, while not MYP-specific, has clear parallels to what may happen there also. Meanwhile further evident in the description is the role played by emotional intelligence in the conduct of the school leader:

> The consistent way the principals dealt with staff challenges offers important insights into leading the professional learning community process. In every case, the principal met with the teacher privately, stated concerns

very directly, and identified the specific steps the teacher needed to take to remedy the situation. Finally, the principal asked how he or she might help the teacher make the necessary changes. The teachers did not always respond positively to these discussions. Some became quite emotional and defensive. The principals, however, did not hedge. They made it clear that the teacher's behavior was unacceptable and that the need for change was imperative. They did so without rancor, but they left no doubt about their expectations (DuFour, 2004a, p64).

The account vividly illustrates the 'personal discipline' inherent in successful difficult conversations of a kind not infrequently called upon within an MYP implementation context. Sanderson talks of initiating a 'difficult conversation' as 'an act of bravery to put your body in the room, ready to become a part of the solution to the problem at hand', and of the need to be 'fully present' – then, 'we are visible and people know where we stand on important issues. Our communications are clear…' (2005, pp14-5); all of which are on display in DuFour's narrative, and have direct relevance to MYP implementation conversations needed at times. Evident too in the context of some teacher responses described is Goleman's 'emotional competence' in play, with its requirement for 'being able to pilot through the emotional undercurrents always at play rather than being pulled under by them' (Goleman, 1999, p166).

The wisdom inherent in the manner of address, meanwhile, is further illustrated by a glimpse into an alternative world, drawn by Dale Carnegie in once asserting that: 'If you and I want to stir up a resentment tomorrow that may rankle across the decades and endure until death, just let us indulge in a little stinging criticism – no matter how certain we are that it is justified. When dealing with people, let us remember we are not dealing with creatures of logic. We are dealing with creatures of emotion' (2006, p13).

Robertson concludes from his study of MYP coordination challenges that teacher engagement with implementation of the programme has 'practical as well as political, social and emotional dimensions'; indicating a need for MYP leadership to devote as much attention to relationships as to material and structural factors involved in developing productive and meaningful collaborative and adult learning cultures. Consideration of relationships should, meanwhile, include those which exist among the leaders themselves. Relationships do, as the key concept definition states, affect 'large networks and systems such as human societies and the planetary ecosystem'. They therefore certainly possess the firepower to impact significantly on the MYP.

The art or otherwise of communication

Communication is the exchange or transfer of signals, facts, ideas and symbols. It requires a sender, a message and an intended receiver. Communication involves the activity of conveying information or meaning.

Effective communication requires a common "language" (which may be written, spoken or non-verbal). (IB, 2014a, p56)

Originally one of the three 'fundamental concepts' of the programme, the concept of communication has made its way into the post 'Next Chapter' programme in starring roles such as that of a key concept, an entire approaches to learning category, and a subject objective for some subject groups, such as Individuals and Societies, and Mathematics. The *Programme Standards and Practices* (IB, 2014b) meanwhile, contain several stipulations for communicating aspects of the programme to all and sundry involved.

Businessman and CEO Richard Branson acclaims communication as 'the most important skill any leader can possess', describing it in terms which resonate in the context of implementing the MYP: 'It facilitates human connections, and allows us to learn, grow and progress. It's not just about speaking or reading, but understanding what is being said – and in some cases what is not being said' (2015). Branson asserts that communication 'make[s] the world go round', and such is certainly true of the MYP world in which communication suffuses every aspect of the programme.

Communication and change

The importance of this concept resonates from the earliest moments at which schools contemplate introducing the MYP, particularly as they embark on a process of communicating with all stakeholders via a mandated feasibility study (IB, 2015b). This provides the means for discussion and communication of possible reasons for adopting the programme, and any potential benefits and challenges it may bring. Kotter and Schlesinger observe that 'One of the most common ways to overcome resistance to change is to educate people about it beforehand. Communication of ideas helps people see the need for and the logic of a change' (2008, p134), comments very much reflected in the need for communication in what is termed the 'consideration' phase of MYP adoption.

Communication represents a key consideration throughout programme implementation too, where, as has been seen, progress may be dependent on the meaning and value of the 'innovative programme features' which lead schools frequently to adopt the programme being communicated successfully to those who carry out its implementation. A note might be added too about the somewhat innovative terminology which can provide something of a communicative barrier at the outset, with challenges of grappling with an array of 'key' and 'related' concepts, 'global contexts', 'service as action' and the like leading one MYP teacher to be heard inquiring if 'MYP jargon' might be added to the offerings in the Language Acquisition subject group. Elsewhere, a suggested contribution to a humorous list of 'You know you're an MYP teacher when…' statements took the form of 'You begin speaking in a language that only you and cats can understand'. Both, aside from their humorous intent, provide some insight into perceptions of teachers at times in engaging with the language of the MYP. The programme may have a 'common language' as the key concept definition of communication suggests is required for 'effective communication', but bringing about familiarity with and understanding of that language represent an early task in a school's endeavours to begin its implementation of the MYP.

Communication and communities

The importance of communication within an MYP community context is evident from the earliest stages of a feasibility study, and the need for reaching out communicatively with all stakeholder groups on an ongoing basis reverberates throughout *MYP: From Principles into Practice*, and around IB practices and documentation generally. Communication is essential in various ways within a school as has been seen, and outside of its physical environs, too, the IB school must ensure that its external stakeholders, particularly in the respective forms of a governing body and parents, are well-served in this respect.

The former group are cited in the MYP publication as essential for successful implementation of the programme, with school leaders being 'responsible for informing and securing ongoing support from their governing body' (2014a, p30), and ensuring in turn that said body 'understands the principles of the programme' (2014a, p35). Mattern (cited in Hayden, 2006) states that a governing body is 'the employer, the maker of policies to be administered, the arbiter of performance' (p114), and such 'support' in relation to the MYP often reflects the first two of those elements in particular. Support in the case of hiring for the MYP generally relates to budgeting, with a critical need thus to keep a governing body informed about teacher, coordination, role specialist (for languages and/or special educational needs, for instance) requirements and other contextual MYP needs, along with associated considerations such as the requirement for teachers to have appropriate teaching qualifications; the impact of mandated collaborative planning time on teacher scheduling and thus potentially number of teachers hired; and the not insignificant professional development commitments involved in implementing the programme.

A governing body may well also have a role in the creation and formal adoption of school policies, mandated in the case of the IB for language, assessment, academic honesty, and inclusion/special educational needs; and in practice an admissions policy is needed also. These set out philosophy statements, principles and practices, and as such represent a potentially valuable means of communicating insight into some fundamental areas of the MYP to board members involved in drawing up the policies. As policies must be accessible and available to all within a school community, and reviewed regularly, they should continue to form an important communicative tool in regard to these areas on an ongoing basis for stakeholder groups, but may be particularly helpful for those outside of the day-to-day life of the school.

Communication with a governing body is thus an essential consideration, although ways in which members may be involved with the programme in practice and in which communication may consequently need to take place, are very much dependent on who and where that body actually are. Governance of a school can take a vast array of forms from the owner-head who is the governing body, to a group of appointed or elected members attached to an individual school, to a possibly remote educational board overseeing a large group of schools scattered around a region, or even the world; and very many more possible forms in between. In such a scenario, communication with the board is, in reality, highly contextual across the MYP world; and its purposes and means have to be determined locally.

Whatever form such channels may take, however, opportunities to use them tend to be relatively constrained compared with other stakeholder groups, and thus establishing most effective lines for this in the context, and ensuring quality in the communication which takes place, represent especially important considerations for school leadership. Opportunities which may arise can include programme presentations and reports at board meetings, provision of in-school training for the board, and inviting members to MYP-related special events, such as themed days or Personal Project fairs (IB, 2014a, p35). Schools are also able to avail themselves of IB governance workshops now offered for school board members, which provide communication about IB programmes from an alternative source.

As with the governing body, the involvement in the programme of a second external group of stakeholders in the form of parents is actively sought by the IB: 'In all schools offering the MYP, parents are informed, involved and welcomed as partners with a clear role to play in supporting the school and their own children' (IB, 2014a, p74). Parents are expected, among other things, to 'understand the central importance of the community or Personal Project' (IB, 2014a, p6); 'have a clear understanding of the purposes of assessment and its practical application in the programme' (p36); and be 'important partners in promoting academic integrity' (p38).

Lee *et al* suggest that parental engagement of such kinds within an IB school needs a willingness on the parts of leadership 'to devote significant resources towards 'educating' parents about the rationale and process of IB programmes' (Lee *et al*, 2012, p298). Such 'education' tends in schools to involve a variety of communication methods, typically information sessions of various kinds, website information, emails, information in newsletters, the reporting system and parent conferences, and, quite often, an 'open door' policy on the part of the school. Such has been the proliferation of means of communication at times, in fact, that concerns expressed on occasion in the course of school visits have focused on too much communication rather than too little, dissipated around too many platforms, and providing overall relatively fragmented information which may need quite considerable piecing together.

This may suggest too, at times, investment in a communicative approach providing 'access to more and more information', a strategy termed 'entirely wrong' by Fullan, and one which may simply lead to an 'information glut' (Fullan, 2001, p78). Parents undoubtedly require information on an ongoing basis, but in the same way as with teachers a need exists also for conveying 'meaning', as the definition of this key concept states. Information alone may give rise to conflicting understandings and expectations between parents and a school, as illustrated in findings reported from a study by Lee *et al*: 'the educational philosophies of East Asian parents (*eg* orientation towards exam results, teacher-directed instruction and focus on learning subject content) often conflict with the student-directed, process-oriented, 'deep learning' approach embraced by the IB programmes, especially the PYP and MYP' (Lee *et al*, 2012, p298).

One particular area in which expectations often part company is that of assessment, frequently of especial interest to parents, but not always readily familiar or comprehensible in the nature of its different elements. Assessment practices in the MYP, founded on knowledge-building through factual to conceptual levels, require more complex summative assessments in the forms of 'performances of understanding', and the more complex reporting systems this involves; while formative assessment also plays a multi-dimensional and prominent role in the programme – all of which may differ quite significantly from personal examination-based experiences. Assessment represents in fact the third of the 'three main strands' stated by the IB to 'initiate and drive school change' (IB, 2014a, p29); and communicating understanding of its various facets is often a pressing concern for both schools and parents.

The degree to which understanding of this may be facilitated is dependent on the modes and nature of communication used – email and newsletter, for instance, might prove convenient for conveying information, but have limitations in their capacity to convey understandings. Face to face 'parent information sessions' (as seems a popular title) are a popular choice in this regard, though as with professional development sessions held for teachers, the content of these need to extend beyond informational presentations and embrace active learning strategies which can facilitate understandings, if more than 'instrumental knowledge' is to result; and if parents are to engage fully as 'partners' who can play the role of 'supporting the school and their own children' (IB, 2014a, p74) in the manner envisaged.

There thus exists considerable onus on IB schools to communicate effectively with all stakeholders, very much including those external groups who do not so readily provide a live audience on a day to day basis. A significant premium thus rests on determining what may represent 'effective' communication in respect of such groups, and by what means that may be achieved within the context of the challenges and opportunities which may exist in communicating with them.

Communication and cultures

Communication also plays a key role within the cultures which support MYP implementation, underpinning to a significant degree the nature and value of those within an adult learning culture. It has a particular part to play in knowledge-building and sharing, named by Fullan as among five 'core competencies' by which 'leaders will be empowered to deal with complex change' (2001, pii), and perceived to be crucial to the success of such cultures: 'Schools are beginning to discover that new ideas, knowledge creation, and sharing are essential to solving learning problems' (Fullan, 2001, pxi).

Fullan asserts that 'Effective leaders understand the value and role of knowledge creation, they make it a priority and set about establishing and reinforcing habits of knowledge exchange among organizational members' (2001, p87). In pursuit of this, Fullan advocates the setting up of 'mechanisms and practices that make knowledge sharing a cultural value' (2001, pp77-8), providing examples of activities used in business organizations which help catalyze the sharing and building of knowledge, which are often fundamentally based on communication, and which have clear applicability in an MYP context:

Peer assist: a team may ask for assistance from another team or group of individuals with experience in the same kind of work or task, and the two teams meet for between one and three days 'in order to work through an issue the first team is facing' (Dixon, 2000, cited in Fullan, 2001, p88).

After Action Reviews (AARs)/'lessons learned' sessions: short meetings of between 15 minutes and an hour which address three standardized key questions: What was supposed to happen? What happened? And what accounts for the difference? Notable in the process is the communicative need stated for all involved to be able to 'call it like you see it' in contributing to the discussion and its purposefulness yet relative brevity.

Fishbowl: where leadership may assume a position in the centre, along with a team of questioners, while other faculty form an outer circle to watch and listen: 'Everyone is watching as the group in the hot seat talks about what they're going to do, and what they need from me and my colleagues to be able to do it' (Pascale *et al*, pp188-189, quoted in Fullan, 2001, p91). Garvin further emphasizes the different communicative elements needed for success in such a process; on the one hand, '[the leader] must personally lead the process of discussion, framing debate, posing questions, listening attentively, and providing feedback and closure' (Garvin, 2000, pp190-191), and on the other, the 'calling it as one sees it' expectation which aids accountability.

A principal's video reflection: 'two hours were spent examining a video of one of the principals in the group as she conducted one of the monthly staff conferences with teachers. The principal on tape viewed segments of the video and discussed them with the instructional leader and other principals ... The principal in question was appalled at what she saw: "My goals were not clear", "I can't believe I said what I said", "When I looked at my video there was nothing I could see that was likely to motivate teachers"' (Fullan, 2001, pp98-9).

The above represent specific ways in which communication may be used to generate purposeful and meaningful knowledge-sharing, within the frameworks of the collaborative, adult learning, and inquiry-based cultures schools may seek to nurture. Branson describes communication as something which 'allows us to learn, grow and progress' (2015), and nowhere may that be more apt than in such cultural environments, where communication may be utilized in such ways by the various players involved to share and build knowledge.

Communication and relationships

Such cultures and their knowledge building and sharing outcomes are dependent too, however, on the nature of the relationships which exist there, which can both impact and be profoundly impacted by communication considerations. Von Krogh *et al* talk of the communicative outcomes of 'constructive relations' which "allow individuals to be more open about their ideas and freely discuss various matters" (Von Krogh *et al*, 2000, p45); while Fullan similarly suggests that 'Good relationships purge a knowledge-creation process of distrust, fear, and dissatisfaction, and allow organizational members to feel safe enough to explore … unknown territories' (Fullan, 2001, p82). Both suggest a causal link between 'constructive' or 'good' relationships, therefore, and the productive communication which represents a feature of successful knowledge sharing processes.

'Constructive relations' do not, as has been seen (DuFour, 2004a), necessarily preclude disagreement, conflict, and tension in the pursuit of productive collaboration, and may even embrace these: 'To be high functioning, teams must embrace disagreement and encourage individuals to voice their perspectives while acknowledging others' viewpoints. Doing so encourages active participation, which brings forth thoughtful, relevant, and forthright contributions from group members' (Strathman, 2015, p60). Such is the nature of knowledge sharing activities such as the 'After Action Reviews', and 'calling it as one sees it' responses to plans presented in the fishbowl scenarios.

Such discussions tend to remain externally focused on professional outcomes, however, emanating as they do from relationships which are constructive in nature. As such they form a contrast to those which may be predicated possibly on micropolitical considerations, where, for instance, a 'desire to dominate, to intimidate, to control' may be the intention. In such cases, the danger exists that they may 'block any possibility of open, trusting, professional communication' (Starratt, 1991, p196 – cited in Blase and Blase, 2004). Salin on the other hand considers how communication issues may influence relationships in the first place, citing even more pessimistically how 'deficient internal communication' such as 'poor information, lack of mutual conversations about tasks and goals, and a poor communication climate have been shown to correlate with bullying (Vartia, 1996)' (Salin, 2003, p1222).

Hoyle's description of the micropolitical environment of a school as – far from being a concern of limited applicability – 'an organisational underworld which we all recognise and in which we all participate' (1982, p45) underlines a need for active consideration and possible intervention by those overseeing such processes, as part of efforts to facilitate more productive communication and 'constructive relations'. Fullan's descriptions of relationships within an organization as 'almost everything', and 'paramount'; with the development of these being 'essential' (2001, pp.75-6) to the cause of knowledge sharing, all underline the importance of maintaining an active interest in the nature of relationships and manner in which communication may influence or be influenced by those. Such an interest may extend to a use of norms in collaborative environments (Kohm and Nance, 2007; Strathman, 2015), and of cultivating 'the proper tone, fostering desirable norms, behaviors and rules of engagement' (Garvin, 2000, p190-191). The more assertive declaration that 'Not everyone on a team or committee will want to be best friends, but personal attacks, criticisms, and judgments cannot be tolerated. It's important for leaders to take action when they hear [such] comments' (Strathman, 2015, p61) nonetheless serves to illustrate the potentially double-edged nature of the role communicative factors may play, both positively and negatively, in affecting relationships and cultures in a school; and thus indeed an MYP implementation process as a consequence.

As can be seen, communication represents a concept which underpins all of the work carried out in the course of implementing the MYP, and all of the conceptual lenses through which that might be considered. The nature communication can take, and uses to which it may be put, can impact that work substantially, for better or for worse; lying as it does at the heart of developing or not understandings on the parts of all stakeholders, and of nurturing or otherwise healthy relationships of all kinds, with consequent impact on the cultural norms of a school. It should thus form a powerful and frequently explicit consideration in the context of any of the many and varied aspects of the MYP which must be addressed in the course of an implementation process.

Reflection

Concepts represent pertinent lenses through which to consider leadership implications for the MYP, inviting exploration as they so appositely do of strategic leadership domains and complexities of these within the context of an MYP programme. Five were chosen for inclusion in this discussion, though many if not all of the MYP's 16 key concepts may have provided equally substantial and relevant food for thought on this topic. Those chosen, meanwhile, form part of a complex relationship of components involved in the process of change which implementing the MYP involves, and relating to the various personnel who form a part of that.

Meanwhile Collins' thoughts on the need, in striving from 'good to great', to commit to the 'long haul', and to excellence, and for putting one's 'shoulder to the flywheel', in the course of change processes, are all highly redolent of the experience of a 'slow and challenging' (IB, 2014a, p29) MYP implementation process, which 'requires a lot of work'; and in which progress occurs 'by experimenting, and sometimes by learning from failures' (Robertson, 2011, pp138-9). Former actor and mayor Alan Autry is credited with that saying the "Leadership demands that we make tough choices" (QuotationOf, 2016). That can be as true of the MYP as it is of other contexts.

References

Ashworth, G. L., 2013. Articulating the gap: the International Baccalaureate Middle Years and Diploma Programmes. In Hayden, M., Thompson, J., eds. *Exploring Issues of Continuity: The International Baccalaureate in a wider context.* Woodbridge, John Catt Educational Ltd.

Bennett, N., Wise, C., Woods, P., and Harvey, J. A., 2003. Distributed leadership. Summary of a literature review carried out for the National College for School Leadership (NCSL) Available from: http://oro.open.ac.uk/8534/1/bennett-distributed-leadership-full.pdf [Accessed 18 December 2015]

Blase, J. and Blase, J., 2004. The Dark Side of School Leadership: Implications for Administrator Preparation. In *Leadership and Policy in Schools* 3(4): pp.245-273.

Branson, R., 2015. *My top 10 quotes on communication.* Available from: https://www.virgin.com/richard-branson/my-top-10-quotes-on-communication [Accessed 24 January 2016].

Carnegie, D., 2006. *How to Win Friends and Influence People.* London: Vermilion.

Codrington, S. 2002. The pain of curriculum change: The challenges of implementing the MYP. In *IB World* 32, pp.18-21.

Collins, J. 2001. *Good to Great.* http://www.jimcollins.com/article_topics/articles/good-to-great.html [Accessed 12 December 2015].

DuFour, R., 2003. Building a Professional Learning Community. *American Association of School Administrators.* http://aasa.org/SchoolAdministratorArticle.aspx?id=9190 [Accessed 22 December 2015]

DuFour, R., 2004a. Culture shift doesn't occur overnight – or without conflict. *Journal of Staff Development* 25(4), pp.62-4.

DuFour, R., 2004b. What Is a Professional Learning Community? In *Educational Leadership: Schools as Learning Communities* 61(8): pp.6-11.

Fahey, K. 2013. Principals Who Think Like Teachers. In *Educational Leadership: The Principalship* 70(7), pp.66-68.

Fullan, M. 2001. *Leading in a Culture of Change.* San Francisco: Jossey-Bass.

Fullan, M. 2002. The Change Leader. In *Educational Leadership: Beyond Instructional Leadership* 59(8), pp.16-21

Fullan, M. 2007. *The New Meaning of Educational Change.* Abingdon: Routledge.

Garmston, R. J., 2007. Results-oriented agendas transform meetings into valuable collaborative events. *Journal of Staff Development.* 58(2), pp.55-7.

Garvin, D. A., 2000. *Learning in Action: A Guide to Putting the Learning Organization to Work.* Boston: Harvard Business School Press.

Goleman, D. 1999. *Working With Emotional Intelligence.* London: Bloomsbury.

Gronn, P., 2008. The future of distributed leadership. *Journal of Educational Administration.* 46(2), pp.141-158.

Hallinger, P., and Lee, M., 2012. A Global Study of the Practice and Impact of Distributed Instructional Leadership in International Baccalaureate (IB) Schools. *Leadership and Policy in Schools.* 11(4), pp.477-495.

Hayden, M. 2006. *Introduction to International Education.* London: Sage.

Hoyle, E. 1982. Micropolitics of Educational Organizations. *Educational Management and Administration.* 10, pp.87-98.

International Baccalaureate. 2010. *History of the Middle Years Programme.* Cardiff: International Baccalaureate.

International Baccalaureate. 2014a. *MYP: From principles into practice.* Cardiff: International Baccalaureate.

International Baccalaureate. 2014b. *Programme standards and practices.* Cardiff: International Baccalaureate.

International Baccalaureate. 2015a. Pedagogical leadership. *Diploma Programme: Approaches to teaching and learning.* [online] International Baccalaureate. Available from: https://xmltwo. ibo.org/publications/DP/Group0/d_0_dpatl_gui_1502_1/static/dpatl//guide-pedagogical-leadership.html [Accessed 2 November 2015].

International Baccalaureate. 2015b. *Guide to school authorization: Middle Years Programme.* Cardiff: International Baccalaureate.

International Baccalaureate. 2015c. *Find an IB World School.* [online] International Baccalaureate. Available from: http://www.ibo.org/programmes/find-an-ib-school/ [Accessed 2 January 2016].

International Baccalaureate. 2015d. *IB leadership certificates.* [online] International Baccalaureate. Available from: http://www.ibo.org/professional-development/professional-certificates/ib-leadership-certificates/ [Accessed 29 December 2015].

International Baccalaureate. 2015e. *IB leadership workshops for aspiring leaders.* [online] International Baccalaureate. Available from: http://www.ibo.org/professional-development/ib-leadership-series/ [Accessed 29 December 2015].

International Baccalaureate. 2015f. *Key facts about the MYP.* [online] International Baccalaureate. Available from: http://www.ibo.org/programmes/middle-years-programme/what-is-the-myp1/key-facts-about-the-myp/ [Accessed 14 December 2015].

International Schools' Review. 2015. *How did you get your International School career started?* Available from: http://internationalschoolsreview.com/v-web/bulletin/bb/viewtopic.php?f=1&t=4885&p=32913&hilit=MYP#p32913 [Accessed 30 December 2015]

Keltner, B. R., 1982. *Funding Comprehensive School Reform.* Santa Monica, CA: RAND.

Kohm, B., and Nance, B., 2007. *Principals who learn.* Alexandria: Association for Supervision and Curriculum Development (ASCD).

Kotter, J. P., and Schlesinger, L. A., 2008. Choosing Strategies for Change. *Harvard Business Review July – August 2008.* Pp.130-139.

Lee, M., Hallinger, P., and Walker, A., 2012. Leadership challenges in international schools in the Asia Pacific region: evidence from programme implementation of the International Baccalaureate. *International Journal of Leadership in Education: Theory and Practice.* 15(3), pp.289-310.

197

Machiavelli, N., 2006. *The Prince* [Online]. Salt Lake City: Project Gutenberg. Available from: http://www.gutenberg.org/ebooks/1232 [Accessed 22 December 2015].

McCarthy, D., 2010. Establishing a Culture of Distributed Leadership. *Great Leadership.* Available from: http://www.greatleadershipbydan.com/2010/06/establishing-culture-of-distributed.html [Accessed 18 December 2015].

Mayrowetz, D. 2008. Making sense of distributed leadership: Exploring the multiple usages of the concept in the field. Educational Administration Quarterly, 44(3), 424-435.

Nonaka, I., and Takeuchi, H. 1995. *The Knowledge-Creating Company.* Oxford University Press: New York.

Porter, W. A., 2011. *The role of leadership in developing and sustaining collective efficacy in a professional learning community.* Dissertation (M.Ed.). University of California, San Diego.

QuotationOf.com. 2016. *Alan Autry's Quotes.* Online: http://www.quotationof.com/alan-autry. html [Accessed 28 January 2016].

Robertson, J. E., 2011. *The role of the MYP coordinator.* In Hayden, M., Thompson, J., eds. *Taking the MYP Forward.* Woodbridge, John Catt Educational Ltd.

Salin, D., 2003. Ways of explaining workplace bullying: A review of enabling, motivating and precipitating structures and processes in the work environment. *Human Relations.* 56(10), pp.1213–1232

Sanderson, B. E., 2005. *Talk It Out!* New York: Eye on Education.

Sperandio, J. 2010. School Program Selection: Why Schools Worldwide Choose the International Baccalaureate Middle Years Program. *Journal of School Choice: International Research and Reform.* 4(2), pp.137-148.

Spillane, J. P., 2005. Distributed Leadership. *The Educational Forum.* 69(2), pp.143-150.

Strathman, B., 2015. Making Team Differences Work. In *Educational Leadership: Communications Skills for Leaders* 72(7), pp.60-64

Supovitz, J. A. and Christman, J. B., 2003. Developing Communities of Instructional Practice: Lessons From Cincinnati and Philadelphia. *CPRE Policy Briefs.*

Von Krogh, G., Ichijo, K., and Nonaka, I. 2000. *Enabling knowledge creation: How to unlock the mystery of tacit knowledge and release the power of innovation.* Oxford: Oxford University Press.

Watts, A. 2002. Adapting to change, with the MYP. In *IB World* 33, 6.

Woods, P. A., Bennett, N., Harvey, J. A., Wise, C., 2004. Variabilities and Dualities in Distributed Leadership: Findings from a Systematic Literature Review. *Educational Management Administration Leadership.* 32, pp.439-457. ISSN 1741-1432